14 September 2021

Best Wishes,

PRAISE FOR
THE BRAINS AND BRAWN COMPANY

"If you're still wondering whether your company is destined to be a disruptor or an incumbent, you may be asking yourself the wrong question. Robert Siegel's *The Brains and Brawn Company* is a must read for any leader looking to fearlessly embrace the advantages of both mindsets—and push the boundaries of what their organization can accomplish."

—**Alex Gorsky**, Chairman and Chief
Executive Officer, Johnson & Johnson

"In this timely book, Robert Siegel brilliantly challenges the common wisdom about competitive advantage, providing a new, essential roadmap for emerging stronger, creating value, and achieving success. *The Brains and Brawn Company* is a must-read for both established and future company leaders."

—**Julie Sweet**, CEO, Accenture

"Simply put—a masterful work by Robert Siegel. His writing reflects the real world of trade-offs, technology, and truths. Digitalization matters, innovation matters, creativity matters. But ultimately what matters most to every business is its focus on customers and clients. An intense focus on clients paired with a commitment to put the interests of clients at the forefront of every decision is the ultimate winning approach in business. I found myself reading chapters multiple times as I marveled at the way Siegel's experience, expertise, and insights come to life in the text. *The Brains and Brawn Company* is an ideal presentation of balance that every business leader can benefit from."

—**Walt Bettinger**, CEO and President,
The Charles Schwab Corporation

"*The Brains and Brawn Company* is a thoughtful exploration of what it takes to succeed as a company in the digital world. Drawing on extensive research and conversations with business leaders, Robert Siegel provides actionable insights from new innovators and well-established titans who focus a disruptive lens on their own industries."

—**Anne Wojcicki**, CEO, 23andMe

"Robert Siegel has done an outstanding job of clarifying that success in today's world will require a unique blend of both digital and physical skills and capabilities. It's not an either/or decision, the future winners will embrace the power of brains AND brawn."

—**Brian Cornell**, Chairman and CEO, The Target Corporation

"We are in a new era of unmistakable disruption, and every business must change how they operate to survive and thrive. Robert Siegel's *The Brains and Brawn Company* couldn't have come at a better time as start-ups and incumbents alike are now positioned to rewrite traditional rules of business in the digital age."

—**Aaron Levie**, Chief Executive Officer,
Co-founder and Chairman of Box

"*The Brains and Brawn Company* provides the blueprint for succeeding in our ever-evolving modern economy and society. It shows leaders how to build productive companies where digital and physical realities coexist in mutually beneficial ways."

—**Dara Treseder**, SVP, Head of Global
Marketing & Communications, Peloton

"We live in an increasingly fast-paced business world. Platforms dominate several industries and separation between digital and physical is no longer possible. Consequently, companies must measure themselves against new criteria. Robert Siegel has defined the most relevant attributes for companies to assess their competitive strength. Every CEO in the world should evaluate their own company along the Brains and Brawn framework."

—**Mathias Döpfner**, CEO, Axel Springer SE

"Transformation in these times has moved from buzz word to a strategic necessity. But it is easier said than done. Legacy companies must change technology and culture; start-ups often lack scale and logistics. In *The Brains and Brawn Company* Robert Siegel offers ideas for both. Unlike other books on the subject, Siegel offers a compelling framework for change and vivid examples of practitioners. Siegel brings an engaging style, bringing his academic talent to the real world. *Brains and Brawn* is a must read for all who are engaging in the most important change of their lifetime."

—**Jeff Immelt**, Venture Partner NEA,
former Chairman and CEO of GE

THE
BRAINS
AND
BRAWN
COMPANY

THE BRAINS AND BRAWN COMPANY

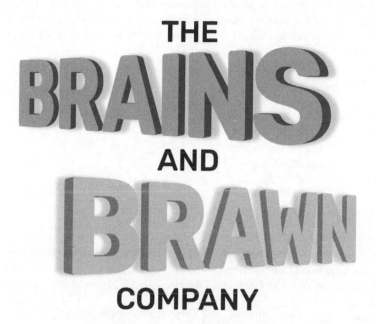

HOW LEADING ORGANIZATIONS BLEND THE BEST OF DIGITAL AND PHYSICAL

ROBERT E. SIEGEL

New York   Chicago   San Francisco   Athens   London   Madrid
Mexico City   Milan   New Delhi   Singapore   Sydney   Toronto

1 2 3 4 5 6 7 8 9   LCR   26 25 24 23 22 21

ISBN   978-1-264-25777-5
MHID   1-264-25777-5

e-ISBN   978-1-264-25778-2
e-MHID   1-264-25778-3

Library of Congress Cataloging-in-Publication Data

Names: Siegel, Robert E., author.
Title: The brains and brawn company : how leading organizations blend the best of
    digital and physical / Robert Siegel.
Description: New York : McGraw Hill Education, [2021] | Includes bibliographical
    references.
Identifiers: LCCN 2021011619 (print) | LCCN 2021011620 (ebook) |
    ISBN 9781264257775 (hardback) | ISBN 9781264257782 (ebook)
Subjects: LCSH: Strategic planning. | Information technology—Management. |
    Industrial management. | Success in business.
Classification: LCC HD30.28 .S4338 2021 (print) | LCC HD30.28 (ebook) |
    DDC 658.4/012—dc23
LC record available at https://lccn.loc.gov/2021011619
LC ebook record available at https://lccn.loc.gov/2021011620

Dedicated to Lil' Deb-Deb,
Lolly Bear, Oovan, and Süm

CONTENTS

PART IV

THE POWER OF SYSTEMS LEADERSHIP

PART I
THE BIG IDEA

The incessant drumbeat that digitization is driving global corporate transformation often feels overdone. But the worldwide COVID-19 pandemic showed that while digitization remains important, companies that can bridge the digital and physical domains will have an advantage in coming years.

In Part I of this book I'll set up the Brains and Brawn framework, and I will introduce the 10 attributes required for successful companies to lead in the new world order. Then I'll walk through a detailed analysis of both a famous mobility company and also an upstart that is attempting to disrupt the healthcare industry. I'll analyze how each is performing as they navigate the blending of physical and digital skill sets.

CHAPTER 1

TODAY'S TRUE COMPETITIVE ADVANTAGE

A re you tired of hearing that digital transformation is the most important issue facing companies today? Me, too. Sometimes, while someone is going on and on about it in my classroom at the Stanford Graduate School of Business, or in a pitch meeting at my Silicon Valley venture capital firm, I feel like banging my head against the wall.

Don't get me wrong—of course, digitization is a massive and massively important trend. Leaders in every industry need to wrestle with it. But despite fervent preaching from the Silicon Valley faithful, it's not the only kind of competency that matters. The less flashy, more grounded aspects of business, such as logistics and manufacturing, are still crucial to the success of any company, large or small. Amid the insistent drumbeat of digital transformation, those traditional, old-fashioned competencies are easily overlooked and underappreciated.

A cultural gulf has opened up between the realms I call brains and brawn. Others may call this dichotomy digital versus physical, the disruptor mindset versus the incumbent mindset, start-up world versus the Fortune 500, or tech culture versus industrial culture. Whatever terms you prefer, it's time to bridge the gulf and reframe the dichotomy.

The sheer luminescence of digital breakthroughs exerts such a strong hold on our imaginations that many of us can't even relate to companies that actually make stuff or move stuff around. Would most young, ambitious leaders rather take a job at Google or Ford? At Twitter or John Deere? At Netflix or Home Depot? Do we even have to ask?

This way of looking at the world is misguided. You can't assume that the legacy giants are doomed. Some so-called dinosaurs will fail, of course, but others will thrive by blending their existing skills at making and moving products with brainy new competencies unleashed by digital technology. Likewise, some of the digital disruptors will win, but certainly not all of them.

Today's true competitive advantage, for your career or your entire organization, is understanding how digital and physical excellence can reinforce each other, achieving more in coordination than either kind of mastery can in isolation. The idea that these worlds are in fundamental conflict is dangerous and shortsighted. Instead, think of brains and brawn as the business version of chocolate and peanut butter, or Lennon and McCartney: valuable individually, but infinitely better together. Building that powerful partnership is the most important issue facing companies today.

Hearing from the Horses' Mouths

I reached this conclusion after some surprising observations while wearing my two hats, as an academic and a venture capitalist.

First came a series of surprises during one of my Stanford courses, The Industrialist's Dilemma, which I've co-taught since 2016 with Max Wessel, the chief learning officer of enterprise software giant SAP, and Aaron Levie, the CEO of cloud company Box. When we launched the course, we planned to invite top executives from tech companies to share their insights on how they were rewriting the traditional rules of business. We also wanted some forward-thinking leaders of incumbent firms that were embracing digital transformation. And we wanted a couple of CEOs from old-line industrial firms that were struggling to respond to disruption.

But that's not how things played out. Over the past six years, I've been surprised again and again by the 70-plus distinguished speakers who've spoken to our The Industrialist's Dilemma class, or to the Systems Leadership class that I co-teach with former General Electric CEO Jeff Immelt. On the incumbent/Fortune 500 side, these speakers have included Home Depot CEO Craig Menear, Johnson & Johnson CEO Alex Gorsky, former Caterpillar Group President Rob Charter, AB InBev Chief Disruptive

Growth Officer Pedro Earp, GlaxoSmithKline CEO Emma Walmsley, and former AT&T CEO Randall Stephenson. On the disruptor/start-up side, we've hosted 23andMe CEO Anne Wojcicki, Lyft CEO Logan Green, Stripe CEO Patrick Collison, and former Google Nest CEO Tony Fadell, among many others.

Over and over, these leaders confounded my assumptions about which companies are set up for future success and which are in serious trouble. While the disruptors continue to innovate, many established companies are finding creative and aggressive ways to counter them. These heavyweights are turning their size and resources, historical market presence, and institutional knowledge from surviving many boom-and-bust cycles into competitive advantages. Yet few people in the wider business community are aware of how they're doing it.

My second key observation grew out of my work as a partner at XSeed Capital and as a venture partner at Piva Ventures, both of which are enthusiastic flag-wavers for disruption. I've noticed that many of the tech companies we work with, while bursting with innovation, are unable or unwilling to navigate the tedious steps that lead to long-term customer relationships. Many also struggle to build systematic management processes. As a result, their performance is often wildly inconsistent. I realized that these brainy disruptors are missing some of the key competencies that drive consistent long-run profits—and that the best way they could master those brawny skills was by studying the very incumbents they were trying to destroy.

Then very suddenly, these trends became personal.

Lessons from Lockdown

On the evening of Friday, March 6, 2020, I was having a group dinner with seven of my MBA students when we saw a news alert: due to the COVID-19 pandemic, Stanford University would be moving all instruction online as of Monday. For the rest of the academic year, all of my classroom skills, honed over 20 years of practice, would be irrelevant. I'd have to figure out how to hold the attention of up to 100 students at a time via Zoom and try to approximate their classroom experience.

Traditional teaching requires a deeply physical set of skills. You learn to read the room by looking into the eyes of your students, decoding which ones are engaged, bored, or completely lost. You also learn how to read body language—who's slouching, who's leaning forward—and the auditory clues of laughing or groaning, depending on how terrible my jokes are that day. But now my only feedback was 100 tiny faces on a monitor that I couldn't see clearly while looking into a camera. And they were on mute, except for a tiny icon of a blue hand that would light up when someone wanted to ask a question or respond to one of my prompts.

This was a shock not just to me but to our entire faculty, as it was to teachers at every level worldwide. We all had to adapt, far more quickly and completely than any of us were comfortable with. We had no choice.

After grinding it out for a week, I was grateful to have a two-week break without classes before the next quarter would begin. I devoted that time to improving my virtual game. I invested in a bigger computer monitor, a higher-quality camera, and backup internet connections in case one went down during a class. I huddled with my teaching assistants about how we could keep the energy levels up and encourage more participation. I rearranged my home office so I could stand up and roam around a bit without stepping out of camera range. I redecorated to turn the space into a Stanford-themed studio. I prepped our upcoming guest speakers on how to make the most of their video sessions.

As our classroom experiences improved during the following quarter, I had an epiphany: the digital teaching skills that my colleagues and I were learning would come in handy for the rest of our careers, not merely during the pandemic. I also ran several remote sessions for global companies based in South America, Europe, Southeast Asia, and the Middle East. These experiences convinced me that education will never fully return to the days of one person standing in front of a lecture hall. Video and communication technology will continue to improve, and people will keep finding creative new ways to apply them. Within a few years, teaching will probably be seen as a hybrid profession, requiring the ability to hold attention and communicate effectively both in a classroom and over video.

Every week—sometimes every *day*—I saw a new phase in the metamorphosis of my field. I watched a transformation blending the best aspects of digital and physical. And as my frustrations at adapting to the new world gave way to excitement over its possibilities, I realized that my own experience was an "up close and personal" lesson in exactly what I'd been teaching. I had joined the hundreds of companies and organizations that were rewriting the traditional rules and embracing digital transformation.

The Best of Both Worlds

What's true for teaching is increasingly true for every industry: nothing is exclusively digital or physical anymore. Brainy fields like biotech, video games, and software depend in part on their mastery of channel partnerships, supply chains, customer service, and quality control. Brawny fields like scrap metal recycling, physical retail, and construction now have to process and act on mountains of data and coordinate complicated machinery via artificial intelligence and cloud computing.

At the individual level, someone with a traditionally brainy job, like a product manager for Apple's AirPods, needs a strong grasp of the details of global manufacturing and distribution. And someone with a traditionally brawny job, like a factory floor supervisor at General Motors, now needs the skills to handle more sophisticated technology than a NASA engineer was given a few decades ago.

At the organizational level, similarly, success increasingly demands the best of both worlds: the speed, nimbleness, and risk tolerance that are the hallmark of digital start-ups, and the attention to systems, best practices, and long-term customer relationships that are more natural to large incumbents.

If you're still not convinced that we're living in a brains *and* brawn world, consider this question: What's the most powerful, most disruptive, most dangerous company on the planet? The only one that can cause sheer terror among the incumbents of *any* sector (healthcare? banking? groceries? television?) merely by considering entering it? It's Amazon, of course—which happens to be the only company with nearly perfect mastery of all 10 of the Brains and Brawn competencies that I'll explore more deeply in the chapters ahead.

The Brains and Brawn Basics

The Brains and Brawn framework analyzes a company's core capabilities along 10 attributes—5 each for the digital and physical worlds. Here's a quick preview of the five competencies on the brainy side.

The Left Hemisphere: Using Analytics

With big data increasingly available for all kinds of products and services, every company needs a strategy to use all this information to serve customers better, improve their offerings, and control costs. I'm calling this capability the left hemisphere, after the brain's center of logical thinking.

The featured example is mammoth financial services provider Charles Schwab. With over $7 trillion in assets under management, Schwab has access to a staggering amount and variety of customer data. It has found smart ways to draw insights from all that data, while also taking a cautious, values-driven approach to protecting privacy and promoting customer trust.

The Right Hemisphere: Harnessing Creativity

As companies grow, they usually develop systems and processes that enable efficient scaling and operational excellence. Unfortunately, these systems often make it harder to innovate consistently. But some growing companies keep finding creative ways, large and small, to meet customer needs and anticipate new trends. The right hemisphere is shorthand for harnessing this kind of creativity in developing new business models along with new products.

The featured example is Align Technology, the inventor of Invisalign, a method for straightening teeth using clear plastic aligners instead of traditional braces. Align's key innovation was combining digital imaging with 3D printing to customize removable, unobtrusive, easy-to-wear aligners. Just as important, Align found an innovative business model by partnering with dentists as well as orthodontists—a previously untapped way to reach many more potential customers.

The Amygdala: Tapping the Power of Empathy

Empathy is symbolized by the amygdala, the seat of emotional processing. A management team with a strong amygdala will be good at understanding and connecting authentically with customers, employees, and outside partners alike.

The featured example is Kaiser Permanente, the managed care titan that was led brilliantly by CEO Bernard Tyson until his death in November 2019. While the managed care industry is usually depicted as inflexible and cold, Tyson always projected warmth and generosity. He inspired employees to focus on empathy for patients, reminding them that they were really selling health, not healthcare. Kaiser uses technology to study what its doctors and nurses really need and aligns incentives for all of its stakeholders to deliver the best possible care.

The Prefrontal Cortex: Managing Risk

The prefrontal cortex is the part of the brain that evaluates and makes decisions about risks. Humans are naturally risk averse because our hunter-gatherer ancestors lived in a world full of mysterious dangers, where any novelty might reveal a new threat. But for many companies today, especially the biggest, risk aversion is a serious disadvantage. Incentives like promotions and raises tend to reward those who support the status quo, instead of doing something bold but uncertain.

The featured example is AB InBev, the world's largest producer of alcoholic beverages. When CEO Carlos Brito realized that the company had become too risk averse, he took the unusual step of appointing a chief disruptive growth officer—a rising star named Pedro Earp. Interestingly, Earp's metric of success was how fast he could make his own job obsolete, by spreading a culture of risk-taking across AB InBev.

The Inner Ear: Balancing Ownership and Partnership

Every company faces a fundamental strategic question: Which functions should it own and manage directly, and which should it pay outsiders to manage? The rise of mobile computing, the cloud, data analytics, and AI have made it impossible for any company to provide all parts of a technical solution. Owning more aspects of the technology stack can increase customer intimacy, while owning fewer makes it easier to master the ones that matter most. My metaphor for this balancing challenge is the inner ear, which controls our ability to balance. (Technically the inner ear is outside the brain, but please cut me some slack.)

The featured example is Instacart, the gig-economy start-up that has jumped into the lead in home delivery of groceries. Under the savvy leadership of founder Apoorva Mehta, it has developed a sophisticated approach to balancing its many partnerships, especially with the supermarket chains that can make or break the quality of Instacart's offerings. The company has had to keep recovering its balance in the face of repeated disruptions, such as Amazon's acquisition of Whole Foods (which removed a key Instacart partner) and the sudden, exponential surge in home delivery orders during the coronavirus pandemic.

Now here's a preview of the five competencies on the brawny side.

The Spine: Logistics

Conventional wisdom holds that being an expert in logistics, supply chains, and getting the right things to the right places at the right times will never get you on the cover of *Fortune*—unless you're Tim Cook and your talents get you promoted to CEO of Apple. But a strong spine is essential to delivering great experiences to customers, even in sectors that are rapidly going digital.

This chapter features three major retail chains—Best Buy, Home Depot, and Target—that have defied the so-called retail apocalypse by adding brains to their brawn. All strengthened their spines by blending the best aspects of physical retail with innovative new approaches to e-commerce. These supposed dinosaurs each have far-sighted leadership teams that have leveraged superior logistics to deliver flexible and satisfying customer experiences, unmatchable by Amazon or other rivals.

Hands: The Craft of Making Things

During the wave of globalization that accelerated in the 1990s, many manufacturing companies moved their factories to lower-cost parts of the world, especially Southeast Asia and Mexico. But with the rise of new technologies such as additive manufacturing, robot assembly lines, and 3D printing, it's now possible to design and make things cost-effectively in a high-wage country like the United States. Smart companies are improving their hands by finding innovative ways to enable high-volume yet affordable production.

The featured example is Desktop Metal, a Massachusetts company that uses 3D printing technology to help its customers make their own high-quality metal parts, from prototyping through mass production. Desktop Metal works closely with its customers to produce customized solutions. It builds long-term relationships as a trusted partner whose services are worth a premium price.

Muscles: Leveraging Size and Scale

Economies of scale are still a huge advantage, but in some ways it's harder than ever to manage a sprawling organization across regions, countries, or continents. It takes strong and agile muscles to act "glocally"—making the most of both global scale and local expertise in challenging, distinct markets.

The featured example is Michelin, a 130-year-old tire manufacturer that operates in 175 countries with 130,000 employees. Michelin benefits from the global scale of its manufacturing and engineering while empowering its local managers to customize offerings for their regions. For instance, its Chinese tires have to be much less expensive to produce than those in Europe and North America, or else Michelin would be priced out of the Chinese market.

Hand-Eye Coordination: Managing Ecosystems

A business ecosystem is an interconnected group of organizations that align for their mutual interests. The relationships among suppliers, channel partners, investors, regulators, and competing firms are frequently in flux, requiring a juggling act to address every ecosystem member's competing needs. Like any juggling act, doing it well requires great hand-eye coordination.

Managing in a fluid and uncertain environment raises a host of questions for leaders. When should you be tough and assertive in attempting to shape the ecosystem? When should you hang back and let others take the lead in how your industry evolves? What can you do if you have a very different vision for the future of your market compared to your channel partners or key competitors?

The featured example is Google's Android division, which makes the operating systems that power about four out of five of the world's smartphones and tablets. While Android is a unique business within a unique industry, its success at managing its complex ecosystem offers powerful lessons for the rest of us.

Stamina: Surviving for the Long Run

Longevity is the ultimate challenge for any business, and no short-term success can guarantee it. It takes stamina to manage an organization's reputation and brand through both good times and bad.

The featured example is Johnson & Johnson, which has evolved continuously since its founding in 1886. Johnson & Johnson still relies on its famous Credo, written by chairman Robert Wood Johnson in 1943, to make decisions in line with its core values. It sees new technology as a tool, never a panacea, as it fights to stay competitive across a huge range of markets—from talcum powder to Tylenol to experimental cancer treatments. The company is now facing some daunting legal and public relations challenges that will further test its stamina.

The Systems Leader: Driving Constant Progress on Brains *and* Brawn

The final chapter of this book explores what I call Systems Leadership—the art of maximizing both the brains and the brawn of an organization.

Traditionally, executives rose to senior management through expertise in a particular function, such as operations, marketing, engineering, sales, or finance. As long as they had teammates who could fill in the blanks in their knowledge, they could succeed while seeing the company and its ecosystem from a limited perspective. But today's leaders need a much broader range of expertise and skills, including the ability to focus on apparent contradictions at the same time: physical and digital, the big picture and essential details, generic solutions that can scale horizontally and customized solutions that can win deep customer loyalty. Systems leaders require the IQ to understand the technical stack as well as the EQ to build effective teams and inspire them to new heights. They hit their financial targets this year while driving changes that may not pay off for five years.

Two additional Systems Leaders are profiled in this last chapter, among them Katrina Lake, the founder and executive chairperson of online clothing retailer Stitch Fix. She has mastered all the major aspects of her company, including fashion, big data, creative branding, and workplace culture. Lake is the driving force behind innovations like detailed questions at checkout ("Why did you *not* purchase that item?") and an HR obsession with both culture fit and "culture add." She also exemplifies a willingness to run toward disruption, even when you might be tempted to run the other way.

Brains + Brawn = Optimism

These are tough times for all kinds of businesses, between the economic turmoil caused by the coronavirus pandemic, ever-increasing global competition, and never-ending technological changes. But my research for this book has reinforced my natural impulse toward optimism. It's simply not true that every old, established company will end up like Blockbuster Video, disrupted and destroyed by a digital start-up. Nor is it true that every hot start-up will end up like WeWork, overextended and struggling with an unclear path to sustainable profitability.

Instead, the door is open for traditionally brawny companies to vastly improve their brainy competencies, while brainy companies boost their brawny competencies. I hope that the chapters ahead will convince you that no person or organization need be trapped in an old mindset. At any level—as individuals, teams, departments, companies, or entire industries—there are opportunities to bridge the gap between brains and brawn, creating a durable competitive advantage.

CHAPTER 2

TWO ATTEMPTS AT RADICAL TRANSFORMATION

We talked about what would happen if you could get the world's DNA. And he said it would change the world.

—Anne Wojcicki, CEO of 23andMe

The Brains and Brawn framework enables us to evaluate a company along 10 competencies that usually don't get as much attention as traditional metrics. To show how this process works, let's dive into two companies that are facing make-or-break inflection points. One is huge, world famous, widely acclaimed for its brawny mastery, and now urgently trying to compete with brainy disruptors. The other is a brainy Silicon Valley start-up that's trying to add the brawny competencies it needs to achieve long-term profitability. Both are attempting to find the happy balance of brains and brawn, although they are approaching that point from opposite directions.

First is Daimler, an automotive icon that has been selling cars since 1885. Its 300,000 employees are committed to the ongoing excellence of one of the world's most prestigious brands, Mercedes-Benz. Daimler sold more than 3.3 million vehicles worldwide in 2019, but the next few years will be extremely challenging, due to multiple, simultaneous upheavals in the global auto industry. Electric cars are a huge battleground, as flashy competitors like Tesla grab market share. Ride-sharing companies like Uber, Lyft, and DiDi will continue to reduce total demand from individual consumers. China is a huge market, but often maddeningly difficult to navigate. And the race is on to produce autonomous vehicles that are both safe and affordable. With so many threats and so much at stake, Daimler is strategizing its priorities, investing billions in research and development (R&D) and acquisitions, and retooling its culture to stay competitive.

Then I'll evaluate 23andMe, which has sold home DNA testing kits to 12 million people since 2006, yet still has fewer than 700 employees. After compiling an enormously valuable database of human genomes, the company is betting its future on turning all that information into blockbuster new drugs. Its CEO, Anne Wojcicki, is attempting nothing less than a reinvention of the healthcare industry, in partnership with brawny, established players like GlaxoSmithKline. But if 23andMe's drug development initiative fails, and if DNA home testing turns out to be just a fad, it could easily burn through its capital and go out of business.

After describing the challenges each company is facing as well as their responses, I assign a 0-to-10 score for each of the 10 benchmarks of the Brains and Brawn framework. The total score summarizes how well the company is blending digital and physical competencies, and provides a clear indication of how competitive it might be in the coming years.

Daimler: Protecting and Extending a Legacy

In 2017 I went to Stuttgart to interview several senior executives at Daimler, including Wilko Stark, the CEO of a recently formed business unit called CASE—an acronym for *connected, autonomous, shared, electric*. Reporting directly to then-Daimler Chairman Dieter Zetsche, Stark was responsible for leading the company into a future that would be far less friendly to vehicles with internal combustion engines, its core competency.[1]

Stark was reminded of the urgency of his mission every time he looked through his window. His office building in Stuttgart was surrounded by several sprawling Daimler factories—nice-looking, eco-friendly factories with greenery planted on their roofs. These factories never allowed him to forget the 300,000 workers who depended on CASE's success.

Another powerful symbol nearby was the Mercedes-Benz Museum, the leading tourist attraction in Stuttgart. This beautiful building, shaped like a spiral with nine levels, allows visitors to marvel at more than 160 classic cars from the company's 135-year history, starting with those built by pioneers Carl Benz and Gottlieb Daimler.[2] The museum isn't just about corporate pride; it's a statement of German national pride. The auto industry contributes about 5 percent to German GDP and even more to the country's sense of its place in the world. To the German people, a future without great car companies like Daimler, BMW, Audi, and Volkswagen is literally unthinkable.

Stark never expressed any fear that Daimler might fail, but he was honest enough not to downplay the extreme challenges it faces—not merely from its traditional competitors in Europe, Japan, Korea, and the United States, but new threats that seemed to be coming from all directions at once.

Before CASE launched in 2016, Daimler had been growing steadily for several years and had just experienced its all-time best financial results. It seemed like a good time to establish a separate unit with several hundred employees, most of them younger than the average age of a Daimler employee, and an independent budget of $10 billion. Stark had the full support of top management to craft a multiyear strategy to build and acquire whatever resources were necessary to compete on all fronts. As an added challenge, CASE was urged to avoid (as much as possible) cannibalizing the profits generated by the core business. Traditional vehicles weren't going to vanish anytime soon, and they were still the key to Daimler's profitability.

Let's examine how this tension between the present and the future played out with each major challenge, as Stark sought to combine Daimler's well-established brawn with its newly expanding brains.

Electric Vehicles

The auto industry has been working toward electric vehicles (EVs) for about two decades. In 2004, Tesla raised its first $7.5 million in venture capital. Just a year prior, General Motors discontinued production of the EV1, its failed first attempt at a mass-market electric vehicle. A GM spokesman explained that electric cars were not "a viable business proposition for GM to pursue long term."[3]

Three years later, Tesla launched the Roadster, the first EV to drive more than 200 miles per charge, and it introduced the first car based on lithium-ion battery cells. By 2017, with its post-IPO stock price soaring after the launch of several more models, Tesla had become the global leader in electric cars. Analysts projected a total EV market of 530 million vehicles by 2040, surpassing the number of traditional vehicles. Even sooner, by 2025, electric cars were expected to match the cost-effectiveness of internal combustion cars.[4] Every major automaker in the world would have to join the EV boom, ready or not.

Daimler's first stab at producing an electric car started in 2010, when it established a joint venture with BYD Auto in China, but it sold only about 4,000 EVs per year until 2016. Stark's new goal was to launch at least 10 electric models by 2022 and have 15 to 25 percent of its global sales be electric by the end of 2025. Daimler budgeted more than $11 billion to develop electric versions of every model, with an integrated ecosystem that would include batteries, recycling programs, and charging stations. Daimler also made plans to electrify its vans, trucks, and buses.

The key hurdle would be finding ways to reduce production costs enough to make EVs affordable to a broad market. This would include reorganizing factories to enable production of both combustion cars and electric cars on the same line—expensive investments that would take a few years to pay off. A second strategy involved proprietary production of lithium-ion batteries. A new 50-acre, carbon-neutral facility would be built in Kamenz, Germany, quadrupling Daimler's capacity.

The company also announced a $1 billion investment to expand its manufacturing plant in Tuscaloosa, Alabama, so it could start making electric SUVs, as well as building a new battery factory nearby. Elon Musk mocked the announcement on Twitter: "That's not a lot of money for a giant like Daimler/Mercedes. Wish they'd do more. Off by a zero."[5]

Daimler's Twitter account responded the next day: "You're absolutely right @elonmusk. Here's the missing zero: Investing >$10bn in nxt gen EVs & >$1bn in battery prod." [6]

Autonomous Vehicles

A second key trend is the development of self-driving cars, as technologies such as GPS, positioning sensors, and artificial intelligence became mature enough to bring this sci-fi premise within reach. But so far, doubts remained about high costs, unenthusiastic consumers, tough regulators, and especially safety. In May 2016, a Tesla driver died while using his car's Autopilot feature. And in March 2018, a self-driving Uber car struck and killed a pedestrian without even slowing down. Despite these hurdles, optimists predict that the benefits of autonomous cars—fewer traffic collisions due to human errors, increased quality of life for passengers, and reduced traffic congestion due to being able to gradually raise speed limits—make their eventual adoption inevitable.

Tesla announced in October 2016 that all of its future cars would be equipped with "the hardware needed for full self-driving capability at a safety level substantially greater than that of a human driver."[7] Also in the chase were traditional automakers (BMW, Audi, Fiat Chrysler, Ford), tech giants

(Apple, Intel, Baidu, Uber), and new start-ups (Waymo, nuTonomy, Zoox, Drive.ai). Waymo, which became an independent subsidiary of Alphabet (Google's parent company) in December 2016, recorded over three million self-driven miles in its first year. GM, which acquired Cruise Automation in 2016 to develop its own autonomous car, announced in 2017 that it had finalized "the first production design of a self-driving car that can be built at massive scale."[8]

As early as August 2013, a Mercedes S500 Intelligent Drive car drove itself more than 100 kilometers between Mannheim and Pforzheim, the first successful long-distance drive of an autonomous car. Stark envisioned future autonomous vehicles that would not only self-drive, but also manage their own refueling and even car washing. He expected Daimler to have fully operational autonomous cars by late 2021, to be introduced first in the ride-sharing industry. The company announced a partnership with Uber to develop a network of autonomous Uber cars. This arrangement followed similar moves in 2016 by GM, which partnered with Lyft, and by Ford, which acquired the ride-sharing start-up Chariot.

Another piece in the autonomous driving puzzle was access to mapping data and location services. Daimler invested in HERE, a company that had begun as a division of Nokia that now designed wireless mapping systems. Gaining independence from mainstream map providers was crucial so that Daimler wouldn't be at the mercy of Google Maps or a similar service.

Ride-Sharing

Meanwhile, ride-sharing companies like Uber and Lyft were starting to reduce global demand for individual car ownership. In cities like San Francisco, where Uber launched in 2009, it made less and less economic sense to buy and maintain your own car. By 2017, Uber was operating in 630 cities worldwide and serving 40 million customers per month. The success of its ride-sharing model spawned new competitors like Lyft and Sidecar in the United States, DiDi Chuxing in China, and 99 Taxis in Brazil. As fewer and fewer people want the hassles of car ownership, automakers need ways to make up for lost revenue.

As part of its response, Daimler began to buy and invest in enterprises that offered ride-hailing, transportation booking, delivery services, and short-term rentals. The first such investment was in car2go, a start-up that offered flexible car rentals for urban areas, making it easy to prebook via smartphone for any length of rental. As of 2017, car2go was the largest and fastest-growing car-sharing platform in the world, with over 2.5 million members and 14,000 vehicles.[9]

Moovel, another wholly owned subsidiary of Daimler, allowed users to compare and book rides with various car-sharing and bike-sharing apps. As of 2017, Moovel had 3.4 million users worldwide. Daimler also bought mytaxi, a successful German start-up that connected taxi drivers and riders via a smartphone app. Mytaxi merged with London-based Hailo in 2016, with Daimler retaining 69 percent of the combined entity. When Uber lost its license to operate in London in mid-2017, mytaxi responded aggressively by announcing 50 percent off fares.[10] CASE executives anticipated additional investments in shared mobility.

Connectivity

Drivers worldwide now want to use their smartphones or similar technology in their cars, using apps to check fuel levels remotely and access services like Spotify, Waze, and Google Maps on the dashboard. This demand for all-around connectivity requires advanced integration with a car's telematics. If car companies don't offer ways to satisfy these customer demands, tech giants like Apple are happy to step in.

The CASE team had three options to develop connectivity. The first, adopted by many carmakers, was connecting the driver's smartphone to a dashboard screen using a system like Apple's CarPlay. The second would be to license a third party's software to control an interface. The most ambitious option would be for Daimler to develop its own, proprietary operating system and interface. They picked the third alternative, developing the "Mercedes me" system that would be exclusive to Mercedes-Benz cars. By controlling the design of the interface, the CASE team believed it could offer a more complete and sophisticated experience. Mercedes me could also become a platform for additional premium services that might be designed in the future.

Mercedes me launched in 2017, with software that could locate parking spaces, lock and unlock the car, or visualize fuel and systems data remotely from a smartphone, among other features. Through its Concierge Services, the system could suggest restaurants and book tickets for events via audio commands. It also came equipped for "Car-to-X communication," an innovation that would eventually let cars from all manufacturers alert each other via radio signals to avoid accidents and traffic jams. As the Mercedes website put it: "What would it be like if you could see past the next bend in the road to the bend after and even farther? You could adjust your driving behavior and defuse dangerous situations."[11] It's an exciting sci-fi vision, but still not a reality as of 2021.

China

With almost 26 million vehicles sold in 2019, China is the largest car market on the planet.[12] It also is the world's largest car-producing country, making almost 23 percent of all cars produced globally in 2019. More than 1.2 million EVs were sold in China in that year, which was 57 percent of total global EV sales—more than in the United States and Europe combined.[13,14]

The Chinese government was determined to leapfrog the global auto industry on EVs, a new playing field where long-established manufacturers wouldn't necessarily have an advantage. Sustainability was another reason for focusing on EVs; with 1.3 billion people, rising per capita income, and air pollution problems, China would face disaster if it kept building internal combustion engines. The question for Daimler was how to get a substantial share of this huge, rapidly growing, yet uniquely challenging market. One executive described China as "a market of 1.4 billion . . . whose language we didn't speak, whose culture we didn't understand, whose customers are much younger than U.S. or European customers, and with whose historical, social, and commercial context we were unfamiliar."[15]

Daimler also wasn't used to dealing with a government that exerted so much control over its economy and industry. China was investing significantly in EVs by way of various subsidies, while placing strict guidelines on non-Chinese manufacturers, such as requiring them to form joint ventures with local companies to do business in China. Worse, the rules sometimes changed unexpectedly, as one Daimler executive reported: "First, we developed a hybrid vehicle three years ago, with a 30-kilometer range. When we finished the car, they said, 'To get an incentive, you have to do a 50-kilometer range.' Now we have a 50-kilometer range hybrid vehicle and they say, 'Fine, but not with a Korean battery cell. You have to use a Chinese battery cell.'"[16]

Even more troubling, Daimler had to worry about defending its intellectual property in a country known for very lax protection of IP. There was no way to know what its Chinese joint venture partners might do with Daimler's technical specs, but also no way to do business in China without those partners. As one executive put it, "If you're trying to build a wall around your IP, it's not going to work long-term. The only recipe that works is to develop innovations much faster."[17]

Culture and Talent

Beyond all these technical and financial challenges, Daimler also faced a cultural crossroads. The company's obsession with excellence and precision, which had helped it lead the industry for more than a century, might now hinder its reinvention. How could 300,000 Daimler employees learn to embrace dramatic changes while also preserving their renowned quality control standards?

The CASE team sought out younger employees more in tune with the new trends, but finding and hiring them wasn't easy. As one executive told me privately, "We build great cars, but Elon Musk is talking about going to Mars! If you were a brilliant young engineer, who would you rather work for?" For some specialized positions in the CASE initiatives, Daimler launched a global search effort, hiring from as far away as India, the United States, Israel, and Singapore.

Another dilemma was dealing with the restrictions of Germany's protective labor laws as well as pressure from its powerful labor unions. In June 2017, 19,000 workers at the Untertürkheim plant protested against the decision to establish the new battery factory in Kamenz, instead of making it a subdivision of their existing plant. After the union disrupted production of two Mercedes models at Untertürkheim, Daimler gave in and agreed to set up another battery factory there.[18] This would surely not be the last labor dispute triggered by the CASE initiatives.

Dealerships

How would all these changes affect the traditional sales model of the auto industry, built around powerful, independent dealerships? Dealers worried that electric cars would cut their after-sales revenues by an estimated 20 percent, due to reduced maintenance requirements.

Stark's strategy to maintain peace in the dealer network relied on Daimler's ability to keep growing steadily. He explained, "We are currently growing by 10 percent per year on a global basis, and therefore, as long as we do not build up additional dealer network, the revenue stream is actually going up for our dealers."[19] Despite Tesla's successful direct sales model and a few similar experiments around the world, Daimler remained convinced that most customers still want to experience a car in person before buying it, so dealerships won't be extinct anytime soon.

Daimler's Future

Daimler knew how to compete with its traditional rivals around the world, but Tesla posed a unique set of challenges. Its customers seemed to forgive any mistakes, which gave Tesla the freedom to take big risks—unlike Daimler, which had to protect its brand and reputation at all costs. Tesla's investors seemed infinitely patient as it slowly approached profitability;

Daimler's investors would punish any quarterly underperformance. And while Daimler had to focus on both traditional and EVs, Tesla had no distractions from its goal of dominating the EV market.

Meanwhile, Daimler also had to worry about tech powerhouses that had no previous place in the auto industry. Waymo and Baidu were dedicating massive investments to autonomous cars, while Apple and Alphabet were competing in connectivity software. These giants could afford to throw 10 times as many engineers at any problem as Daimler could.

To Stark, the best response was to make sure Daimler stayed number one in its core mission: designing and manufacturing great cars. Yet he also feared that Daimler was at risk of becoming the equivalent of Chinese electronics manufacturer Foxconn, which had very little market power and much lower profit margins than its customers such as Apple, because Foxconn offered low-value, commodity-like hardware manufacturing services. Daimler had to avoid becoming merely the fulfillment partner for other people's cool new technologies.

As 2021 dawned Daimler's challenges did not seem to be getting any easier. Amazon acquired Silicon Valley autonomous vehicle company Zoox in 2020 for $1.2 billion, and Apple was reported to be in talks with major car manufacturers in Asia as part of its own automotive efforts.[20, 21] Even Microsoft was increasingly active in providing cloud services to many global car companies.[22] The competitive landscape for Daimler was becoming more complex to navigate.

Evaluating Daimler

How will the company manage all of these simultaneous changes while still preserving its traditions of manufacturing excellence and industry leadership? It's too soon to know for sure, especially since the automotive sector greatly depends on the health of the global economy and was badly hurt by the recession of 2020. But based on its fundamentals, not the economy, here's how I evaluate Daimler using the 10 benchmarks of the Brains and Brawn framework:

The Left Hemisphere: Analytics = 5
Daimler is getting better at mastering customer data. But Tesla already has every car it sells sending usage data back to the company every night, and it fixes software bugs remotely via wireless upgrades. Daimler is barely halfway there.

The Right Hemisphere: Creativity = 6
Daimler is working hard, investing, and experimenting in many kinds of innovation, but not yet dominating.

The Amygdala: Empathy = 4
Daimler is still a fact-driven company that doesn't put a high priority on empathy for outsiders. But it's getting better at working with partners who come from very different backgrounds and perspectives, as in China.

The Prefrontal Cortex: Risk-Taking = 5
Daimler is taking significantly more risks than ever before, but I'm not convinced that those risks are aggressive enough or fast enough.

The Inner Ear: Balancing Ownership and Partnership = 5
Daimler is trying to own many kinds of tech, perhaps too many. For instance, it may have made a mistake building a proprietary connectivity platform, now that customers seem to prefer connecting to their cars via their smartphones. To quote Max Wessel of SAP, who co-teaches with me at Stanford, "If your strategy is to do everything, you don't have a strategy."

Total Brain Score = 25/50

The Spine: Logistics = 9
Shipping cars around the world is one of Daimler's core competencies. They have it down to a science.

Hands: Making Things = 9
As we've seen, they refuse to cut corners or compromise on excellence in production.

Muscles: Leveraging Scale = 9
They also excel at adapting their products for major countries on every continent.

Hand-Eye Coordination: Managing Ecosystems = 5
Daimler is still not great at finessing relationships outside the company and participating in a broader ecosystem of partners.

Stamina: Surviving for the Long Run = 8
Historically, Daimler has been outstanding at this, but it's unclear how well their reputation and brand will survive the next decade.

Total Brawn Score = 40/50

Combined Score = 65/100

23andMe: From DNA Tests to World-Changing Drugs

Now let's dive into a very different company that's also facing a make-or-break inflection point.

I interviewed Anne Wojcicki, CEO of 23andMe, in her Mountain View office in May 2019. It had the classic feel of a brainy start-up, where the CEO works out of a cramped, nondescript fishbowl with two glass walls, in a hallway adjacent to the elevator. No mahogany furniture or luxury trappings in sight.[23]

Since founding the company in 2006, Wojcicki has grown it into one of the world's largest databases of genetic information (close behind their biggest competitor, Ancestry.com). Her original concept of a direct-to-consumer genetic testing kit has scaled to more than 12 million customers, most of whom agreed to allow their ancestry, health history, genotype, and phenotypic information to be used for potentially lifesaving research. Since 2015, 23andMe has been exploring the best ways to turn all this genomic data into powerful new drugs, targeting everything from cancer to asthma. Wojcicki's ambition couldn't be bigger: "using genetic data to revolutionize healthcare."[24]

The company's expansion into drug development has created major new challenges for the leadership team. They have to establish a foothold in developing and launching pharmaceuticals before the boom in home DNA testing ends; demand for their testing kits peaked in 2019. Drugs might mean the difference between a bright and profitable future for 23andMe or a painful demise in a few years.

From Zero to 400,000 in Six Years

After receiving her bachelor's degree in biology from Yale in 1996, Wojcicki worked as a healthcare analyst for a Wall Street hedge fund. But the more she learned about healthcare, the more unsettled she became. Many of the industry's main players—physicians, insurance companies, hospitals—were so mired in structural and financial complexities that they lost sight of the patients they were supposed to serve. After attending a dispiriting health-care conference in Washington, DC, she decided to leave Wall Street and pursue ways to improve the system. As she recalled, "I just realized that so many people are making money on healthcare's inefficiencies, it's not going to change from within."[25]

A few months prior, Wojcicki had met Rockefeller University scientist Markus Stoffel at an investment dinner. He had described a genetics project he was working on to study the causes of a handful of conditions in a small population on the Micronesian island of Kosrae. As she recalls, "He said they had so much data it was overwhelming . . . but also not enough data to make sense of things. We talked about what would happen if you could get the world's DNA. And he said it would change the world."

At the time Wojcicki was dating Sergey Brin, the cofounder of Google. Brin, knowing Wojcicki's interest in DNA, invited her to a meeting he was having with Linda Avey, an executive at Affymetrix and an early pioneer in genetic research tools. (Brin's mother was suffering from Parkinson's disease, and Affymetrix was working on a Parkinson's-related initiative.) Wojcicki and Avey shared a passion for both genetics and consumer empowerment. Together with Avey's former boss, Paul Cusenza, the trio hatched the idea for 23andMe, named for the 23 pairs of chromosomes in human DNA. The company launched with seed funding provided by Google and shipped its first consumer genetic test for $999 in November 2007.

Upon ordering a 23andMe test, customers were asked to fill out a health history, with the option to allow the company to study their de-identified genetic information and survey answers for research purposes. They could also grant permission for 23andMe to recontact them for future research. The customer then received a DNA kit in the mail, provided a saliva sample, and mailed it to a lab for genotyping and analysis. Within four to six weeks, customers could access their health and ancestry results.

People loved these reports, which included information on more than 263 factors, from their status as a carrier of genetic diseases, to likely reactions to various drugs, to ancestral origins. After just six years, 23andMe became the world's leading genetics testing platform, ahead of competitors like deCODE Genetics, Navigenics, Pathway Genomics, and Counsyl Genetics. By late 2013, its database included results from more than 400,000 people, 80 percent of whom had agreed to contribute their health and genetic infor-mation to research.

The firm's scientists began to publish peer-reviewed academic papers, including one that revealed three genetic variations associated with

Parkinson's and another that linked genes related to breast size to increased breast cancer risk. 23andMe also published groundbreaking evidence about more than 180 genetic associations using self-reported medical data, a significant departure from traditional research methods.

The Heavy Hand of the FDA

With all this good news on both the consumer and research fronts, 23andMe was able to raise nearly $90 million to fuel its continued expansion. But then came a major setback in November 2013, when the Food and Drug Administration ordered the company to stop selling its health reports in the United States. The FDA said it had failed to meet the government's requirements for regulatory approval and warned of the public health consequences of inaccurate results.

23andMe relaunched a more limited set of health reports with the FDA's blessing in October 2015, at a price of $199. The test now allowed healthy individuals to be notified if they carried a genetic variant related to just 36 hereditary conditions, including cystic fibrosis, sickle cell anemia, and Tay-Sachs. But the transition to selling a regulated product was costly, as the company was forced to overhaul its compliance and quality control processes. In April 2017, the FDA approved some additional health reports, including testing for risks of Parkinson's and Alzheimer's diseases.[26]

In 2018, the company received two further FDA authorizations, one to report genetic risk factors associated with breast and ovarian cancer in certain populations, and a second to report information about how genetic variants might affect reactions to certain medications. In early 2019, they also received regulatory clearance to warn customers about their genetic risk for a hereditary colorectal cancer syndrome.

But just when they seemed to be in the clear with the FDA, an April 2019 study by diagnostics competitor Invitae claimed that nearly 90 percent of participants who carried BRCA gene mutations would have been missed by 23andMe's BRCA testing. Some breast cancer experts argued that this study meant that customers were unable to grasp the limitations of 23and-Me's tests. Dr. Mary Claire King, who discovered the BRCA1 region of the genome, told the *New York Times*, "The FDA should not have permitted this out-of-date approach to be used for medical purposes. . . . Misleading, falsely reassuring results from their incomplete testing can cost women's lives."[27]

This criticism seems unfair. 23andMe specifically and repeatedly warned customers that it tested for only three specific variants that were prevalent among Ashkenazi Jews, not all known variants. As part of the FDA's review process, the company had been required to submit user comprehension studies, which showed that its customers understood the test's limitations. 23andMe also conducted its own study and found that 44 percent of people carrying one of the three variants the company tested for had no family history of BRCA-related cancer. Another 21 percent did not self-report any Jewish ancestry, meaning that they wouldn't have been caught by traditional guidelines for BRCA screening. The company stressed that any warnings from its tests required follow-up testing by a doctor.

Wojcicki found this controversy frustrating but not surprising. 23andMe was not only disrupting traditional genetics labs; it was also displacing genetic counselors by directly arming consumers with their own health information. It challenged the traditional paternalism of healthcare and the assumption that patients couldn't deal with the stress of receiving their own results, requiring doctors to make sense of the data. Of course, the establishment would push back.

Paths to Profitability

Wojcicki's passion and bluntness made her an outstanding fundraiser. Here's how she recalls starting a mid-2017 pitch to Sequoia Capital, which had declined to join 23andMe's first funding round and instead backed a competitor, Navigenics. She said: "I'm here to tell you about what we're doing, but I'm not here to try to win you over. We are going to win. We have been through a lot and everyone dismissed us. If you are looking for an IPO or a short-term exit, you are not the right match for us. I'm looking for people who genuinely buy into the vision and want to be along for the ride, but it's going to be super bumpy. I can't promise you timelines. I can't promise you exactly how things are going to happen. But I promise you the vision is stable."[28]

To Sequoia, 23andMe's exponential user growth was impressive, but it was Wojcicki's pitch that sealed the deal. They agreed to lead a $250 million investment round. As Sequoia partner Roelof Botha put it, "For me, the founder following their moral authority, their vision and their passion, that's what you want to back." [29]

But venture capital (VC) funding would soon have to be replaced by consistent profitability. The consumer tests alone—a $99 "Ancestry" report (not to be confused with competitor Ancestry.com) and a $199 "Health and Ancestry" report—were still losing money, although margins were improving. The management team had to decide whether to raise prices to turn a profit with the downside of slower growth, or to keep growing the dataset via cheap testing. The answer followed from Wojcicki's original vision: using genetic data to revolutionize the healthcare industry. They had to keep expanding because their database of genotyped individuals—already 8.5 million—would keep getting more valuable to drug researchers as it grew. There were no diminishing returns in scientific impact. So they decided to keep prices low on the home tests while seeking other paths to short-term or medium-term profitability.

One was monetizing their amazingly high user engagement rates, including the statistic that 48 percent of their longest-held customers opened their 23andme profile at least once every 90 days to explore the implications of their genomes. Given this strong user engagement, Wojcicki was convinced that some users would pay for incremental services beyond their initial health and ancestry reports. Her team began exploring subscription options that could add revenue.

Another path was a 2019 partnership with the disease management platform Lark, to integrate genetic information into Lark's health programs. Wojcicki stated in the partnership press release: "Access to your genetic information is really just the beginning—using that information to prevent serious health consequences is the next critical step. Our collaboration with Lark enables 23andMe customers to use their genetic information in a clinically validated program to help them make lifestyle changes to improve their health."[30]

A third promising option was entering the clinical trial recruitment business. Patient recruitment for high-value clinical trials often costs thousands of dollars per eligible patient, lengthening clinical trial timelines and increasing trial costs. Millions of customers in 23andMe's database had consented to email contact, so the company was well-positioned to match them with clinical trials that needed people with specific health conditions.

But ultimately, none of these revenue sources would diminish the make-or-break importance of drug development.

Moving into Brawny Drug Development

Wojcicki had hired Dr. Richard Scheller, former executive vice president of R&D for biotech pioneer Genentech, to explore ways to use the genetic data to discover new drugs. He recruited an experienced team and set up a state-of-the-art lab in South San Francisco. 23andMe also began research collaborations with Genentech and Pfizer.

A much bigger deal followed in July 2018: a fifty-fifty drug development joint venture with GlaxoSmithKline (GSK). It gave 23andMe $300 million in funding and established a four-year exclusive partnership, during which the partners would each bear 50 percent of the cost of developing new drugs and own 50 percent of any commercialized therapies. Researchers from both could use the massive dataset to discover safer, more effective "precision" medicines; target narrower patient subgroups; and identify and recruit the ideal patients for clinical studies.

Both companies believed that this joint venture would lead to break-through treatments for a wide range of diseases. But massive capital and human resources would be required to pursue many research programs at the same time. Drug development is a high-risk business, with typical approval rates of just 9 to 14 percent for programs that reach Phase I clinical trials, and it takes tens of millions of dollars just to get to that point. Companies need only one hit product—one Lipitor or Advair—to deliver tens of *billions* of dollars in revenue. But every failure along the way is incredibly expensive.

23andMe Vice President of Business Development Dr. Emily Conley summarized this partnership of brains and brawn: "We brought this incredible database and some really great genomics science, the ability to find these novel targets that we believe are more likely to be effective as therapies. And GSK brought a 100,000-person organization, with a proven track record of actually going from a target to a therapy."[31] In August 2020, 23andMe and GSK announced that they were entering clinical trials for their first jointly developed cancer drug—a huge milestone on the road to a commercial product.

23andMe's Future

23andMe has until 2022 to decide if the GSK joint venture is delivering enough development, production, and marketing value to firmly establish the pharmaceutical side of their business. If not, they will have to explore other options, such as nonexclusive deals with multiple drug companies.

Organizational concerns loom on the horizon as well. The risk profiles of the consumer and therapeutics arms of the company are vastly different. The consumer business is trying to become sustainable and profitable, while drug development will always be hit-and-miss, high risk–high reward. Yet the two are strategically intertwined; drug development depends on the continuing growth of the consumer dataset. Internal competition for resources may lead to increasing tension between the two sides.

Despite all these challenges on her plate, Wojcicki is excited about the opportunities ahead. She noted that chronic diseases trigger the majority of healthcare spending, and many of these diseases are highly preventable. She believes that 23andMe's health reports can help consumers change their lifestyles before it's too late. For instance, everyone hears about the importance of a healthy diet and exercise, but finding out that you are genetically predisposed to diabetes is a huge motivator to finally hit the gym and eat more salads.

23andMe has a potentially limitless future, but the next phase of its success will be even harder. As Wojcicki told me, "We'll make lots of wrong decisions . . . you only figure that out by trial and error. But I believe in the long run that the right thing to do will pay off. Part of the challenge in healthcare is that so many of the incentives are fundamentally wrong. We have to swim against the current for now, but ultimately, in time, things will change."[32]

Evaluating 23andMe

Here's how I evaluate this brainy tech start-up that has expanded into an extremely brawny new line of business.

The Left Hemisphere: Analytics = 10
Data analysis is 23andMe's core competency, the source of all of its value.

The Right Hemisphere: Creativity = 9
The company is built on creativity at all levels, from its founding idea to its business models to its marketing messages.

The Amygdala: Empathy = 8
Wojcicki says that building trusting relationships with patients is a top priority. She criticizes the healthcare industry for not caring enough about patients and was furious when the FDA blocked 23andMe from warning women who carry the BRCA marker for breast cancer.

The Prefrontal Cortex: Risk-Taking = 9
23andMe stuck with their risky vision for business-to-consumer genetic testing even when the FDA shut down their reports, which frightened some of their competitors out of the business. Now they're taking even bigger risks in drug development.

The Inner Ear: Balancing Ownership and Partnership = 8
So far their key partnerships seem to be working well, especially their make-or-break joint venture with GSK.

Total Brain Score = 44/50

The Spine: Logistics = 9

They are efficient in managing shipments, deliveries, and customer service for their testing kits.

Hands: Making Things = 5

This is a big question mark for the future. Manufacturing drugs is a lot harder than making home testing kits.

Muscles: Leveraging Scale = 7

23andMe deserves credit for managing their huge and growing customer base, and scaling further by partnering with Walgreens and others to sell more testing kits.

Hand-Eye Coordination: Managing Ecosystems = 9

They've built a strong ecosystem of product suppliers, physical and online retailers, and partners like GSK and Lark. Even relations with the FDA are now much improved.

Stamina: Surviving for the Long Run = 8

They did a great job recovering from the bad publicity of the FDA shutdown, but their stamina is a question mark for the future. Their brand may suffer as more people worry about data privacy and as the novelty of DNA testing wears off.

Total Brawn Score = 38/50

Combined Score = 82/100

So What Have We Learned?

You might think I was too hard on Daimler. How can a legendary company with so much influence, capital, prestige, and profitability score so low, especially when it's pouring billions into innovations that will pay off in the future? It's true that in a few years, Daimler's brain scores may be significantly higher. But as admirable as the CASE initiatives are, none of them are guaranteed to pan out. Given the fundamental disruptions in the global automotive industry, it's possible that a decade from now Daimler could be a minor player, or perhaps even gone via a merger or bankruptcy.

Likewise, despite my admiration for 23andMe, I have no idea if it will still be around in 5 or 10 years. Demand for personal genomics testing is already starting to show signs of saturation. What if it was a fad all along? What if their researchers never actually discover a commercially viable block-buster drug?

As we go through the next 10 chapters, we will dive deeply into each of the brains and brawn attributes and show how different kinds of companies are applying them. These explorations will help us understand some best practices your company can follow and some mistakes to avoid. We'll finish each chapter with a few key takeaways for our Systems Leader's Notebook, which will inform our analysis in Chapter 13 of how leaders can drive change in organizations.

PART II

WHAT IT MEANS TO HAVE BRAINS

When older, nontech organizations are told that they need to "digitize" or "embrace digitalization," what that means is often unclear and ambiguous. Are they being urged to automate manual processes, thus driving cost savings? Does it mean acting like a Silicon Valley tech company, being more agile in product development? Does it mean wearing casual clothes to work and talking about "failing fast," as young founders do around the world?

Over the next five chapters we will drill down more deeply on the digital and emotional aspects that are often associated with the brain: using analytics (the left hemisphere), harnessing creativity (the right hemisphere), developing empathy (the amygdala), taking risks (the prefrontal cortex), and finding balance between ownership and partnerships (the inner ear). Each chapter will look at several companies along each of these dimensions, with a deeper analysis of one organization.

At the end of this section you should be able to evaluate your own company on these five Brainy competencies, give your company an overall brain score, and identify which areas you might need to work on improving.

CHAPTER 3

THE LEFT HEMISPHERE: USING ANALYTICS

Disruption occurs when someone listens more carefully to customers, or better anticipates what customers might want before they even realize it themselves. Most companies are disrupted because they lack the will and courage to disrupt themselves first.

—Walt Bettinger, CEO of Charles Schwab

We're still in the early days of an analytics revolution. Vast amounts of data are increasingly available for all kinds of companies, from the oldest incumbents to the newest disruptors, from high tech to low tech, in industries ranging from products to services. Data has enormous potential to improve your offerings, enhance your customer service, and sharpen your marketing messages, while simultaneously helping you slash unnecessary costs. It's no exaggeration to say that data powers the engines of modern businesses. In the Brains and Brawn framework, I call the capability to analyze and employ data "the left hemisphere," after the brain's center of logical thinking.

But there's a catch: while gathering data has never been easier, using it wisely has never been harder. Everyone needs a strategy to manage the flood of incoming information. You can get distracted by focusing on the wrong metrics—perhaps those that are easy to track but not the real drivers of the success of your business. Or you can be tempted into abusing your data to exploit your own customers in ways large or small, thereby damaging their loyalty and trust. Leaders who can balance mastery of the power of data with the insight and ability to use it wisely will have a huge advantage. But it's possible to be too smart for your own good.

Amazon: The Power of Analytics

As in so many respects, Amazon is the gold standard on data mastery. Amazon Prime, its free shipping program, which now includes countless perks such as free video and audio content and discounts at Whole Foods, is first and foremost a data play. Free shipping encourages Prime members to engage more and more with Amazon, in every aspect of their lives—from restocking toner cartridges to watching original TV shows such as *The Marvelous Mrs. Maisel*. Each purchase, click, or Alexa command adds to the massive amount of granular data the company has about its customers. This, in turn, allows Amazon's artificial intelligence (AI) and machine learning technology to make better predictions about what they'll want next and promote those items, which drives even more sales.

Anticipating needs is a far more powerful way to attract and retain customers than waiting to fulfill their needs. Prime customers love the service and don't complain much about Big Brother knowing so much about their daily lives. Amazon combines big data with machine learning to lock in customers. The longer you subscribe to Prime, the less likely that you will ever give up Prime.

Compare the huge advantage of Amazon's left hemisphere to any old-school company, such as a hypothetical umbrella manufacturer. The latter gets customer demand data secondhand, via the wholesalers and retailers it partners with, and usually in the aggregate rather than broken out into segments. It's likely to be guessing about the demographic of its customers, which makes marketing harder. If there's a change in demand trends, the manufacturer will find out days or weeks later than a retailer that can instantly see point-of-purchase data. The same is true for interpreting price sensitivity, such as how customers will react if a $19.99 umbrella goes up to $24.99.

Even scarier for smaller companies, Amazon (as well as other major retailers) can produce their own generic umbrellas, using their data mastery to choose the exact features and prices that are most in demand. It's been repeatedly accused of doing so, against the interests of its own suppliers.[1]

Without some serious brand loyalty or deep pockets, our umbrella company might have a very hard time competing.

Facebook: The Perils of Analytics

Another huge risk is unleashing machine learning and AI without considering how your customers or users might feel about being turned into fodder for analytics. Companies that focus on optimizing data at all costs risk alienating the very people who drive their business model. The ultimate cautionary example is Facebook, which spent its first decade building up an enthusiastic and massive user base, then spent the next half decade blowing up its reputation and angering its users. Although Facebook is still growing and extremely profitable, many business leaders I know see it as a case study of the consequences of being careless, complacent, and greedy about the power of data.

Early on, Facebook users were fine with targeted ads based on their interests. It made sense that if you loved to garden, you'd see ads for gardening supplies in your news feed. It seemed like a small and reasonable price for the benefits Facebook offered as a free platform for connecting friends and family. And sometimes those gardening ads would actually show something you wanted.

But over time, by focusing relentlessly on optimizing revenue, Facebook violated user trust. It sold private information to third parties, including unscrupulous political organizations like Cambridge Analytica, without warning users or giving them a fair chance to opt out. That led to a 2018 data breach that was the largest known leak in Facebook history.[3] News headlines about data insecurity and abuse of privacy drove some people to abandon the platform. It didn't matter whether Facebook had upheld the letter of the disclosure laws in the fine print of its baffling user agreement. Its lawyers and compliance experts missed the bigger picture of trust and customer service.

It may sound easy to monetize the golden eggs of data analytics without killing the goose of trust, but it's not. For a deeper look at the complexities involved, let's dig into our featured example, Charles Schwab & Co.

Charles Schwab: The Rise of a Financial Powerhouse

Schwab's approach to analytics has been at the heart of its almost uninterrupted success since 1975, and especially since Walt Bettinger took over as

CEO during the financial crisis of 2008. The financial services giant has set a gold standard for smart, empathic, ethical use of a staggering amount of customer data.

Chuck Schwab (the man) launched his company right before the Securities and Exchange Commission deregulated the cozy world of traditional stock-brokers, who had never before competed on price. Once the regulations were changed, Schwab positioned itself as one of the first discount brokerages, offering low-cost, no-frills trading for middle-class-investors, rather than expensive services for high-net-worth investors. Within a decade, Schwab had 100 branches, 1.2 million customers, and $7.6 billion in client assets.[3]

Technology was always a key to its success. In 1979, Schwab became the first discount broker to bring automation in-house. Chuck Schwab risked $500,000 (equal to all of the company's revenue that year) on a back-office settlement system with proprietary software.[4] He wanted to own as much tech as possible, as a competitive advantage. Schwab soon had the first online order entry system in the business. "Almost overnight, Schwab order-takers could handle twice as much volume, at less cost, with greater accuracy than any broker in the business," wrote John Kador in his book about the company.[5] As a side benefit, the system generated reams of data about customers and transactions, which Schwab could mine to uncover trends and patterns.

Bank of America purchased Schwab in 1983 for $55 million, but Chuck bought the company back in 1987 and took it public, just before the October market crash. At that time, Schwab was serving not just solo investors, but also independent investment advisers, providing them with asset custody and back-office operations. It also launched its own money market mutual funds. During the dotcom boom, it spent $2.4 billion to acquire U.S. Trust, a financial advisory firm that catered to 7,000 extremely wealthy clients. Things were going so well by 1997 that Chuck began planning his transition away from running the day-to-day business, promoting David Pottruck to co-CEO.

"Schwab couldn't do anything wrong in the late 1990s," recalled Bettinger. "But when the Internet bubble burst in 2000, Schwab couldn't do anything right, for a period that went through about 2004."[6] As the market tanked, Schwab saw a 50 percent drop in trading volume and had to implement major layoffs and cuts to employee benefits. Instead of focusing on the small investors who had made the company, Pottruck, who became sole CEO in 2003, began raising fees on lower-value accounts while scaling up services for wealthy clients. But with revenue continuing to drop, the board ousted Pottruck in 2004 and brought back Chuck as CEO.

Chuck shifted Schwab's focus back to middle-class investors, many of whom had jumped to newer, low-cost online brokerages like E*Trade and

TD Waterhouse. He cut average trading fees by over half, taking a short-term revenue hit, and began to shed noncore acquisitions like U.S. Trust. This strategy meant that Schwab had to rely less on fees from trading, which had driven as much as 50 percent of its revenue before the dotcom crash. By 2005, 79 percent of Schwab's revenue was coming from asset-based products and services, and only 17 percent from trading fees. This shift enabled the company to further reduce its trading commissions, which made Schwab even more attractive to small investors. Things were looking up again, until the 2008 financial crisis.

Steering by the Same Star

Walt Bettinger met Chuck Schwab in 1995, when Schwab acquired his Ohio-based 401(k) plan record-keeping company. As Bettinger tells the story of negotiating the deal, "I had never met a multi-billionaire before in my life. I was very nervous. I walked into his office and he had this torn, hideous orange carpet, ratty old chairs, kind of a disheveled look. Just a normal guy." Chuck's down-to-earth nature put Bettinger at ease. "Chuck treats everybody the same way, with honor, with respect. We just had a natural connection."[7] After the sale, Bettinger stayed on to run his company as a division of Schwab, then took on increasing responsibilities within management.

A key meeting between the two happened in 2005, when Bettinger was leading Schwab's core retail business. The banking unit was about to offer its first checking accounts, and since Schwab didn't own any ATMs, it had to decide what to charge customers for using ATMs at other banks. Bettinger prepared an 80-page PowerPoint analysis of various options, including buying or cosponsoring their own ATM network. Bettinger's research noted that not a single major US bank was eating the ATM fees it was charged by competing banks; they all passed those fees on to customers. But as he recalled 15 years later, "It seemed like the puck would be headed in that direction, due to ongoing consolidation in banking."[8] Bettinger concluded that despite a short-term cost spike, the best long-term move would be to cover all fees from other banks, essentially turning every ATM in the world into a Schwab ATM.

Bettinger didn't get past slide three before Chuck interrupted to ask what clients would prefer. The answer, of course, was free withdrawals from any ATM. With his decades of experience, Chuck probably just needed only a second or two to estimate how many millions of dollars Schwab could save by passing along those withdrawal fees. But he could also intuit the vastly greater long-term value of a customer who smiled every time she made a free withdrawal at a Chase or Wells Fargo ATM, instead of frowning and reconsidering whether it made sense to have a Schwab checking account.

While Chuck was a strong advocate of data collection and analysis, he didn't need Excel to know the value of making customers happy. He also knew that every happy customer would tell other potential customers, and that word of mouth was more powerful than any advertising campaign. Since Chuck's intuition led to the same result as Bettinger's net present value analysis, there was no need to go through the other 77 slides. That meeting crystalized Bettinger's embrace of Chuck's North Star principle: Customer satisfaction is the most important metric. "It was a pure eureka moment. Who cares what the competition does? Long term, it's the best decision."[9]

Recognizing Bettinger as a kindred spirit, Chuck promoted him to COO and then to CEO in 2008, just as the financial crisis worsened. Like most financial services firms, Schwab took a big hit when the markets tanked and people cut back on investing. But unlike other firms, Schwab didn't accept any government bailout funds. When the recovery began, account growth started to accelerate, while Schwab relied more and more on revenue other than trading fees. As of early 2021 the company is managing almost $7 trillion in assets in more than 29 million brokerage accounts.[10]

Through Clients' Eyes

Schwab isn't merely big, it's extremely complicated. Various business units offer mutual funds, stocks, ETFs, options, futures, closed-end funds, bonds, CDs, money market funds, IRAs, foreign securities, savings and checking accounts, mortgages, home equity lines of credit, credit cards, life insurance, disability insurance, and much more. No CEO could possibly master every detail of all those products and services.

Bettinger made sure that his executives were guided by Chuck's North Star: taking care of customers is the key to long-term success. He launched an initiative aimed at getting everyone to see every aspect of the business "Through Clients' Eyes." Staffers were urged to judge each decision, large or small, based on its impact on customer satisfaction and loyalty. And they were frequently reminded of the company's five core principles:

1. **Trust is everything. Earned over time. Lost in an instant.** We will focus on anything we do or don't do that builds or undermines trust and our relationship with clients.
2. **Price matters. More than ever. And in our industry more than most.** We will leverage our scale to deliver industry-leading pricing without prospects or clients having to ask or negotiate.

3. **Clients deserve efficient experiences. Every time.** We will respect our clients' time by ensuring that every interaction a client has with us is simple and easy.
4. **Every prospective or existing client is critical to our future growth. No matter how large or small.** We will value and delight them at each possible opportunity.
5. **Actions matter more than words. Clients, press, influencers and employees will give credit to what we do vs. what we say.** We will challenge everything we do to ensure it is consistent with what we believe and say about ourselves.[11]

Bettinger stressed that focusing on the customer would sometimes require cannibalizing an existing line of business in pursuit of new growth. "Disruption occurs when someone listens more carefully to customers, or better anticipates what customers might want before they even realize it themselves. Most companies are disrupted because they lack the will and courage to disrupt themselves first."[12]

Most of Schwab's surveys and other forms of direct feedback focus on tactical improvements that would make life easier for customers, online or off. Those efficiencies are a win-win, helping both Schwab and its customers. But sometimes the surveys reveal demand for a new product or service that would generate little or no profit but is justified by the five principles. In those cases, an analytic process follows *after* a values-driven and customer-driven decision to move forward.

Bettinger is especially proud of how this worked for Schwab Stock Slices, a fractional investing program that debuted in June 2020. Now that fewer companies are doing stock splits, it can be hard for small investors to afford shares of a stock like Amazon, which trades above $3,000 per share as I write this. "We could have ignored the demand for fractional shares among our less wealthy customers, but helping the little guy is Schwab's original purpose. So, we did three months of research and usability studies to design Stock Slices, then spent millions to implement it, even though it won't bring in any extra commissions."[13]

Using Analytics to Boost Services and Lower Costs

Bettinger is a data junkie who checks on Schwab's most important metrics literally before he gets out of bed each morning. But how does he know which numbers to look at, to gauge the true health of the business? Schwab's computers collect a staggering amount of data: every financial instrument bought or sold; every click on every page of schwab.com; every tap on its mobile app; every one of the 60,000 phone calls placed daily to its customer service center; every transaction by the 13,000 independent financial advisors who use Schwab for back-end support and asset custody.

A Systems Leader needs to surf on top of that ocean of data without drowning, by focusing on a manageable number of variables that truly matter. Bettinger zeroes in on just three daily metrics: the number of new accounts, the value of net new assets, and the net value of assets transferred in and out. As he explained, "New accounts tell us the level of engagement by the general population in investing. Net new assets tells us how healthy the business is overall—are people bringing more and more money to us? And net transfer of assets [from other institutions] is the measure of where we stand from a competitive standpoint; our market share."[14] This information shows up on a dashboard on his phone, so between his alarm clock going off and beginning his morning routine, Bettinger already knows how good or bad the previous day was for Schwab's competitive position, its bottom line, and the country's overall investing climate.

That's just the start of his day. While Schwab's computers can calculate how much revenue is generated by each product and service, they can't tell Bettinger and his team what to do with all that information. Every day requires a series of value judgments about what should get priority in the allocation of resources, staff, and marketing. It's easy to repeat Chuck's North Star—"Our priority is giving our customers better and better services at lower and lower costs"—but the devil is in the details:

- ► How much cost can be taken out of any given service without wrecking it?
- ► Will adding a new technology justify its cost?
- ► Do we really need to match every fee cut from every competitor? Conversely, do we need to match every competitor's new product or service?
- ► How much can we afford to spend to optimize every detail of the customer experience—on the website, on the app, on the phone, or in person?
- ► Out of all the variables we track, which ones do customers *really* care about? The time spent on a call to customer service? The number of clicks needed to accomplish a task on the app or website? The waiting time before seeing a rep at a customer center?
- ► As our size and scale allow us to operate at a greater and greater efficiency, do we really need to pass all these operating cost savings on to customers? If we don't have to match the rock-bottom fees of the no

frills, online-only services that have sprung up in recent years, how close do we have to get?

▶ On the other hand, just how high-touch do our services have to be to make customers feel well taken care of at every point of connection (on the web, on the app, on the phone, in person)?

A great example of how Schwab applies human perspective to these questions is its response to Robinhood, an app-based financial services start-up that launched in 2013. By going 100 percent virtual, Robinhood was able to offer free trading on equities and funds, generating revenue instead through interest on cash balances, margin lending, and commissions from the high-speed trading firms that processed its orders—a controversial but legal practice called "payment for order flow." According to the *Wall Street Journal*, Robinhood also charges customers a bit more than the market prices it gets from those high-speed traders. "Unlike E*Trade [and] Charles Schwab Corp.—which also take payment for order flow—Robinhood doesn't publish data on how much price improvement it gives customers. The upshot: When you buy or sell shares on Robinhood, the app is likely executing your trade at a slightly worse price than another broker would, market veterans say."[15]

Even though Robinhood customers were paying higher prices for "free" trades, their costs were nearly invisible. Schwab customers, in contrast, got the best possible market prices, thanks to its status as a giant market maker, but paid a transparent $4.99 per trade. Schwab had actually anticipated the threat of zero-commission competitors long before Robinhood existed; Bettinger remembers his first meeting on the subject as early as 2004. "We knew that was our Achilles heel, so we constantly asked ourselves if any new step would get us closer to or farther away from zero commissions."[16] By the spring of 2019, when commissions had fallen below 10 percent of Schwab's total revenue, he was prepared to make a big move whenever the time felt right.

That time came just a few months later, when Schwab knew that E*Trade and TD Ameritrade were about to make the same dramatic change. Schwab's announcement of free equity and ETF trades via the web hurt its stock price initially. But Chuck Schwab personally defended the decision on CNBC: "We make our money on other relationships—you might want advice, you might want fixed income or things like that. . . . What we try to do is offer things that customers really want, and they definitely want lower prices."[17] Because Schwab had spent 15 years steadily reducing its dependence on commission revenue, it felt the impact far less than competing brokers that were caught off guard by the industry-wide race to zero.

Using Analytics to Preserve Trust and Strengthen Loyalty

During my interviews with Bettinger and his visits to my Stanford classes, he must have mentioned trust a hundred times. It's his biggest obsession, because he knows that anything that damages customer trust in Schwab is potentially catastrophic, and threats can come from multiple directions at any time.

The first threat is that people will lose faith in the financial services industry as a whole, as they did for a while after the financial crisis of 2008. Despite regulatory reforms, there are still enough unscrupulous practices and conflicts of interest that the industry has a trust level, as Bettinger put it, "maybe just one or two levels below used-car sales." He added, "Without trust, everything else you do to a certain extent becomes irrelevant. Because this is not like buying shoes, or cars, or neckties, or a cup of coffee. This is your future, this is your family's future, this is what you work for, and so trust is at the core of everything you do."[18] On this standard at least, Schwab benefits from its clean reputation since 1975. Whenever it rolls out a new product, its brand equity as the good people of financial services goes a long way toward reassuring customers.

A second key threat is technical—the risk of hacking or cyber-sabotage, whether by individual hackers, organized crime, terrorists, or foreign enemies of the United States. Joe Martinetto, Schwab's CFO from 2007 to 2017, noted that "you can spend an infinite amount of money, but if anybody tells you that they can give you a 100 percent guarantee that their systems are impermeable, they're lying."[19]

Schwab's technical experts consider a wide range of possible new security technologies, but it's hard to calculate their ROI. Should Schwab move aggressively on voice authentication? Facial recognition? Retina scanning? Thumb-print technology? Other biometrics? As Martinetto observed, "There's very little that's not affordable in technology anymore. I would love to have some of this better authentication stuff in place, because . . . once we know it's really you, it just makes it a whole lot easier for us to deliver better, faster experiences to you."[20]

Perhaps the biggest and most frightening threat to customer trust, because it's the most tempting, is the potential misuse of customer data. It would be extremely easy for Schwab to follow Facebook and others to the dark side by exploiting that ocean of data it collects every day. The more a company knows about customer behavior, the more it can deduce via AI, which opens up countless opportunities for customized offers at low marginal cost. But where do you draw the line between targeted marketing and an invasion of clients' privacy? Machine learning can't answer that question, nor can the legal department. It requires a strong, company-wide sense of mission and values.

Consider an example Bettinger brought up. "If you're on schwab.com and you click on the 'life events, divorce' section, we might know something before your spouse does." It would be easy to autosend an email saying something like, "We noticed that you're researching the financial impact of a possible divorce. Here are links to some articles and online calculators that can help you plan. . . ." Even customers who rarely worry about data privacy would consider that the worst kind of "Big Brother is watching you" scenario. Any incremental profit generated by that email would be dwarfed by customer departures and bad publicity.

In 2021 trust was raised as an issue yet again in the financial services industry with the volatile and erratic surge in stock trading around the company GameStop.[21] Robinhood was at the center of the controversy when it restricted trades in certain companies, including GameStop, which prevented people from selling their positions as the stock was falling. Some asserted that Robinhood was hurting individuals by not allowing them to make trades, but large hedge funds were still able to sell their shares and get out as the company's stock price dropped. While it was later revealed that Robinhood needed to raise additional capital to cover their customers' trading activity, and thus limited the trades as it was necessary for the company to operate its business, the lack of trust in the company's actions led to the CEO being summoned to testify in front of Congress. The company's opaqueness in why it limited trades caused intense blowback for several weeks. In an industry that sells something as vitally important as financial well-being, Robinhood's approach stands in stark contrast to Schwab's relentless obsession with customer trust.

Bettinger says that Schwab executives almost never have internal disagreements about trust-related decisions. "Those five principles go a long way toward preventing debate, because they're so simple and clear. We think of them as both a road map to growth and a set of guardrails to keep us out of trouble."[22]

Using Analytics to Reframe the Competitive Landscape

"Who is your competition?" isn't always a simple question, especially in financial services. Schwab started out as a low-cost competitor to traditional, full-service broker-dealers ("wire houses") such as Morgan Stanley and Merrill Lynch, and later faced off with online brokerages like E*Trade, mutual fund companies like Fidelity, banks, and financial supermarkets that combined all of the above services. More recently, new digital innovators such as Robinhood and Betterment (a robo-advisor) are trying to steal market share on the low-end, slicing off pieces of Schwab's business. As Tim

Heier, Schwab's CTO, told me, "A lot of the [financial technology] companies are doing rapid experimentation. They're looking at incumbents like Schwab and unbundling us, saying, 'I can do free trades. I can do automatic asset allocation.' They're not trying to replicate the whole elephant, but they're biting us off one part at a time."[23] Heier added that Schwab is willing to "trade punches" with those small disruptors, as it did when it moved to free trading to counter Robinhood.

But what if one of the tech giants such as Amazon or Google decides to expand into financial services, or if some other disruptive force is lurking around the corner? Heier said he worries about "disruption with a capital D. . . . Somebody goes into a new market, offers a new service, something that's pretty dramatically different, like Google did with search. . . . That would probably be harder to defend against. It would be a company that, by definition, would have money for investment. And if they're deciding to do this, they're going to make a real go of it."[24]

While Bettinger's team prepares for all these potential threats, they can take comfort in their analysis of Schwab's standing among its competitors. The executives estimate that the total "investable wealth" in the United States is about $45 trillion, down from $55 trillion before the recession of 2020. Even including Schwab's acquisition of TD Ameritrade (a $26 billion deal, announced in November 2019),[25] it still has only 12 to 14 percent of the country's investable assets under management. That still leaves significant opportunities for growth. "We continue to take market share from the big wire houses and banks," said Mike Hecht, senior vice president for corporate development, planning, and strategy. "That drove our growth over the last 40 years, and we think it's going to drive our growth over the next 10-plus years, if not more, because six out of every seven dollars in the U.S. is still with the wire houses."[26]

Using Analytics to Follow Fast

Chuck Schwab considered cutting-edge technology one of his competitive advantages in the 1970s. "There was an era where we built everything," said Joe Martinetto, the former CFO. "I think we have gotten a lot more rigorous in our thoughts around what's really a competitive advantage and what's a commodity. We buy commodities. We only build things that we think are differentiated."[27]

One reason for that policy is that Schwab faced complex legacy issues from owning so much tech early on. For instance, Martinetto's group spent 10 full years untangling and upgrading the company's early computer systems. "We licensed a broker-dealer platform 40 years ago and brought it in-house, then went off of their upgrade path. We had been doing our own enhancements and customization and maintenance for 40 years. You can only imagine the complexity that has built up. The mainframe code base was around 39 million lines of code."[28]

Instead of chasing proprietary technology, Bettinger's team embraced a "follow fast" strategy to keep an eye on which innovations were worth adding, then emulating them quickly with all the advantages of Schwab's scale. The advantages of being first out of the gate are often short-lived, while a fast follower can get virtually the same benefits with a fraction of the resource investment. It's like cruise control in a car: whichever automaker invented that feature didn't have very long to brag about it, before everyone else offered cruise control as well. The challenge is figuring out which new offerings will become permanent and what's just a passing fad.

As Heier, the CTO, observed: "Expectations keep changing, which puts pressure on our software development teams. You have to think about how people will interact with us with voice—not necessarily about picking up the phone and going through a call center or call tree. They can use a virtual assistant. That's a different kind of software. Do we write it? Do we buy it? Do we partner with another company? . . . Is it too early to partner? If we wait too long, are we behind? . . . It's expensive to be first on everything, so we've honed our skill and our process of watching, learning, innovating."[29]

Perhaps the best example of Schwab's "follow fast" strategy is how it responded to the "robo-advice" trend. Personalized portfolio management used to be an expensive, high-end service for clients with at least $250,000 or $500,000 to invest. Then Wealthfront, a start-up founded in 2008, offered asset allocation by automating the investment strategies of great wealth managers and stock pickers. You could input all of your relevant information—age, family status, goals, risk tolerance—and get a recommended portfolio based on whatever those rock stars were currently telling their high-end clients. Wealthfront pitched the service as almost everything a great planner could give you at a fraction of the cost, for a minimum investment as low as $5,000. Smaller investors loved it. A similar start-up, Betterment, followed in 2010. By mid-2019, an estimated $440 billion was being managed by robo-advisory services.[30]

In 2014, after concluding that robo-advising wasn't a fad, Schwab began working on its own product, which it calls Schwab Intelligent Portfolios. Despite some resistance and concern from the roughly 7,500 advisory firms that use Schwab as a custodian, the data convinced Bettinger's team that there was plenty of room in the market for both high-cost, high-touch human advice and low-cost automated advice. Just two years after its debut in 2015, Schwab Intelligent Portfolios reached $25 billion in customer assets. By 2020, it had $41 billion under management in 360 million accounts.

While robo-advice shifted some Schwab customers away from higher-fee advice, which hurt revenue, Bettinger's team believes the long-term impact on the bottom line is positive. Robo-advice has led many new customers to Schwab, including millennials who wouldn't choose a financial services company that didn't offer the service.

Following the Data Wherever It Leads—Ethically

Schwab is a role model for combining the agility of a bold disruptor with the resources and scale of a strong incumbent. Bettinger's management team never rests on their reputation or assumes that they can't learn from start-ups like Robinhood or Wealthfront. They're always on high alert for complacency. They never assume Schwab is too strong or well-established to crash and burn.

In terms of analytics, they are committed to following the data about what customers really want, wherever it may take them. If investors in 2030 want to do their transactions via AI voice interfaces such as Alexa and Siri, Schwab will be ready for them. But the company will still focus on ensuring data privacy and preserving customer trust. It knows that mastering big data isn't worth much if you don't combine it with human insight and empathic decision-making. It aspires to transparency about how it uses data—not on line 397 of the fine print of the terms of service, but in plain English in a visible location. It knows that most customers are fine with sharing their personal information, as long as a company treats them with respect and delivers real benefits in exchange for their trust.

Bettinger's team rejects the Silicon Valley cliché of "Move fast and break things"—style is more like "Move as fast as you can without breaking things." They study the competitive landscape, evolve with the times, and cannibalize parts of the business when necessary. They learn from upstarts instead of ignoring them. But they never risk the trust of the customer base or nickel-and-dime customers to inflate profits. And they never forget that doing the right thing is still the best path to long-term loyalty.

Of course, Schwab has a huge advantage even beyond its resources, reputation, and 45 years of brand equity. It has an 83-year-old founder and chairman whose values are hardwired into the company's DNA and who owns in the high single digit percent of the stock in case his management team ever needs a reminder about those values. I asked Bettinger if he thinks the company's strong culture will endure after Chuck is no longer there to inspire everyone:

> I think when Chuck is gone someday, what he has built cultur-
> ally will remain. The risk will be when big decisions have to be
> made that demand big-time courage. If the company gets in
> trouble 15 years from now, can someone walk into the board of
> directors and say, "We need to give up 20 to 25 percent of our
> revenue to fix this, and trust that in doing so consumers will
> reward us by bringing more money." If nobody owns more than
> 1 or 2 percent of the company, it may be a tougher decision.

THE SYSTEMS LEADER'S NOTEBOOK

Using Analytics

- Build up your data by measuring every possible interaction. You won't necessarily know which variables are significant to your business until you analyze many of them.

- Use size to your advantage. Disruptors might seek to scale quickly by building data moats; incumbents can use their large data sets to aggressively defend their turf.

- Be patient, knowing that the transformation of existing industries rarely happens overnight. Don't assume that big data will reveal immediate insights. You might need months or years before data collection and analysis really pays off.

CHAPTER 4

THE RIGHT HEMISPHERE: HARNESSING CREATIVITY

It never dawned on anybody that it was a decision between digital and analog. And once you get there, you have to think, when did analog ever win?

—Joe Hogan, CEO of Align Technology

Popular mythology suggests that innovative ideas require a sudden flash of insight: a "light bulb moment" when your brain clicks on and illuminates a radical vision— such as for a phone that doubles as a computer, a better way to search the Web, or a theory of gravity (granted, Newton required the assistance of a serendipitous apple). In fact, the cliché of the light bulb moment was dismissed by no less a brilliant thinker than Thomas Edison, the actual inventor of the light bulb, who is credited with the aphorism "Genius is one percent inspiration and ninety-nine percent perspiration."

I have nothing against visionaries, but it's much more common that bold ideas and innovative business models come from looking at existing products, services, and markets in new ways. Step by step, one increment at a time, ideas emerge and evolve. The end result could be a more efficient supply chain process, a brand extension that opens a previously overlooked source of revenue, a bold business model, or a never-before-seen product. The more ideas you consider seriously, the more likely that your organization will endure and thrive.

I think of this use of the right hemisphere as "grinding" creativity, because you are literally grinding out ideas, refining and polishing them until their brilliance shines through. The grunt work involved in grinding creativity will probably never get you written up in the *Wall Street Journal* or *Fast Company*. But it will help you find new markets for old products, or new products for old markets that had seemed resistant to anything different. The possibilities are truly endless.

Let's look at a few brief examples before we delve into our main case study.

Lego: New Markets for Old Products

The Lego Group began in 1932 as a Danish family business that made wooden toys. After World War II, when plastics became more available in Europe, the toymaker introduced the interlocking plastic bricks that would spread around the world by the 1960s. Those bricks were Lego's original burst of creativity, and they made the company a part of virtually every home in America.

Lego continued to improve and refine their core product over the next few decades, adding myriad special features and customized kits. By the 1990s, many Lego products were based on licensing pop culture intellectual properties, such as *Star Wars*. By 2009, about 60 percent of Lego's American sales were linked to licensing deals, which was double the share in 2004.[1] More and more sales were also driven by adult hobbyists who wanted to build intricate Lego projects, such as a huge replica of the Millennium Falcon from *Star Wars*—an example of adapting an old product for a new market.

The company continued to find and invest in more creative ways to expand. Over the past two decades, Lego has successfully reframed its entire identity, from merely a toy company to an entertainment company for all ages. That included building more Legoland theme parks around the world—there are now eight parks in operation plus another three under construction.[2]

As the *New York Times* noted in 2009,

> Even as other toymakers struggle, this Danish maker of toy bricks is enjoying double-digit sales gains and swelling earnings. In recent years, Lego has increasingly focused on toys that many parents wouldn't recognize from their own childhood. Hollywood themes are commanding more shelf space, a far cry from the idealistic, purely imagination-oriented play that drove Lego for years.[3]

Other kinds of Lego-branded entertainment wouldn't have been imaginable even 20 years ago. *The Lego Movie*, a 2014 computer-animated adventure, earned rave reviews and $468 million in global box office, making it one of the biggest animated movies of all time.[4] *The Lego Batman Movie* and other sequels also reached huge audiences. Lego even launched a TV game show for adults called *Lego Masters*. As the *New York Times* described it, "The competition pits teams from around the country against one another in a variety of brick-building challenges. The contestants' first assignment: to create a model theme park. Their time limit? 15 hours. The prize for winning the competition at large is $100,000—though surely any contestants who make it through without stepping on a brick can be considered successful."[5]

In March 2020, the Lego Group reported that for the previous year, consumer sales, revenue, and profit all grew, outpacing the industry.[6] But where would it be if it had stuck to making plastic building blocks for children?

Adobe: Signing Up for a New Business Model

Since 1982, Adobe has developed some of the world's most widely used and influential software, including Photoshop, PageMaker, InDesign, PostScript, and many other programs. For its first three decades, the company applied a straightforward business model:

1. Design a great new software tool for PCs and Macs.
2. Sell it for hundreds of dollars, as physical disks packed in shrink-wrapped boxes. Offer discounts for companies that buy software licenses in bulk for their employees.
3. Every two years or so, release an improved version that forces customers who depend on the software to purchase the update, often frustrating them in the process.
4. Rinse, repeat, profit.

But in 2013, Adobe took a bold leap into an entirely new business model for them: software via subscriptions only. If you were a graphic designer who relied on Photoshop, you'd now be billed $30 a month, or $240 a year, which would include automatic upgrades via web downloads. You could also save money by subscribing to the entire Adobe suite (which included Illustrator, InDesign, Premiere, and more) for $600 a year.[7] You might hate the change, as many customers did, especially since it wasn't optional. But sooner or later, if you needed Adobe products, you'd have to accept the new normal.

Adobe didn't invent subscriptions for software; some of the leading software companies in the world were already offering a subscription option. Microsoft was already offering Office 365 for $100 a year. But Adobe was the first established software giant to see the advantages of shifting 100 percent to subscriptions.

For starters, the new model would eliminate all the resources and labor that went into producing and distributing millions of shrink-wrapped boxes. More profoundly, it would change the way Adobe worked toward upgrades. Instead of releasing a new version every 18 to 36 months that included many improvements, Adobe's engineers could constantly tinker with smaller ways to improve the user experience. Since upgrades were included in the subscription price and were easy to release over the Web, customers wouldn't mind getting new versions more often. Any bugs that emerged in Adobe software could be fixed for the entire user base within days or weeks, not years. And the company could smooth out its revenue stream, instead of experiencing dramatic ups and downs tied to releases of major software upgrades.

While this might seem in hindsight like an obvious shift in strategy, it took creative vision and guts for Adobe to make that drastic change ahead of the competition. A more cautious management team would have tested a subscription option for a few years, which would have prevented Adobe from reaping the benefits of a full embrace of the new model and would have allowed competitors to jump ahead. Instead, Adobe got there first and reshaped its industry.

Nike: Running to New Customers

Nike, like Lego, built up a dominant position in its core business, then got creative to expand that business far beyond the original goals of its founders, Phil Knight and Bill Bowerman. From its earliest running shoes in the 1960s (when the company was called Blue Ribbon Sports) through the 1970s, Nike focused on making and marketing high-performance gear for serious athletes. It grew steadily and profitably, but it was clear that future growth in that market could only go so far. As Knight recalls in his memoir, *Shoe Dog*, "Bowerman was forever griping that people make the mistake of thinking only elite Olympians are athletes. But everyone's an athlete, he said. If you have a body, you're an athlete."[8]

After a successful IPO in 1980, Nike began focusing more on "weekend warrior" athletes, teenagers, and even nonathletes who just wanted to look cool. One key moment in this strategic shift was the 1984 signing of NBA rookie Michael Jordan for a series of Air Jordan branded shoes, which quickly became the biggest selling and most coveted sneakers in the world. Another was the 1988 debut of the inspirational "Just Do It" advertising campaign, which launched with a commercial about 80-year-old running icon Walter Stack, shown jogging across the Golden Gate Bridge.

By the early 2000s, Nike seemed unstoppable as a global lifestyle brand. Its most passionate fans even got the "swoosh" logo tattooed on their bodies. But the need to keep thinking boldly never ends. In 2018, Nike unveiled a new ad campaign featuring the controversial quarterback Colin Kaepernick, who had essentially been kicked out of the NFL and denounced by President Trump for his protests against police brutality and his support for the Black Lives Matter movement. Nike knew that embracing Kaepernick would alienate many conservative customers, and sure enough, pictures and videos flooded social media of people throwing out or even burning their Nike gear.

But Nike gambled that losing those customers was a small price to pay for winning the respect of younger, more progressive customers who supported Kaepernick's protests against systemic racism. By embracing him in 2018, Nike's management made a bold statement about its corporate values and the kind of customers it wanted. If they had played it safe and waited for 2020, when support for #BLM became much more mainstream, the Kaepernick ads would have seemed tame and crassly opportunistic. Their value and impact came from taking a chance, before the risk-reward tradeoff of supporting #BLM became clearer. By continuing to push boundaries, Nike signaled that it was still the same scrappy company that Knight had founded on a shoestring, even as it became a global behemoth with more than $39 billion in annual revenue.[9]

Align Technology: Creativity on Every Dimension

Now let's dig into this chapter's featured case study, one that exemplifies "grinding creativity" in an industry that's far less sexy than athletic gear, toys, or even software: teeth straightening. By combining digital treatment planning, mass-customization, and the power of computer-aided design and manufacturing, Align Technology revolutionized the orthodontic industry. By learning from a massive database that now totals more than nine million cases, Align has made continuous innovations in its aligner materials, software algorithms, logistics, and processes.[10]

Zia Chishti and Kelsey Wirth founded Align Technology in 1997, while getting their MBAs at the Stanford Graduate School of Business. Neither had any background in dentistry or orthodontics, but they saw the huge potential market for a better way to treat orthodontic problems, by using 3D computer-aided design (CAD) software and 3D computer-aided manufacturing (CAM). They didn't invent clear plastic aligners, but they were the first to attempt to market them at scale by digitizing the process. They believed that aligners would be more appealing than traditional metal-and-wire braces in every respect—easier to wear, easier to take care of, and much less obvious in social settings—while still accomplishing their orthodontic goals.[11]

After Chishti used CAD/CAM systems to design prototype aligners, he and Wirth began to raise money from some of Silicon Valley's premier venture capital firms. They launched the product as "Invisalign" in 1999, with a team of just five employees working in a small duplex in Redwood City. The founders were right about demand from orthodontists and their patients. By 2001, Align had already manufactured one million unique clear aligners, helped treat hundreds of patients, and trained over 10,000 orthodontists in how to use them.[12] By 2002, having grown to $46 million in revenue, the start-up was big enough to hire a more experienced CEO, Thomas Prescott.

Over the next dozen years, Align continued to grow, to $845 million in revenue. As impressive as that was, the board felt that Align was far from reaching its potential, so in 2015 it recruited a new CEO, a GE veteran named Joe Hogan. He agreed that there was something holding Align back and set out to vastly increase Align's share of the rapidly growing global market for orthodontic services, a total market that might eventually climb as high as 300 million new cases per year.[13]

Later in this chapter we'll see how Hogan more than doubled Align's revenue to more than $2 billion, in his first five years as CEO. But before we get to his ambitious growth strategy, let's look at the different kinds of creativity that put Align on the map to begin with.

Creative Technology

The first and most obvious kind of creativity was technical—the better mousetrap that disrupted a very traditional industry. Conventional braces move the patient's entire bite and smile, starting the moment an orthodon-tist tightens the wires and brackets. Invisalign aligners could move just one individual tooth, several teeth, or an entire bite, which enabled much greater customization. And they could be removed for eating and drinking, elimi-nating a big part of the frustration that teenagers had always experienced. But beyond the actual aligners, Invisalign never would have gotten a foot-hold in the market if the aligners weren't part of a comprehensive three-part process.

Step one: Align offered orthodontists a way to measure a patient's mouth accurately for aligners. At first this required a silicone mold; later, this step was done with a digital scanner. Later still, in 2011, Align acquired the company that made the state-of-the-art iTero Element intra-oral scanner. As Align says, iTero offered "a natural extension to our digital treatment processes . . . enabling enhanced patient scans and an improved patient experience."[14]

Step two: Align solved the logistical challenge of turning those measure-ments into actual aligners, then delivering them to the orthodontist quickly and cost effectively. Early on, the silicone mold was shipped to an Align 3D printing facility; later, the digital scans could simply be emailed. Facilities would spread over time to locations in Mexico, Pakistan, Costa Rica, China, Germany, Poland, Spain, and Japan.

Eventually more than 3,000 CAD engineers would be on staff to turn the scanned images of each patient's smile and bite into a detailed treatment plan—one that would adjust each individual tooth along six dimensions of possible movement. Goals might include anything from eliminating a gap between teeth, to correcting an overbite, to creating space for teeth that had grown in behind the primary bite. Each treatment plan was as unique as each person's mouth. The orthodontist (or later, the dentist) would have a chance to review and adjust the plan before it was finalized.

Step three: CAD engineers forwarded the plan to one of Align's CAM facilities, where 3D printers created molds of the patient's teeth designed for each step in the digital treatment plan—a new mold for every two weeks of treatment. Then the actual aligners were vacuum-printed into those molds, using a patented 3D printing process. The aligners had to be both flexible and sturdy, capable of comfortable wear while being firm enough to move the patient's teeth. As described by Align's senior vice president for global operations, Emory Wright, "The aligners must have memory."[15]

After production, each patient's trays were shipped to the dentist or orthodontist. The patient returned to pick up their first set of aligners and began wearing them for 20 to 22 hours a day for one to two weeks before moving to the next set. All told, the process lasted around a year, with the patient returning every six to eight weeks to check on progress.

Creative Business Models

It's fairly easy to measure creativity in technology by counting patents. Align has earned 1,068 patents worldwide as of September 2020 for its treatment software, aligners, scanners, and other technical innovations.[16] But I'd argue that Align's creativity in business strategy was just as impressive as its technical breakthroughs.

At its inception, Align focused on a channel partnership strategy with orthodontists, setting up long-term contracts in which the orthodontists would buy the aligners at wholesale prices, with extra discounts for high-volume and long-term commitments. Orthodontists had an incentive to recommend Invisalign because they could see more Invisalign patients per day compared to wire and bracket patients, who need a lot more time in the chair to attach, adjust, or remove their braces. If you've ever visited an orthodontist's office on a weekday after school hours, you'll see how hard the staff works to maximize the flow of young patients in and out. Anything that enables an orthodontist to take on more patients is a big advantage.

But patient count wasn't the only draw for orthodontists. Before Invisalign, very few adults sought orthodontic treatment if they didn't have access to it in their teens. Some would risk the embarrassment of wearing braces in their twenties or thirties to improve a smile that had always bothered them, if they could afford to spend thousands of dollars. But those were rare exceptions, until Invisalign began marketing to adults about its more convenient and less obtrusive clear aligners. Soon orthodontists were being approached by more and more adult patients.

Then came an even bigger burst of business model creativity. By federal regulation in the United States, orthodontists could only practice their specialty and couldn't do general practice dentistry. But there was no regulation stopping general practice dentists from performing orthodontics. It was only by convenience and custom that dentists had always automatically referred patients to local orthodontists. Traditional braces were so challenging and time-consuming that it didn't make business sense for the typical dental practice to offer them.

But not quite four years after Align's launch, a group of dentists realized that Invisalign's process was simple enough for them to offer patients basic orthodontic treatments. They filed an antitrust lawsuit against Align in February 2001 for working exclusively with orthodontists.[17] The case never reached trial. Instead, Align seized the opportunity to shake up the orthodontic industry by settling the lawsuit and reaching out to dentists as a new channel.

This shift was a big deal because in the United States there are about 15 dentists for every orthodontist.[18] But it was much more than a numbers play. Dentists have regular visits with adults who might not love their smile, but who would never think to set up a consultation with an orthodontist. Now, millions of potential Invisalign customers could hear about the product from their dentist during a semiannual checkup. They would be a captive audience while sitting in a dentist's chair—an amazing opportunity to reach exactly the right customers at the exact moment when they were focusing on their teeth. Out of the approximately 150,000 dentists in the United States, Align has now trained about 65,000—and 40,000 of them are active Invisalign providers.[19]

Creative Marketing

Align's rise also depended on a dramatically different and creative approach to marketing orthodontic services directly to end users. No previous maker of orthodontic equipment had tried that before; the common practice was to sell and market equipment exclusively to orthodontists. "This was both the first product in dentistry other than toothbrushes or toothpaste and the first medical device company to employ direct-to-consumer advertising to drive demand among consumers and therefore adoption by doctors," remembered Shannon Henderson, Align's long-time communications consultant. "This was a really big deal."[20]

This is a great example of "grinding creativity"—continuing to iterate to come up with new ideas and breakthroughs, as opposed to being struck by a bolt of lightning. In this case, Align borrowed a tactic from one industry and applied it to another in a new way. Pharmaceutical companies had pioneered direct-to-consumer advertising for prescription drugs in the late 1980s and early 1990s, driving blockbusters like Prozac, Zoloft, and Claritin. If a public awareness campaign could get people to ask their doctors about an antidepressant or antihistamine, why not get them to ask their dentists about aligners?

Align invested in all kinds of marketing in the 2000s, including glossy magazine ads with smiling models, upbeat TV commercials, and cutting-edge banner ads and search ads on the Web. The sales pitch to adults was simple: Invisaligns were comfortable to wear, easy to maintain (because you took them out to eat), and nearly invisible to other people. They were less likely than traditional braces to be damaged. They didn't require long visits to an orthodontist while surrounded by middle-school kids. The whole process could usually be done in a year. And in most cases, Invisaligns would cost about the same as braces. The ads encouraged customers to learn more via a toll-free phone call or a visit to Align's website, or to find orthodontists or dentists nearby who could provide the treatments.

The marketing campaign worked for adults, as awareness of Invisalign's brand grew to as much as 80 percent in some surveys. While the market for orthodontics had traditionally been an 80/20 split of teens versus adults, Align has flipped that to about 75/25 in favor of adults.[21] And its brand name has come to be used as the generic term for clear plastic aligners— what might be called the "Kleenex problem" for Align, but a bigger problem for other makers of aligners that were trying to catch up to the leader.

Creative Reframing of the Market

When Joe Hogan arrived from GE in 2015 to become the new CEO, he inherited a successful, profitable company, with $845 million in revenue and a strong brand image. But the GE management system had taught Hogan how to think big and reframe the definition of market penetration. He's the archetype of a Systems Leader who understands both products and commercialization at incredible depth. While respecting the company's progress so far, Hogan envisioned a radically bigger future, driven by a creative approach to growth.[22]

For starters, he saw that while Invisalign was dominating adult orthodontics, it still had only a 4 percent share of the vastly bigger market for teens and tweens. Clearly, the typical American orthodontist still wasn't urging kids and their parents to choose aligners rather than traditional braces. What could be done to change that?

In the adult market, Align had almost no direct visibility into the effectiveness of its marketing efforts. It couldn't measure how many people saw its advertising, how many were prompted by the ads to visit the website, or how many made dental appointments specifically to ask about Invisalign. Some large share of new patients were simply being pitched by their dentists during routine dental work. Hogan referred to this problem of incomplete information as "the leaky bucket." Improving Align's understanding of what was or wasn't driving new cases could be a massive win-win for the company, its dentists, and their patients.

He also wanted to expand Align's international sales. How many more people around the world could afford and benefit from Invisalign treatment? How could the company market to them? How hard would it be logistically to ship aligners to different regions?

After studying the entire landscape and crunching the numbers, Hogan set a goal that challenged Align veterans: doubling overall revenue within three years.

Creative Domestic Growth

Getting more teens and tweens on Invisalign would require improving the pitch to traditional orthodontists. As Hogan explained, "Orthodontists are like jewelry makers. For them, everything has to be perfect. They forced us to be perfectionists [too]."[23] This professional ethic of perfection meant orthodontists were initially reluctant to embrace clear aligners. But as Align's products improved, orthodontists grew more comfortable prescribing them. Said Hogan, "For years, orthodontists thought they were making a decision between wires-and-brackets and plastics. It never dawned on anybody that it was a decision between digital and analog. And once you get there, you have to think, when did analog ever win?"[24]

Improving the pitch to dentists would be harder, because orthodontics was just one relatively small part of a dental practice's business. Orthodontic treatments accounted for less than 9 percent of the total $130 billion dental industry.[25] Align's head of strategy, Raphael Pascaud, detailed some of the complexity of selling to dentists: "If you only offer them Invisalign, it's hard to be relevant, and it's hard to pitch in the five minutes you may get from them."[26] But the more Align could sell to dentists beyond just the core Invisalign offering, the more value Align could provide and the deeper their relationship could become. Digital technology permitted greater customization and customer segmentation of all dental services.

Align made the case for this evolution in workflow beyond antiquated analog systems, by stressing the performance of its new digital intra-oral scanner. It offered dentists and orthodontists innovative software that would help them "sell in the chair" by taking fast, accurate scans that would enable consumers to visualize their post-treatment smile.

In mid-2019, it also launched pilot programs of consulting packages that would help dentists make their entire practices more digital. The first few practices that signed on each committed to hit certain targets for Invisalign sales in exchange for the consulting services. While it was too soon to gauge success when I interviewed the Align team, they were optimistic about this path to growth. As Pascaud said, "Until we can make a practice turn into a fully digitized ecosystem, we will never get to the full potential for Invisalign."[27]

From Align's perspective, these digital tools served as obvious progress toward a more digital future. But for dentists, the transformation to digital was not so simple. Many agreed that a digital practice with better customization and tailored services would lead to higher margins and throughput. But dentistry was still a cottage industry, and investing in the wrong platform or IT system could badly hurt a small practice. As Henderson noted, "Dentists are not technologists. They may own a business, but they are clinicians first and businesspeople second. And practice consultants preaching digital transformation for dental practices are very hit-and-miss [because] it's so new. How do you coach people on total digital transformation? I think [dentists] just don't know what to do."[28]

Creative International Expansion

From its earliest days, Align Technology was a global company. Shortly after its founding it opened a CAD/CAM design studio in Pakistan, taking advantage of an abundance of low-cost engineers there. Align also established manufacturing facilities in Juarez, Mexico, just across the border from El Paso, which was much less expensive than California.

After the September 11, 2001, terrorist attacks, Align sought an alternative to its engineering hub in Pakistan, to reduce possible disruptions due to rising volatility in the region. It settled on Costa Rica, a much safer country with a surplus of engineering and dental professionals. Align's operation in Costa Rica has grown from 32 employees in 2001 to more than 3,000 now. It designs treatment plans and handles customer support and some corporate administrative functions like finance, HR, and IT. Meanwhile, Align's 3D printing and manufacturing facility has continued to grow in Juarez, which is ideally situated for manufacturing due to its access to mass transportation in the United States.

Though Align initially targeted only American patients, Hogan made connecting with global customers a major priority, especially in Europe, Korea, Japan, China, and Brazil. He believed that international expansion was both a "quick win" to grow market share in large economies and strategically necessary to grow the Invisalign brand and get out ahead of competitors.

Each country that Align expanded into had its own local logistical and regulatory complexities. More surprisingly, each also had its own preferences on the customer demand side, local cultural preferences that helped define what an "optimal" smile would look like for each consumer. For example, Americans and Europeans tended to prefer a wider, fuller, "Hollywood smile," while Align's East Asian consumers tended to prefer a narrower, less prominent smile.[29]

Align managed this cultural customization with heavy reliance on local orthodontists and dentists in each country. To fully support them, Align decentralized its sales and marketing teams, empowering them to make their own decisions on what local dental professionals needed. "Getting closer and closer to the customer—that is hugely important," as Pascaud put it.[30]

As part of this localization initiative, Align also opened new facilities in China, Spain, and Germany, a research center in Russia, and a digital scanning manufacturing facility for its iTero intra-oral scanners in Israel. Today, it serves customers across every global region with strategically placed manufacturing operations.

Creative Self-Defense: When the Innovator Becomes the Vulnerable Incumbent

Hogan kept his eyes open for whoever might try to disrupt Align, including new entrants from other parts of the world or any 3D printing or materials science company. He knew how easy it can be for yesterday's bold disruptor to become tomorrow's vulnerable incumbent—especially with several of Align's key patents starting to expire October 2017. This would open the door for lower-margin, generic competitors, including direct-to-consumer start-ups such as Candid Co., Smilelove, and SnapCorrect. As Pascaud summarized the challenge, "We've spent our lives convincing people that clear aligners work. I think everybody's convinced now. The next five years is about convincing them that our clear aligner is better than everybody else's."[31]

But as Clay Christensen taught us in *The Innovator's Dilemma*, the company with the best mousetrap doesn't always win. Sometimes the good-enough mousetrap wins by slashing costs and making an irresistible offer to price-sensitive consumers. "We disrupted the marketplace. We are now being disrupted," Pascaud stated matter-of-factly. "That innovator's dilemma is here."[32]

One threat was ClearCorrect, which launched in 2006 but struggled to grow until it was acquired by the Straumann Group, a Swiss dental supply company, in 2017. With Straumann's resources and extensive sales relationships in the dental industry, ClearCorrect had a direct pipeline to offer dentists and orthodontists a cheaper alternative to Invisalign.

An even more dangerous competitor was SmileDirectClub, which launched in 2013 and immediately started growing faster than Align. Instead of a channel partner strategy, SmileDirectClub relied on a small team of remote orthodontists to review scans and approve case initiations, so consumers never needed to visit a local orthodontist or receive aligners from a dental professional. Patients could simply have their teeth scanned in a "SmileShop" retail location. According to SmileDirectClub, its services cost 60 percent less than "other types of teeth-straightening treatments," and its treatments last just six months on average. SmileDirectClub infuriated the American Association of Orthodontists, but its direct-to-consumer business model was legal. And its rocket-ship-growth drew investments from venture capital and then private equity firms. By 2018, SmileDirectClub had more than $1 billion in revenue and a private valuation of $3.2 billion.[33]

In addition to continuing to invest in R&D to maintain its innovation advantages in materials science and 3D printing, Align went after SmileDirectClub with a patent infringement lawsuit in 2015. As part of a deal the following year to settle that suit, Align invested $46 million to buy 19 percent of SDC, with a noncompete provision and a supplier agreement for Align to manufacture a portion of SmileDirectClub's clear aligners. The investment received a cold reception from the orthodontists' trade association and trade publications, but subsequently skyrocketed in value.

In February 2018, however, SmileDirectClub sued Align for a breach of the noncompete provision from their deal. Align had begun a pilot program of showroom locations to support its consumer marketing efforts. These showrooms didn't sell Invisalign products, but they would offer consultations to consumers with referrals to Invisalign-trained dentists or orthodontists. As Henderson noted, "I think [showrooms] were the way to have a really important conversation. . . . It doesn't have to be either you're the ortho in the office with the *Highlights* magazine on the coffee table, or you're bypassing the doctor's office and going straight to consumers. There's a way to be consumer-friendly and still provide doctor office-driven treatment."[34]

SmileDirectClub's lawsuit went to arbitration, and in March 2019 the arbitrator decided against Align on all claims. It would need to close all 12 of its pilot showroom locations within the month and couldn't reopen them until 2022. Align was also ordered to divest all of its SmileDirectClub investment at its October 2017 valuation—far below the valuation based on its most recent fundraising round.[35]

Hogan had seen SmileDirectClub coming, but his plan to ward them off with investment and collaboration had now been derailed. This inferior, lower-margin competitor was now a serious threat, just as The Innovator's Dilemma had warned.

The Creative Battle Is Never Over

When I interviewed him in March 2019, Hogan reflected on his decisions and Align's accelerating success since his arrival. Revenues were up to a record $2.4 billion for the year that had just ended, and the stock price had increased nearly 700 percent.[36] But for these encouraging trends to continue, Hogan knew that his team would have to keep pushing deeper into new markets. They would need to grow "share of chair" with both orthodontists and dentists. They would have to ramp up marketing to parents, with the message that Invisaligns were a great option for teens. And they'd need to keep supporting the digital transformation of the entire dental industry, perhaps by moving into other adjacent products and services.

Above all, Align would have to remain vigilant and keep innovating in all directions, especially now that many of its original patents had already expired or would soon expire, increasing the risk of cheaper, generic competitors. Hogan believed that the best strategy wasn't to compete with those upstarts for the low-end of the market; it was to maintain Align's status as the market leader with the highest-quality products and customer service, while expanding into underserved markets.

Like any great Systems Leader, he knows that the battle is never over and the need for ongoing creativity never ends.

THE SYSTEMS LEADER'S NOTEBOOK

Harnessing Creativity

- Study the forces shaping technological invention and innovation, and try to find new ideas at the intersections of existing ideas. Look for previously unnoticed connections to other industries or markets.

- Focus your creativity on improving customer outcomes, especially for how your product or service can improve the income statement, balance sheet, or quality of life of your customers.

- In times of volatility, resist the temptation to play it safe. Instead, rush *toward* the disruption; embrace it to discover how it might work for you. The opposite of creativity is standardization. In times of great uncertainty, urge your people to be even more creative than usual.

CHAPTER 5

THE AMYGDALA: TAPPING THE POWER OF EMPATHY

In our brief time together, you might agree with me, you might disagree with me, but you will never forget me.
—Bernard Tyson (1959–2019), former CEO of Kaiser Permanente

E mpathy is defined as "the action of understanding, being aware of, being sensitive to, and vicariously experiencing the feelings, thoughts, and experience of another . . . without having the feelings, thoughts, and experience fully communicated in an objectively explicit manner."[1] Traditionally, empathy hasn't been taught as an essential business skill. Most companies try to measure customer needs and wishes objectively, by looking at sales patterns, as well as through surveys and focus groups. Similarly, most set policies for their employees by focusing on the company's needs. But some companies have always had a more intuitive, right-brained approach to optimizing experiences for both customers and employees. Because they truly care about both groups, they listen closely to subtle cues that might not show up in sales data, survey results, or other traditional metrics.

A 2018 research study by Fleishman-Hillard showed that Americans have a strong affinity for companies that embrace and display empathetic qualities. "Rather than viewing empathy as a soft skill, companies must regard it as a hard and essential skill from the CEO on down."[2] The survey asked consumers about specific organizational behaviors that signal a culture based on real empathy, not artificial or pretend empathy. They found that most Americans feel that all of the following qualities are extremely or very important for considering a company as empathetic:

- Kindness—lead from the heart in how to treat and think about people. (59%)
- Active communication—communicate as a two-way, collaborative process. (59%)
- Self-control—seek to understand first and react second. (59%)
- Aversion to toxic behaviors—set strict boundaries on staff who violate standards of good conduct. (58%)
- Understanding—continually seek to understand how customers and employees are doing, what they need and how they feel. (57%)
- Self-awareness—transparently lead through management's challenges and fears, while helping employees and customers through theirs. (56%)
- Unselfishness—understand that giving has to come before getting. (55%)[3]

To show how these qualities play out in real situations, let's look at how three iconic companies have applied empathy in different ways. Then I'll share what I learned about empathy from Bernard Tyson, the deeply inspiring CEO of Kaiser Permanente.

Southwest Airlines: "Treat Your Employees Like Customers"

According to JD Power, a leading data analytics and consumer intelligence company, Southwest Airlines has the highest customer satisfaction of any airline in North America, trouncing both the major carriers and the discounters. Travelers find its service "far less surly and prone to power-trips than on other airlines. Their crew members aren't perfect, but it's not uncommon to see Southwest flight attendants smiling, joking and singing as they go about their job. Also, Southwest has some of the nicest phone representatives in the business."[4]

Among the widely cited reasons for Southwest's popularity are its lack of change fees, two free checked bags, free TV and movies streamed to any device, and family-friendly open seating—families with young kids can board right after the priority boarding group, which makes it easy for them to find seats together. These and other distinctive touches aren't very costly to the airline, but they show sincere thoughtfulness for the customers' experience—in strong contrast to other airlines that can seem utterly disdainful about customer frustrations.[5]

Take something as simple as the pre-takeoff safety announcements. Most airlines now show preflight videos that mix in some marketing messages while going over the boring details of seatbelts, oxygen masks, and emergency exits. Many passengers ignore the videos. But Southwest not only still has its flight attendants doing safety announcements—it allows them to go off-script by cracking jokes, singing, or doing whatever it takes to get passengers to pay attention. As one airline critic noted, "This unique approach has had positive results both on the aircraft, where the passengers enjoy the show, and on the web, where videos of the improvised Southwest Airlines safety shows are uploaded by passengers and go viral."[6]

According to consultant Fathi El-Nadi, Southwest's culture can be traced back to its founder: "Herb Kelleher encouraged informality and wanted staff to have fun at their jobs. Employees were valued, with Kelleher acknowledging births, marriages, and deaths by notes and cards. Staff were encouraged to pitch in and help out, especially at check-in, giving Southwest turnaround times less than half the industry average."[7]

Kelleher urged business leaders to "hire for attitude, train for skill." He'd say that you can't train employees to care, because, "That was Mom and Dad's job."[8] Consider this tactic, after the company would gather dozens of applicants for flight attendant jobs:

> Southwest breaks candidates into smaller groups of eight to ten. They ask each to tell the story of the most embarrassing moment in their life. People go around the circle and tell that embarrassing story one by one . . . And you might be thinking they are hoping to learn how people overcome adversity. Or how people don't take themselves too seriously. Or how open-minded they are to tell that embarrassing story in public. . . . No. The interviewers aren't even paying attention to the person telling the story. They are looking on the faces of everyone else in the room . . . looking for empathy. Empathy simply shows up on your face if someone is telling about their most embarrassing moment right next to you. But only if you're an empathetic person.[9]

Kelleher believed that in addition to hiring empathic staffers, Southwest should do everything possible to keep them happy, so their good vibes would spread to customers. Management icon Tom Peters called this dictum by Kelleher the key to success in one sentence: "You have to treat your employees like customers."[10] Countless articles and books have been written about Southwest's remarkably good and consistent results in a tough industry. Much of it traces back to a deep commitment to empathy for both staff and customers, at every level of the company.

Patagonia: "Cause No Unnecessary Harm"

Patagonia makes some of the best outdoor gear in the world, but since its founding by rock climber Yvon Chouinard in 1973, its vison has gone far beyond profit. Every new product, marketing message, and charitable activity has been geared toward protecting and celebrating nature. The company consistently shows empathy for customers who share Patagonia's passion for sustainability, walking the talk of its mission statement: "Build the best product, cause no unnecessary harm, use business to inspire and implement solutions to the environmental crisis."[11]

For instance, a few years ago Patagonia actually encouraged consumers to buy less from them, by promoting its Common Threads Initiative: "We design and sell things made to last and be useful. But we ask our customers not to buy from us what you don't need or can't really use. Everything we make—everything anyone makes—costs the planet more than it gives back."[12] It ran an ad in the *New York Times* on Black Friday 2011, with the eye-popping headline "Don't Buy This Jacket."[13] Today it promotes recycled clothing on its website: "Worn Wear is Patagonia's hub for keeping gear in play. . . . The best thing we can do for the planet is cut down on consumption and get more use out of stuff we already own. Join us to repair, share and recycle your gear."[14]

Paradoxically, these initiatives that stress Patagonia's concern about more than making money keep driving sales upward. As one marketing pundit observed, "Patagonia's branding is clearly based on an empathetic view of the target audience. People who buy Patagonia gear tend to spend a lot of time outdoors. If they're backpacking, camping, and hiking, it's a safe assumption that (1) they'll need equipment and clothing, and (2) they'll prefer to buy from a company that values what they care about. . . . Patagonia found a match between its values and the values of its consumers."[15]

Over the years, Patagonia has turned down affiliate opportunities with other brands that are wasteful or unethical. In 2016, the executive team

donated the company's entire Black Friday profit ($10 million) to environ-
mental charities."[16] The payoff is priceless: Patagonia customers never doubt
that the company shares their values and actually lives those values.

This empathy extends to employees, helping win their long-term loyalty.
Since 2014, Patagonia has been closed each Thanksgiving, in recognition
that everyone deserves a private life. The company was one of the first in the
United States to offer parents of both genders two months of paid parental
leave. It lets workers set their own hours, grants two-month paid sabbaticals
for employees to work on environmental projects, offers on-site childcare,
and covers the full cost of health care.[17] Not surprisingly, Patagonia's staff
turnover rate of 4 percent per year is far lower than the 13 percent average for
the retail and consumer product sector.[18]

SAS Institute: The More You Give, the More You Get

North Carolina–based software developer SAS Institute is another company
that walks the walk on empathy for employees, convinced that happy workers are more engaged and productive, leading to lower turnover and better
long-term results. As founder and CEO James Goodnight likes to say, "95
percent of a company's assets drive out the front gate every night. The CEO
must see to it that they return the following day."[19] SAS consistently scores
highly on lists of "best companies to work for." While that's not the only
reason for its extraordinarily consistent performance, the company enjoyed
a 44-year streak of increasing profits, from its founding in 1976 until 2020.

Leadership consultant Mark C. Crowley identified four key aspects of
SAS's empathy that have made all the difference to its optimal workplace
culture:

▶ **Value people above all else.** During the Great Recession, when
revenues plunged and competitors were doing mass layoffs, CEO
Goodnight announced that none of its 13,000 employees would lose
their job. He simply asked them to be vigilant with spending. As he
later explained, "By making it very clear that no one was going to be
laid off, suddenly we cut out huge amounts of chatter, concern, and
worry—and people got back to work."

▶ **The more you give, the more you get.** SAS employees have free access
to a gym, tennis and basketball courts, a weight room, a heated pool,
and "work-life counseling" to help manage stress. An on-site health
care clinic is also free, and childcare is deeply discounted. While

SAS could simply raise salaries and forgo these benefits, Goodnight believes the perks are a better way to show how highly SAS values its workers. The company's annual turnover is just 2 to 3 percent compared to an industry average of 22 percent.

▶ **Build a culture of mutual trust.** Employees are surveyed annually on the characteristics of a trusting workplace: open communication, respect, transparency, and so on. To get promoted into management, they must demonstrate a natural inclination to support and help people. Managers who display the greatest advocacy for others get rewarded with better assignments.

▶ **Recognize the importance of every contributor.** Goodnight sees part of his job as encouraging staffers to take pride in their work. Programmers have the responsibility for upgrades to the software they produce for as long as they stay at SAS, which adds to their sense of ownership. The same principle applies to everyone; even the landscapers who take care of the SAS campus are given dedicated acreage to care for, so they come to treat it as their own.[20]

While Southwest, Patagonia, and SAS all use empathy as a competitive advantage, none face a playing field as complicated as health care. Let's see how one major company is using empathy to change the fundamentals of its industry.

Kaiser Permanente: Using Empathy to Disrupt Healthcare

Kaiser Permanente is both an incumbent and a disruptor within the $4 trillion a year US healthcare industry. This managed care nonprofit generates $80 billion in annual revenue, and its 305,000 employees serve more than 12.2 million members in eight states plus the District of Columbia. Kaiser integrates a network that includes 39 hospitals, more than 700 medical offices, 23,000 doctors, and 63,000 nurses to give its members everything they need: personal physicians, specialists, hospital care, labs, and pharmacy services.

Kaiser uses its integrated service model to fight the inefficiencies (some would say the insanity) of the piecemeal "fee for service" model that dominates American health care. Kaiser's hybrid status as both an insurance company and a health care provider eliminates the tensions that often arise between those two camps. Traditionally in the United States, doctors and hospitals have a financial incentive to order tests or treatments that might not be fully justified by a patient's condition. And insurance companies have the opposite incentive, because the fewer tests and treatments they approve, the lower their costs.

By filling the roles of both an insurance company and a network of doctors and hospitals, Kaiser controls the entire dollar of a patient's healthcare costs. This maximizes the company's incentive to keep its members healthy with just the right amount of medical intervention. This alignment of goals gives everyone at Kaiser a natural impulse toward empathy for its members.

Kaiser sees its hospitals as purely a cost center, because unnecessary tests and longer-than-necessary stays drive up costs without increasing revenues. When a patient is discharged from a Kaiser hospital, it's not the end of the relationship—he or she goes to a Kaiser doctor for ongoing outpatient treatment or monitoring. On the other hand, Kaiser also has an incentive to make sure patients are properly tested and treated before being discharged from the hospital, because a failure to solve their problem will bring the patient right back again. Repeat hospitalizations don't merely result in frustration for patients; they also drive higher costs to Kaiser without any corresponding increase in revenues.

This structure also gives Kaiser the unique ability to share data between portions of its business that are hidden to competitors that control only a piece of the healthcare dollar. Kaiser sees trends that might not be visible to a company that has data from only hospitals, primary care doctors, or specialists, instead of all of them. Even while respecting the strict laws that govern patient privacy, an integrated company can combine disparate pockets of data to make life better for customers.

I learned much more about the company's strategic use of empathy from the most influential CEO in its history, the late Bernard Tyson.

The Unforgettable Bernard Tyson

Tyson's career at Kaiser spanned more than three decades, during which he successfully managed all major aspects of the organization, serving in leadership roles that ranged from hospital administrator to division president. He was appointed CEO in 2013 and then chairman of the board in 2014. He held both positions until his tragically premature death, at age 60, in November 2019. His influence was felt both nationally and internationally. He was named by *TIME*, *Fast Company*, *Modern Healthcare*, and many other publications as one of the most influential people in health care.[21] While the managed care industry is usually depicted as inflexible and cold, even cruel,

Tyson always projected warmth and generosity. He inspired employees to focus on empathy for patients, reminding them that they were really selling health, not healthcare.

His presentations to my Stanford classes in 2016 and 2019 were among the most gripping and passionate we've ever witnessed. MBA students tend to have excellent "BS" detectors, and they could tell that Tyson's faith in Kaiser's mission was sincere. He didn't merely talk about empathy as a theoretical driver of his business; he actually demonstrated his ability to forge an instant connection with 85 strangers.

He opened his 2019 visit with this attention-grabbing comment: "In our brief time together, you might agree with me, you might disagree with me, but you will never forget me." He told us that he had just come from meeting with the families of suicide victims, to discuss what Kaiser might have done better to protect the mental health of their loved ones, and how it could help prevent future tragedies. As he spoke about the misaligned incentives that plague American healthcare, we watched him process his own grief, anger, and determination in real time. You could hear a pin drop in the lecture hall.

Tyson explained his efforts to make Kaiser's hospitals, doctor's offices, and other facilities as good as they could possibly be, not as a business imperative, but because they really matter to the communities in which they operate. He spoke of his sense of responsibility toward all of his internal and external constituencies: individual customers, institutional customers, doctors and nurses, other staffers, technology partners, and the government regulators who oversee everything from safety standards to patient privacy.

Like any Systems Leader, Tyson was pulled in all directions by these powerful constituencies and had to be very intentional about where he directed his energy. He put a priority on spending time with Kaiser employees, especially the doctors and nurses. While he mastered both the big picture and the small details of his company, he was convinced that protecting and enhancing doctor-patient relationships was the core driver of Kaiser's ongoing success.

During his tenure as CEO, the Affordable Care Act radically changed the game by making it much easier for millions of Americans to join the health care system—including self-employed and gig workers who didn't get insurance from an employer. But it also offered individual consumers a bewildering array of health insurance options, with different levels of coverage, premiums, deductibles, and networks of providers. For Kaiser, this meant that a much bigger share of its business would now be individual consumers who needed a different, more empathy-based approach than institutional consumers. Tyson saw this change as an opportunity to grow Kaiser by promoting its unique advantages.

Using Empathy to Reframe Incentives

As Tyson told my class, "The reason our hospital days are more effective than almost anyone else's in the industry is because when you're done in our hospital, we have a warm handoff to outpatient care."[22] Unlike a traditional hospital that has no incentive to worry about you after you get discharged, a Kaiser hospital is on the same team as your primary care doctors and specialists. It has nothing to gain if you shuttle from hospital to outpatient doctor and back again. He continued, "I'm responsible for everything. So I get to take the entire health care dollar and, with my doctors, look at the best distribution of that dollar along the whole continuum, whether a patient needs to be in a hospital or a nursing home or a medical office building."[23]

He noted that the fee-for-service model doesn't merely pit healthcare providers against each other and against insurance companies. It also creates a massively skewed incentive to overtreat America's oldest and sickest patients, while undertreating everyone else and misallocating the industry's resources. "The health care system is financed towards the last year and a half of a person's life. About 75 percent of health care dollars are spent on about 20 percent of the population. And of that 75 percent, about 90 percent is spent in the last 12 to 18 months of a person's life. What I'm trying to do is transform the industry based on the fundamentals of what Kaiser Permanente is about, which is prevention. The best cure is to prevent or catch something early, so you can treat it in a more efficient and effective way and prolong what we call the healthy life years of an individual."[24]

Tyson argued that Kaiser could be a role model to change the industry paradigm away from "We can fix your problems" to "We can help you stay healthy." He set the company's priority toward reallocating the majority of health care spending from the last 18 months to a member's entire life. This included strongly encouraging members to take more responsibility for their own health, including their diet, exercise, sleep, and use of alcohol and tobacco. So many of the chronic illnesses that dominate healthcare spending, including cancer, diabetes, and heart disease, are tied to those lifestyle habits and choices. If Kaiser could help its members do their part toward increasing their number of "healthy life years," the company would also benefit financially from reduced costs. It would be the perfect alignment of incentives.

How Empathy Helps Patients

Kaiser's marketing is designed to reassure potential members. It hired Allison Janney of *The West Wing* to be the calming narrator of its commercials. As one critic noted, "We would happily listen to Janney's voice all day, and if that means tuning in for Kaiser Permanente commercials, we'll do it. Who else could possibly sound so soothing, so knowledgeable, and so appropriately chipper while chattering about something as confusing and upsetting as health care coverage?"[25]

If you browse the Kaiser website as a member or potential member, you'll see the constant emphasis on seeing everything from a patient's perspective:

- **We're here when you need us, 24/7.** If you have a sudden illness or minor injury, your care starts with a simple call to our 24/7 advice line. We can give treatment advice, schedule a same-day appointment with a doctor, or give you the location of your nearest urgent care center.
- **Personalized care from a team that knows you.** Your allergies are acting up. Your son's earache is back. Your mother forgot to take her diabetes medication. Call our advice line day or night and talk to a caregiver who knows about your family's conditions, medications, and allergies—and what you'll need to feel better.
- **Skip the trip.** Whether you have a minor issue like the common cold or a mysterious rash, you can save time by talking to your care team by phone or video. Or email your doctor's office with a non-urgent question or photo and get a response usually within two business days.[26]

And much of the copy focuses on preventing illnesses, rather than waiting until they become bad enough to require help:

- **Help fine-tuning your lifestyle.** Work with a wellness coach by phone to improve your eating habits, stress less, quit vaping or tobacco, and more—at no extra cost. And enjoy discounts on alternative therapies like acupuncture.
- **A plan to treat the whole you.** If you're dealing with depression, anxiety, or addiction, your doctor can help you find care that works for you—and you don't need a referral for mental health care.
- **A doctor who's your personal advocate.** From tracking your health screenings to coordinating your care in an emergency, your doctor is there to connect you to specialists and help you get the right care.[27]

During his 2016 visit, Tyson was excited about the trend toward wearable monitors like the Fitbit, as a way to keep improving prevention services. He imagined future monitors that could track not just exercise but also sleep, diet, and blood sugar. "Kaiser Permanente wants to have a bigger impact on you when you go into grocery stores, because what you eat is a precursor to what's going to happen. We want to be your digital life coach."[28] In a more rational health care system, everyone would talk this way about prevention, but the forces that shape the industry make it rare.

Tyson also spoke about focusing on the nuances of individuals' needs and differences as part of its service delivery model. "It is the nuances that make all the difference in the world. That's why we have, for example, blood pressure checks in local barbershops. That's a community setting that we can go in with credibility and teach African-American men, for example, about prostate cancer testing and things that you may not be as comfortable with in another environment."[29]

He was referring to a program Kaiser launched in 2016, partnering with Baltimore barbershops and beauty salons to offer flu shots and a range of health and wellness services via a mobile health vehicle. Local residents didn't have to pay anything, regardless of whether they had insurance. This public health program later added two "pop-up shops" in West Baltimore markets, offering not only clinical services like HIV tests and blood sugar screenings but also career support, fitness instruction, and financial counseling.[30]

Tyson's emphasis on these charitable initiatives flowed in part from his own family's experiences. Once he had joined Kaiser as a young man, he and his mother didn't have to worry about access to quality care. "The doctor was always there for her—and the doctor was always there for us . . . I assumed that everybody had that. Then I discovered that that's not the case, which led me to one of my passions, which is disparities of care and the inequity of the healthcare system in our country, where people are not getting equal access and equitable care."[31] Whether those mobile health vehicles and pop-up shops drive revenue or not, they reinforce Kaiser's brand as a company that truly cares about people.

Technology as a Tool to Increase Empathy with Patients and Staff

Tyson kept reiterating the importance of using cutting-edge technology as a win-win-win: convenient for patients, efficient for doctors and nurses, cost-effective for Kaiser's bottom line. He was years ahead of the curve in predicting the boom in telehealth. As he told our class in 2016, "Telehealth is going to be our future, via iPad, iPhone, TV, you pick it. We'll be able to create visits between our members and the physician that are not only more efficient all the way around, because the member does not have to drive across town, park, check in with a receptionist, take off their clothes, wait in a room, and read an old magazine, although we have new magazines."[32] For Tyson, technology was not only about cost efficiency. More important, it was about making a member's life easier and better through convenience and speed.

He noted that while Kaiser had started as a hospital that eventually grew into an integrated system, "If I were building Kaiser Permanente today, I would start with my technology platform and then everything else would follow that. . . . I'm now putting $300 million into building an entire digital platform."[33] That was an especially significant investment because Kaiser didn't charge additional fees for e-visits. But Tyson could see a near future when patients would be much more comfortable with seeing their doctors via video chat.

According to the *Wall Street Journal* in 2018, "In the past year, the percentage of Kaiser's insurance enrollees who used its online prescription refill, scheduling and laboratory-result tools climbed, as did use of secure emails between Kaiser and its patients. The company also is redesigning its hospitals, using technology to make patient visits more efficient, from the check-in process to the interaction between doctors and patients. Doctors have access to a platform that enables video consultations with patients."[34]

I discovered how useful telehealth can be in April 2020, when my annual appointment with my endocrinologist fell during the coronavirus lockdown. This was an unmissable follow-up visit to make sure that my thyroid cancer from a decade ago was showing no signs of returning. While I still had my blood test and ultrasound done in person the previous week, my actual conversation with my doctor was fast and easy over video, with none of the usual hassles of driving to her office.

Tyson also invested heavily in new technology to replace various outdated legacy systems, especially for tracking patient information. "When I put in a new pharmacy system that we completed last year, what was supposed to cost $500 million cost over $1 billion, because we had to plug it into all of our other systems, to create the whole integrated approach for our members." He noted that it was worth that huge expense to be able to combine all key data and alerts to improve patient care. "If we give you 30 days' worth of diabetes medicine and it's now 35 days and you haven't reordered, it's very important that we figure out what's not working, if you aren't taking your medication."[35]

Showing Empathy for Doctors and Nurses

Life as a doctor or nurse at a Kaiser hospital or practice is very different from working for a traditional fee-for-service provider. Instead of being paid by how much healthcare you deliver, your income is based on the number of patients under your care. That helps keep the focus on doing whatever it takes to increase those "healthy life years" for patients, rather than racking up more tests and treatments. As CIO Dick Daniels noted in 2018, "Kaiser Permanente physicians do not get reimbursed per virtual visit, just as they don't get reimbursed per in-person visit. This is because the physician groups receive bundled payments for the overall care for each patient, which promotes a balanced approach of high-quality care with appropriate resource use."[36]

This system creates more financial stability and peace of mind for medical professionals. They don't have to worry about whether an insurance company will change their policies to make it too hard to continue working with them. Their exclusive relationships with Kaiser eliminate the traditional tension and frustration many physicians express toward insurance companies. As Tyson noted, "In my business model, I do the coverage *and* the care. So my doctors sit at the table with me, and we can just talk about the members that we are honored to take care of."[37]

Kaiser uses technology to study what its doctors and nurses really need to make their jobs easier. But many are skeptical about innovation and resistant to changing their tried-and-true practices. Consider electronic health records, which have been widely praised as a major leap forward for capturing and sharing patient information among different providers. Tyson had empathy for "traditionally high-touch, hands-on physicians" who now had to focus part of their exams on putting the right information into the right fields on the computer. He recognized that many of the resisters were older, while younger doctors were more comfortable with digital records. He believed that this generation gap was fixable, if Kaiser could be patient with some of its doctors.

To make these transitions easier, Tyson always tried to include doctors in the planning process for implementing a new technology. While other CEOs might just discuss a new initiative with the tech experts and then impose a decision on the company, he saw the value of giving "the people who are actually doing the work" a seat at the table. If he couldn't get his physicians on board with an innovation and persuade them that it would enhance their ability to deliver great health care, any theoretical boost to efficiency would be irrelevant.

Emphasizing Empathy Among Staff and Colleagues

Tyson extended the same empathy to Kaiser's entire workforce, ranging from his C-suite executives to hospital administrators to the thousands who worked behind the scenes to keep everything running. He also described himself as a "continuous cheerleader inside of the organization."

But like any good Systems Leader, he knew that micromanaging could be fatal. The only way to support the entire company was to focus his time and attention where they could do the most good at any given moment, trusting his team to help him direct his focus. "I view my job as thinking about the future. I don't think that I would leverage my platform in my role if I were knee deep into today's operations. So I have smart executives who work with me, and I do not micromanage. Instead, I micromonitor. That means that at any point when I need to know the details, I get the details that allow me to go deep. And then I look for trends and patterns, and I test whether those are anomalies or in fact represent a problem."[38]

Tyson took feedback seriously and would do one of those "deep dives" when a complaint from a patient or frontline worker reached his desk. He stressed to his staff that it was more important to understand the source of any problem than to hide it or ignore it. Like many empathic leaders, he was strongly opposed to shooting the messenger. "I've built a culture where everyone understands this is about being on the same team. This is not about gotcha."[39]

He taught his executives to promote openness and a culture of free speech within their own teams. "I tell people all the time when they come into my office or the boardroom, 'You have the freedom to speak what is on your mind.' I promote that with my leadership team. Sometimes, they speak up too much, but I respect it, and it's a great way to have transparency and an authentic relationship."[40]

Tyson even showed exceptional empathy around the sensitive subject of race, which affected him throughout his career as a successful Black executive. He once described his experience of failing to connect with an older, more senior White colleague who acknowledged that he didn't know how to relate to Tyson as an African American. "What he painted for me was a picture of when a person just doesn't have a roadmap for relating to someone. And that roadmap has a set of theories and hypotheses based on some history that doesn't reflect the person who's in front of you. Then . . . Bernard Tyson shows up. He's qualified to run a hospital, but you don't have a mental map about how to relate to that person."[41]

Leveraging Empathy for the Government

In addition to the financial, technological, and customer service pressures we've already considered, Kaiser also faces the constant challenge of dealing with the federal government and the state governments where it has operations. American healthcare, in addition to being far more complicated than its counterparts in other countries, is also intensely political. At any moment, depending on the occupant of the White House and the various governorships, healthcare companies can be whipsawed with new rules and regulations. This is especially true for a managed care company that fills the roles of both insurance company and healthcare provider. In addition to being Kaiser's most important regulator, the federal government is also a major customer for its services through Medicare and Medicaid.

Tyson stressed the importance of getting along with government representatives from both major parties. While he had strong opinions on how he'd like to change the laws and regulations, he was extremely diplomatic whenever asked about those topics. Offending either Democrats or Republicans would have been a huge problem for Kaiser, which couldn't afford to be tagged as partisan. Perhaps more important, both parties represent citizens who need healthcare to live happy and productive lives—regardless of political affiliation.

Still, his heart was with advocates for reforming the fee-for-service model, which Tyson saw as the primary culprit for America's astonishingly high health care costs. He didn't blame individual companies or executives—he believed they were behaving rationally by responding to the incentives of the system. While reforms like the ACA improved affordability of *coverage*, which he called "the front door to healthcare," they didn't do enough to improve affordability of *care*. He pointed out that 91 percent of Americans had health insurance by 2019, but if a middle-class family can only afford an insurance plan with an expensive deductible (say $5,000) on top of their premiums, a serious illness is still a major financial burden. This leads to a vicious circle: costs spiral out of control, people can't get the care they need, satisfaction with the whole system erodes, people give up coverage, and providers are forced to raise their fees even further.

But rather than rage against this irrational situation, Tyson worked within the system and maintained good relations with Kaiser's regulators. "We have actually taken the approach to embrace the regulatory environment when we don't have a choice. In many cases, we're doing things to meet regulatory requirements that have absolutely no use in my system because I've put the technology in place to do what the regulation is now asking me to do." For instance, his team made sure that Kaiser's innovations in telehealth didn't run into trouble from the strict privacy requirements of HIPAA.[42] Compliance with government regulations were meant to serve the broader goals of keeping members alive and healthy as long as possible, and ensuring that the government was enrolled in Kaiser's decisions was a key part of his thinking and action.

Tyson's Legacy of Empathy

I don't want to imply that Tyson was a perfect CEO. Like any company, Kaiser during his tenure faced a series of problems and controversies that led to bad press. These included lawsuits about the company's requirement that all malpractice claims had to be addressed via arbitration; several conflicts with labor unions that led to strikes by thousands of Kaiser employees; and criticism by activists and some regulators about whether the company maintained high enough cash reserves.

Tyson dealt with those and other problems head on and discussed them with exceptional candor. Whether we were speaking privately or in front of my class, he never responded to tough questions with mere talking points from his legal or marketing departments. Rather, he shared insightful analysis of the opportunities and challenges facing his company, his personal experiences over his decades in the industry, and the complications of solving America's healthcare crisis. He clearly believed that healthcare is as much a noble calling as a business, and he couldn't have been more passionate about his moral obligations to his patients, as well as his responsibilities as CEO,

When Tyson died suddenly and unexpectedly at age 60, he was almost universally mourned across the industry. He was hailed as a visionary and role model for a better future for health care, the kind of person who would light a candle instead of cursing the darkness. I praised him to my students as the ultimate Systems Leader—able to understand the many changes impacting his industry, willing to reframe goals and metrics to align constituencies (such as Kaiser's use of "healthy life years" as a benchmark), and great at communicating a clear and inspiring vision.

His optimism about the future and empathy for all stakeholders continue to inspire me. "I try to bring clarity to the long-term view of the organization. I don't try to create a vision from blue sky. I look at what we have today in terms of assets, and where I think we need to be ten years from now. What are we going to consciously drive towards in terms of defining our future?"[43]

Doing Empathy Right

After interviewing hundreds of business leaders and writing dozens of case studies about leaders from around the world, I have found that the most successful ones are authentically open to others and excited about confronting the challenges facing their organizations. In additional to their intelligence and business savvy, they share an above-average emotional awareness that forms the foundation for empathy. They're willing to go beyond safe, well-rehearsed talking points to speak from the heart to their employees, partners, and customers. Just as important, they listen from the heart as well.

In contrast, some of the least-effective leaders act as if they have too much to lose by acknowledging the challenges that they, their companies, and their people are confronting. I've concluded that this inability or unwillingness to be open and authentic acts as a barrier to understanding the points of view of others in their ecosystem. When a leader is too entirely focused on her or his message, it prevents a true understanding and connection with all parties—employees, customers, suppliers, and even competitors. It can lead to an inability to read a tough situation and take actions that will benefit the organization in the long run. But when done well, as exemplified by Bernard Tyson, empathy can be a powerful tool to move a company forward.

THE SYSTEMS LEADER'S NOTEBOOK

Tapping the Power of Empathy

- Even when you focus on customer outcomes, be aware that while their goals may remain consistent, how they choose to achieve those goals might change.

- Inspire change not necessarily by being extremely dynamic or flashy, but by providing clear and concise messaging both inside and outside of the organization. Articulate your company's mission in a way that motivates employees and partners. Show empathy even to departments or groups that usually don't get much respect.

- Treat governments as a key part of your ecosystem, worthy of a great deal of attention and empathy, even if you have to deal with political parties or bureaucracies with whom you personally disagree.

CHAPTER 6

THE PREFRONTAL CORTEX: MANAGING RISK

There are things that are potentially big in the future but small today—those need to be on the radar of a dedicated independent team with separate resources.

—Carlos Brito, CEO of AB InBev

Humans are naturally averse to taking risks, not because they are dumb but because they are smart. Our ancient ancestors could die at any time from all sorts of threats, and risk aversion became one of the keys to survival. It's literally hardwired into the oldest part of our brain, the brain stem or "lizard brain," so called because that part of the brain controls the primitive fight-or-flight instincts that we share with reptiles.

Doing things that we know have a high chance of failure is unnatural, requiring willpower, discipline, and determination to ignore our deep need for safety and security. Overcoming those instincts requires a well-developed prefrontal cortex, the part of our brains that evaluates and makes decisions about risks. Only the prefrontal cortex can overcome our more primitive lizard brain.

Risk aversion is just as natural in organizations as it is for us as individuals, perhaps even more so because organizations apply peer pressure against taking unnecessary risks. Ignoring the way things have always been done at a company can open you up to losing your status, or maybe even your job if you ruffle enough feathers. Risk aversion was at the root of a popular slogan in the 1970s: "No one ever got fired for buying IBM." During the early days of the IT revolution, computers from IBM were considered a safer bet than those from any lesser-known competitor. If an executive had to choose between proposals from different vendors, the IBM proposal wouldn't draw internal criticism, even if another might offer a better solution at a lower price.[1]

But for many companies today, risk aversion is more of a threat than an advantage. As they become bigger and more successful, their internal rewards systems of promotions and raises too often encourage people to defend the status quo instead of taking risks to drive change.

Even if you're a CEO with a supportive board behind you, it's hard to model smart risk-taking and get your team to follow your lead. Human instincts and peer pressure are always at work, even among the best executives. It's easy to talk about taking risks as the key to innovation and growth, but hard to walk the walk consistently. The easiest path is always to stick to your core business, especially if that core is still profitable and won't be in serious danger for years to come. It's much more difficult to ignore your lizard brain's risk aversion and open yourself to a rational exploration of options, driven by your prefrontal cortex.

The companies featured in this chapter have found interesting ways to overcome organizational risk aversion. We'll see how a Silicon Valley start-up (Stripe) and an iconic industrial giant (John Deere) are both moving beyond their initial strategies and comfort zones. Then we'll dive more deeply into AB InBev, the world's largest brewer of alcoholic beverages, whose CEO realized that even $55 billion in global revenue wouldn't protect them if people keep drinking less Budweiser each year. How do you keep growing in a low-growth industry after you're already become the dominant player via mergers and acquisitions (M&A)? The only answer is a systematic approach to risk-taking.

Stripe: Pivoting to Bigger Customers

Irish brothers Patrick and John Collison dropped out of MIT and Harvard to launch Stripe in Palo Alto in 2010, because they saw a huge opportunity to make it easy for e-commerce companies to send and receive money around the world via credit card payments. Instead of navigating the convoluted global financial system—setting up merchant accounts, ensuring data security, transacting across borders in multiple currencies, and figuring out how to enable recurring payments or multisided marketplaces—companies could partner with Stripe to bypass all those hurdles. Then Stripe's customers could focus on growing their businesses instead of managing payments.[2]

These entrepreneurial brothers were right about the high demand for their services, which were a godsend for small and medium-sized retailers. Stripe's user-friendly, comprehensive system helped it leapfrog more established competitors in the payments space, especially PayPal. As John Collison explained, "Unlike PayPal, which built products to please both merchants and end consumers, we focused all of our energy on [e-commerce] developers. We learned what [they] wanted, and we gave them the tools to build their businesses."[3]

By 2012, mostly thanks to word of mouth, Stripe had more than 100,000 merchants using its platform. It moved to a bigger office in San Francisco and kept growing, thanks to VC funding from major investors such as Sequoia Capital, Andreessen Horowitz, Peter Thiel, and Elon Musk.[4] But even as their core business was growing rapidly over the next four years, the brothers began taking risks to expand into new markets as well.

Until 2012, Stripe had declined almost all requests for customized products tailored to just one customer, so it could continue to improve and scale its main offering. But e-commerce platform Shopify forced a rethinking, as Cristina Cordova, head of Stripe's business development, recalled: "Shopify was already a customer of ours, but . . . they wanted to build a new type of payment platform. . . . To this point, every merchant that used Stripe had to create a Stripe account, even if they were doing so through an e-commerce platform like Shopify. [Shopify] wanted a white-labeled solution in which their merchants could easily accept payments without creating a Stripe merchant account." (*White-labeling* is jargon for making Stripe's brand invisible to merchants, even though it would supply the technology.) "From a technical standpoint, we were confident that we could build this type of product. The question was *should* we."[5]

There was no doubt that Shopify could drive a lot of business to Stripe, but was it worth the resources to build an exclusive product? And would Stripe set a bad precedent by not requiring every Shopify merchant to have a Stripe account? After weighing the risks against the potential long-term rewards, the Collisons decided to go for it. Stripe built customized software that did *not* require Shopify's merchants to create their own Stripe accounts. When this solution proved tremendously popular, other Stripe customers also began asking for unique products tailored for their businesses.

Instead of getting stuck making an endless stream of unique products for each customer, the Stripe team developed "Stripe Connect," a white-label payments solution for e-commerce marketplaces and platforms that connected multiple buyers and sellers online. It could support a wide variety of uses and helped Stripe focus on customers with high growth potential. As Cordova explained, "The decision to launch Connect helped us think about who we wanted to serve—Internet businesses and technology-forward companies. We decided that the average Shopify merchant—such as Sally's T-Shirt Shop—would not be our core customer. Shopify, on the other hand, was exactly the type of company we wanted to target."[6]

Connect opened the door to more high-potential customers, including Squarespace, Indiegogo, Instacart, and Lyft. Each used Connect in different ways, tailoring it for their individual needs. This, in turn, led to the continued evolution and improvement of Stripe's core service. Soon Stripe was attracting even more prominent customers who needed innovative, customized solutions, including Kickstarter, Postmates, DoorDash, Facebook, Twitter, and Salesforce. Just a decade after its launch, Stripe has evolved far beyond being a convenient payments solution for the likes of Sally's T-Shirt Shop. It even ventured into lending in 2019, offering credit cards and small business loans that could be approved automatically using AI models, with no human intervention.[7] By the end of 2019, the company was processing hundreds of billions of dollars a year in transactions.

In December 2020, Stripe announced an ambitious new offering called Stripe Treasury, partnering with banks to deliver a banking-as-a-service interface that would enable Stripe clients to set up bank accounts for their customers. As TechCrunch reported, "Stripe could take advantage of its existing user base to convince them to use Stripe Treasury for new banking products. For example, Shopify will use Stripe Treasury for Shopify Balance. If a Shopify merchant wants to hold money, pay bills and spend money from their Shopify account, they can open a bank account in Shopify Balance directly. This way, they can skip the traditional bank account. Behind the scenes, Stripe Treasury powers that feature. . . . Slowly, Stripe is building products that cover a bigger chunk of the payment chain."[8]

Stripe may seem like a cliché of a brainy company: two smart guys drop out of elite universities, identify and fill a big gap by designing elegant technology, raise a ton of VC cash, and do media interviews in jeans and T-shirts. But the Collison brothers were better than most of their peers at balancing risk tolerance with risk aversion. Their key decision to expand their mission from serving small customers to pursuing major partnerships could have been catastrophic. Without their highly developed prefrontal cortexes, we might be discussing Stripe as a cautionary tale, like WeWork—a start-up that got too ambitious and tried to expand too broadly and too quickly. The Collisons recognized that it was possible to move into adjacent markets while still growing the core business. They were also smart to delay focusing on profitability, to avoid prematurely slowing their growth phase, which was showing increasing returns as the user base expanded.[9]

John Deere: The 183-Year-Old Tech Innovator

It's hard to imagine a company less like Stripe than John Deere, a Fortune 500 stalwart founded in 1837 by an Illinois blacksmith whose innovative steel plow was perfectly suited for cutting through the thick prairie sod. Deere describes itself as "a world leader in providing advanced products, technology and services for customers whose work is revolutionizing agriculture and construction—those who cultivate, harvest, transform, enrich and build upon the land to meet the world's increasing need for food, fuel, shelter and infrastructure."[10]

Deere is so stable that it's only had 10 chief executives in 183 years. Yet former Chairman and CEO Sam Allen, who led Deere from 2010 through 2019, was a role model of smart risk-taking and vigilance against inertia and stagnation. He helped this very brawny company and its 75,000 employees simultaneously push the envelope on culture as well as technology.

When Allen spoke to my Stanford class in 2018, I was impressed that despite his decades at Deere, which he joined in 1975 as an industrial engineer out of Purdue University, he talked as if he were running a tech company. He believed that advanced hardware and software solutions would drive Deere's future growth by generating more and better data that would help Deere's customers become more successful. He also knew that with trends toward digital agriculture and construction automation accelerating, Deere had to take more risks. As a Systems Leader, Allen could figure out what services customers needed by drawing on his deep domain knowledge, while simultaneously improving processes that scaled across multiple business segments and regions. I call this kind of flexibility "managing both vertically and horizontally"—we'll explore it in Chapter 13, on Systems Leadership.

On the culture side, perhaps Allen's most impressive achievement was how he handled the 2017 acquisition of Blue River Technology, a six-year-old Silicon Valley start-up. Deere spent $305 million for Blue River's advanced robotics, which could identify unwanted plants and shoot them with high-precision squirts of herbicide. Deere's machines were already using GPS to automate the movements of farm vehicles to sub-inch accuracy. By adding Blue River's computer-vision tech, Deere would lead the industry in helping farmers maximize the potential of their crops.

As *Wired* reported, "Many companies are using drones to help farmers by collecting data on crops to plan spraying or other operations. . . . Blue River's technology can make a larger impact on productivity because it makes decisions up close, on the ground. Pesticides and other chemicals are traditionally applied blindly across a whole field or crop. Blue River's systems are agricultural sharpshooters that direct chemicals only where they are needed. . . . Blue River, which has roughly 60 employees, will operate as an independent brand, from its base in Sunnyvale, California."[11]

Preserving Blue River's independence, with founder Jorge Heraud continuing as its CEO in Silicon Valley, was arguably a bigger a risk than the $305 million investment. Instead of trying to indoctrinate Blue River's people into the Deere way of doing things, Allen did the opposite, working closely with Heraud to inject Blue River's risk-taking culture into the rest of Deere. So far the arrangement is working, with Heraud helping Deere compete for young engineering talent.

Now let's dig into a company that's even bigger and more dominant in its field than Deere and found an even more innovative approach to risk.

AB InBev: The Rise of a Global Powerhouse

AB InBev became the world's largest producer of alcoholic beverages through a complicated series of M&A going back to the 1980s; it united many formerly independent beer brands from around the world, including Stella Artois, Beck's, Labatt, Corona, and Foster's. In 2008, Brazil-based InBev completed its biggest acquisition, buying US-based Anheuser-Busch for $52 billion. That deal added iconic American brands like Budweiser, Michelob, and Busch to the approximately 630 beers now sold by AB InBev in 150 countries. The Anheuser-Busch deal was the third-largest acquisition in history, creating a powerhouse with annual sales over $55 billion—$10 billion more than Coca-Cola's.[12]

For a company built through M&A, with about 200,000 employees and production in 50 countries, AB InBev's culture has been surprisingly unified. Tested and developed in Brazil in the 1990s, the cultural DNA of original company, Brahma, remained mostly unchanged through three decades of expansion. That's thanks in great part to CEO Carlos Brito.

Carlos Brito: A True Believer

Brito, a Brazilian, joined Brahma right after getting his MBA at the Stanford Graduate School of Business in 1989 and was soon put in charge of a small production plant outside São Paulo. The plant's excellent results led to bigger assignments, until he became CEO of InBev in 2005. After the 2008 AB merger, he became CEO of the combined global giant and a tireless promoter of what he described to me as the company's four unique strengths:

- ▶ **A strong focus on talent.** Brito stressed the urgency of hiring, retaining, and developing great people; neglecting such focus "would make AB InBev an average company in five years." The company recruited at leading universities around the world and ran a Global Management Trainee Program for more than 200 entry-level employees each year. Its goal is to nurture and promote young executives as much as possible, rather than hiring senior managers from outside. Brito often shows up for these recruiting sessions wearing a Budweiser shirt with his name in script on the front—thus demonstrating to others how important this activity is for the company.
- ▶ **A culture of ownership.** AB InBev teaches its people to think like owners so they'll take their business unit's results personally and always strive to improve. "We are never completely satisfied; the focus is always on the next thing," said Brito.
- ▶ **Cost controls.** AB InBev uses "zero-base budgeting," a process developed by Peter Pyhrr in the 1970s when he was at Texas Instruments. Each department and division starts from zero each fiscal year and justifies every line of budgeted expenses, as opposed to the usual practice of simply modifying the previous year's budget.
- ▶ **Humility.** AB InBev emulates the best practices of top companies in unrelated industries, such as Goldman Sachs, Walmart, and GE, because it sees no shame in learning from others. As Brito noted, "We built the company [by] being always the underdog, always the insurgent. When we started, we were not market leaders anywhere. We had to conquer that position."[13]

But despite AB InBev's global market dominance, operational excellence, consistent culture, and strong financial performance, the decade that followed the Anheuser-Busch deal showed increasing signs of serious long-term problems. The company would need a strong prefrontal cortex to take the necessary risks to confront those challenges.

Craft Beers Come on Tap

In the 2010s, the traditional beer market was stagnating in developed markets such as the United States and Europe, due to rising preferences for craft beers, wines, and other types of drinks. The problem was worse for traditional brands like Budweiser and Coors Light, which consumers perceived as lacking flavor compared to niche craft beers.

The situation was particularly gloomy for AB InBev because consumption trends in the industry traveled from developed to developing markets. In the short term, strong performances in other markets could compensate for stagnation in the United States, but tougher times globally were likely in the near future.

The craft beer movement started in the early 1980s, sparked by upstarts like San Francisco's Anchor Brewing Company, the Sierra Nevada Brewing Company, and the Boston Beer Company. The 1990s and 2000s saw a huge upsurge in craft beers, with hundreds of microbreweries offering alternatives to the light lager beers that had long dominated the US market. Some of these (Samuel Adams, Goose Island, Ballast Point, etc.) had grown into large, profitable companies by the 2010s. By 2017, the craft beer segment accounted for more than 20 percent of America's total beer market, up from just 0.1 percent in 1987.[14]

Global powerhouses such as AB InBev and Constellation Brands had reacted by acquiring some of the most successful craft brands. In fact, AB InBev bought eight of the fastest-growing craft brands in the early 2010s. But by 2017, as a result of excessive competition and a new wave of ultra-localized breweries, even the most promising craft beer brands were seeing slower sales growth.

Meanwhile, just when AB InBev might have ramped up its marketing budget to counter these trends, traditional advertising was becoming less effective compared to online and social media marketing. Companies started microtargeting consumers with personalized content based on their demonstrated interests. Could that approach work for brands like Budweiser, which spent tens of millions every year to reach the widest possible audience, via Super Bowl ads and every other kind of mass marketing?

At first, Brito's team addressed these concerns by trying to reinvigorate some of those core brands. For example, a low-carb beer called Michelob Ultra had launched in 2002 with the slogan "Lose the carbs, not the taste." But soon it shifted its target audience to active people with athletic aspirations, and the company ran ads that showed men and women competing in intense athletic activities. The new tagline became "Brewed for those who go the extra mile." By 2017, Michelob Ultra was one of the fastest growing beers in the industry.[15]

But one-brand-at-a-time upgrades and other incremental initiatives weren't delivering enough impact. In October 2014, Brito had an intense meeting with AB InBev's board of directors, which was disappointed that the company had taken too long to capitalize on craft beers and other trends. Brito had to admit that the company's top executives had been discussing innovation for more than 15 years, but fundamentally not much had changed. It was time to try a more drastic approach, to send a message across the company that disruption was of central importance going forward. "There are things that are potentially big in the future but small today—those need to be on the radar of a dedicated independent team with separate resources," he concluded.[16]

A Home-Grown Disruptor

At the time, Brito had 16 direct reports in a matrix organization: nine zone presidents based on geographical areas and seven global chiefs based on functions (finance, strategy, people, sales, marketing, supply, and procurement). He decided to add another direct report who would lead a new, independent unit: a chief disruptive growth officer (CDGO).

In line with the company's culture, Brito didn't want to hire an outsider. He decided that the best person was Pedro Earp, then vice president of marketing for the Latin America North Zone. Earp had joined Brahma as a Brazilian trainee 18 years earlier and had grown with the company. He was skeptical when he first heard about the CDGO job, thinking "This is a $50 billion company. Even if we succeed in the next five years, the difference that we're going to make is going to be immaterial."[17] He would be giving up a secure rung on the AB InBev career ladder, with no idea what position might be available after his time as CDGO, even if this loosely defined unit succeeded. And if it failed, Earp knew he could easily go from rising star to deadwood.

Despite his concerns, Earp agreed to take the position. Brito made it clear that the new unit was intended to be temporary—an accelerant to spread a new culture of risk-taking and innovation to the whole company. It had a dual mission: making progress on innovations like craft beers, e-commerce, and new marketing approaches, while simultaneously helping all of AB InBev overcome its traditional sluggishness. Paradoxically, the more quickly and completely Earp achieved these goals, the sooner his position would be eliminated, as it would no longer be necessary.

The group launched in February 2015 as "ZX Ventures" (Z for *zythology*, the study of beer, and X for *experience*). It would have its own profit and loss (P&L) reporting and autonomy from the company's management structure, in part to signal to everyone that this wasn't just another department. Here's how Brito described it in his Letter to Shareholders:

> Getting consumers to see beer in new and fresh ways means we must do the same. To encourage this behavior, we have created a Disruptive Growth team to explore opportunities beyond the traditional areas of brands, brewing or marketing campaigns. One area being explored by the team is how technology can enhance distribution, packaging, and other aspects of the consumer's experience. The team has identified a number of 'bets' which, while initially small, could eventually become game-changers in the years ahead.[18]

ZX Ventures immediately began to deviate from AB InBev culture by hiring a mixed team that included outsiders from other companies, and even other industries, along with internal veterans. As Earp noted, "Historically, our success had depended on hiring people that, by default, were not contesting the model because the model worked."[19] But ZX needed creative people with an appetite for risks—and it had to convince those outsiders to think of ZX as a tech start-up hidden within a global giant.

Five Speedboats

ZX was organized into five groups that worked mostly independently: specialties (focusing on craft beers), e-commerce, brand experience (focusing on experiential retail), home brewing, and explore (which managed venture capital investments and acquisitions). Earp used a naval analogy for these small groups: "The best way to make sure that you are the one doing the disrupting is to have a lot of speedboats all over the place. You have a carrier that has its focus, but you also have speedboats with troops to go there and do the work. They know what the mission is, so we just leave them out."[20]

The specialties team was the biggest, with 40 percent of ZX's staff. It acquired and invested in several American craft breweries, aiming to partner with their existing teams rather than impose new management. Earp's goal was to create "an ecosystem for innovation for craft." Thirty-one whole-owned craft brands would be integrated into AB InBev by 2020, along with another five in which the company held a minority stake.[21]

The e-commerce team wrestled with the question of how a bulky, heavy, tightly regulated, hard-to-ship product with low profit margins could get in on the boom in e-commerce. Only 1 percent of all beer sales took place online in 2017. But the team believed that share would rise as e-commerce continued to evolve, and they didn't want Amazon or other e-tailers to get too far ahead of AB InBev. They created different e-commerce platforms in several countries, such as saveur-biere.com in France, emporio.com in Brazil, and bevybar.com.ar in Argentina—all offering a variety of premium beers with options for speedy delivery.

The e-commerce group also invested in Ratebeer, an online platform that tracked the popularity of beers in each geographic area. It had a database of more than 500,000 global beers by 2017, reviewed and rated by both experts and casual drinkers. This kind of real-time preference and demand data had the potential to improve future e-commerce targeting. Another recommendation engine that the group developed internally, Brewgorithm, used big data to predict which beers would most appeal to various groups of consumers.

The brand experience group focused on using digital resources to create memorable offline moments for beer drinkers, through initiatives such as physical retail bars, pubs, and brewpubs, as well as licensing beer-branded merchandise.

The home brewing group pursued growing market of enthusiasts who wanted to try brewing their own beer. In 2016 it acquired Northern Brewer Homebrew Supply, a 20-year-old Minnesota company that sold ingredients and equipment to home brewers. The ZX team believed that there was no harm in encouraging beer drinkers to experiment with home brewing, because the more enthusiastic and knowledgeable they became, the more likely that they would drink more of AB InBev's beers. In the long run, the company was better off supporting any consumers who loved beer.

Finally, the explore team was responsible for non-beer acquisitions and investments. They invested in emerging disruptors such as Picobrew (maker of an expensive home brewing appliance that offered Keurig-style convenience); Owl's Brew (maker of "boozy teas" marketed as healthier cocktails in a can); and Starship Technologies (a robotics start-up specializing in food and package deliveries). This group was also responsible for the ZXelerator, a 10-week incubation program for employees who had ideas to solve some of the company's biggest challenges. Just like a Silicon Valley incubator, the program ended with a Demo Day when teams pitched ideas to AB InBev executives. One-third of those ZXelerator pitches ended up being funded. Several became successful start-ups, including Brewgorithm and Canvas, which produced protein drinks using spent grains from the brewing process.

Smart Risks Require Better Data

AB InBev gave its CFO oversight of data and information analysis, since it didn't have a global chief technology officer or chief information officer. Those roles were decentralized to the various business units, since the company had never fully integrated the data systems of all the brands it had merged together over the years. ZX found this to be a significant constraint, since many of its initiatives depended on having large amounts of data. For instance, the e-commerce group needed sophisticated sales analysis for its craft beer platforms, but the relevant data was scattered and often hard to access.

Another frustration was the difficulty of sharing tools and strategies from developed markets with emerging markets. While the beer business is different in every country, there are enough similarities over time to make it valuable to have easy access to global data, to identify similar trends and deploy tools that might already be working in a different zone. But there was no such global database.

Senior management began hiring more data experts, offering them a chance to make a significant contribution. According to Chief Sales Officer Michel Doukeris, "We have a guy here that used to work for Amazon who said, 'Man, there are 1,000 people like me at Amazon and I'm only one more. But when I joined ABInBev, I realized the power that I could unlock through data and digitalization here.' That's great, because those guys are digital natives and understand the power of information. At Amazon and Google, they would be just one more. Here they are game changers."[22]

It would take years for the company to develop a truly coordinated, unified approach to data; until then ZX would have to make do with whatever data it could get its hands on. As ZX Head of Product Management Alex Nelson put it, "The long-term goal is to transform AB InBev into a vertically integrated data company. If we had real-time, hyper-local demand information on what people want, what they're drinking and where—that could completely transform our entire business, our entire supply chain."[23]

On the other hand, data integration carried some risks. Even ZX's e-commerce data team, which Nelson headed, was concerned about the danger of other parts of the company misusing customer information. As he noted, "Most of our global e-commerce customers are craft beer drinkers. So just imagine if the core started sending them ads for Budweiser or for some product that wasn't considered craft in that market. It would hurt our brand proposition in the channel in which we acquired that customer. So if we acquired them in a craft e-commerce store and then suddenly they're being targeted by one of our brands that don't fit that value proposition, that's a huge no-no."[24]

ZX Versus the Core Business Units

Another frustration for the ZX staff was tension between the new unit and the rest of the organization. Not only did the new hires tend to stand out in style and personality, but they were seen (and saw themselves) as working toward the disruption of AB InBev's core businesses. No one was surprised to find some resentment from people in those core businesses—especially since their revenue was funding ZX's experiments. Who wants to live in the shadow of "the chosen ones," as the ZX team was sometimes mockingly called?

It was hard to deny that ZX was favored by top management in many respects. It had more autonomy and more freedom to work on long-term projects. Its people were rewarded based on different criteria than the rest of the organization. Chief People Officer David Almeida summarized how the situation looked to the core units: "We're going to pull bits and pieces of your business out from under you and create an organization that will be managing businesses within your territory. And we're going to do this separately, with a group of people who have a different incentive scheme, different priorities and a different focus. Okay?" [25]

Some leaders of the core business units were frustrated that top management didn't intervene in this misalignment or even seem to acknowledge it. Others basically shrugged off ZX, because the resources it spent were so small compared to the overall scale of AB InBev. Still others recognized ZX as an ally, because any revenue generated by joint efforts between ZX and the geographic zone teams would go to the P&Ls of the zones, while the costs would land on ZX. That was a big incentive to let go of sibling rivalry, which didn't escalate to a serious problem.

The View from 2021

When Carlos Brito launched ZX in early 2015, he couldn't have predicted a pandemic that, on top of all its other horrible consequences, would devastate the global beverage industry. 2020 became the year without live audiences at sporting events, without parties and business conferences, without thirsty students on college campuses. But while AB InBev sales fell more than 17 percent in the second quarter of 2020, both its top-line and bottom-line results exceeded the expectations of analysts. As one noted about the Q2 results, "The company's investments behind B2B platforms, e-commerce channels and digital marketing have accelerated in the past few months, which is likely to aid growth."[26] The initiatives driven by ZX Ventures had cushioned the blow of the pandemic-driven recession.

Meanwhile, several of Brito's predictions had come true during those five years. Overall sales of mass market beers had gradually but steadily declined, especially in the United States. Traditional advertising continued to be less effective than online marketing. And opportunities for M&A had dried up, after one final huge merger with SABMiller in 2016 (requiring AB InBev to spin off SABMiller's MillerCoors subsidiary as a condition of US regulatory approval). There simply weren't any other huge acquisition targets left to pursue. AB InBev would have to rely on the kind of organic growth that ZX's initiatives had started to deliver.

It's hard to apply specific metrics to ZX because much of its work ends up helping the bottom lines of the regional zones and other units. But the company was pleased enough with Earp's results to promote him to chief marketing officer in January 2019—which meant that his personal risk in accepting the CDGO job had paid off. As his promotion announcement noted, "We are bringing together Marketing and ZX Ventures under one global lead, Pedro Earp. By pairing our industry-leading marketing capabilities with the innovation approach of ZX Ventures, Pedro will build on the success of our global brands and help us anticipate consumer trends. Creating a common global lead for both organizations means we can share best practices to bring together the best of both."[27]

What about Brito's goal of making the CDGO position obsolete, by driving a culture of innovation and risk-taking through the entire organization? That was always likely to be a marathon, not a sprint, in a huge global company dominated by bureaucracy, cultural inertia, and an incentive structure that rewarded short-term execution more than long-term disruption. But in the fall of 2020, Brito noted with pride that "some of these early investments have scaled up and were transferred this year to the main company, like many of the craft investments and e-commerce/direct-to-consumer platforms. Now we are talking about ZX 2.0 for the next five years."[28] Earp agreed that a culture of innovation was spreading to the core business. "Probably two to three years from now, I believe the core will have all the innovation and tech capabilities at full speed, and I believe ZX won't be needed at the capability level."[29]

Doing Risk Right

In theory, the very nature of being a disruptor or start-up should make it easier to take risks. You have relatively little to lose, and the idea of creating something new is the whole point of your venture. But even start-ups face the psychological and social pressures of the lizard brain—the deeply human instinct to play it safe and stick to tried-and-true behaviors.

The common thread among Stripe, Deere, and AB InBev is that their leaders saw problems that weren't urgent crises yet but were likely to become existential threats in the near future. They all responded by running *toward* the forces of disruption, taking big risks rather than making excuses to ignore those threats. Stripe began targeting larger but more challenging customers, while its core business was still growing. Deere embraced new technology and a new culture of disruption, imported from Silicon Valley to Moline, Illinois. AB InBev realized that it couldn't avoid a slow decline by tinkering around the edges of its business or getting marginally more efficient. The leaders of these companies realized that running toward risk was actually safer than running away.

On an individual level, Carlos Brito risked his job by very publicly shaking up a stodgy incumbent and declaring ZX to be critical to AB InBev's future. If ZX had failed, Brito would have failed with it. And Pedro Earp risked his secure rung on the corporate ladder to take an unconventional, vaguely defined position, knowing that even if he succeeded, his new job wouldn't last very long. He needed faith that AB InBev would look out for him after his time as CDGO. While he ultimately delivered great results and got promoted to chief marketing officer, his risk could have easily gone the other way.

That's part of the definition of uncertainty: you can do everything wrong and succeed, or you can do everything right and fail. Systems Leaders distinguish smart risks from dumb risks by focusing on long-term impact, not on what's easiest in the short term. They know that in a world of infinite strategic options, intentionally narrowing your choices is almost always a bigger risk than thinking broadly and boldly. When in doubt, they face their challenges head on.

THE SYSTEMS LEADER'S NOTEBOOK

Managing Risk

- Nudge your people toward welcoming risks and uncertainty as a window of opportunity. Show them how they can personally contribute to an exciting new mission or goal, and why the risks the company is taking are better than accepting the status quo.

- Be mindful of your own biases, which naturally emerge from your personal journey and surroundings. People are shaped by whatever behaviors have been rewarded in the past, reinforcing our urge to repeat old habits and consort with colleagues of similar backgrounds instead of embracing change.

- Become conversant in whatever new tools and technologies are reshaping your industry, including your customers and their organizations. Relying on your subordinates to explain these changes to you will only lead to a superficial understanding of their implications. Get firsthand experience and feedback whenever possible.

CHAPTER 7

THE INNER EAR: BALANCING OWNERSHIP AND PARTNERSHIP

When we started talking to [supermarkets], we realized that there were more and more ways to partner with them.... And we saw Instacart becoming more and more the retailer's best friend.

—Apoorva Mehta, founder and CEO of Instacart

C ompanies must constantly make decisions about what they should develop internally and where they should partner externally. This has become even more complicated as digital competencies become core to products and services that have a physical component, and often the companies that make these solutions do not have a strong digital DNA. Yet, outsourcing digital solutions can become an existential problem as these skills become more important to the value delivered of these goods and services. The metaphor I use for this company challenge is the inner ear, which controls our ability to balance.

Business leaders have wrestled with ownership versus partnership since at least the dawn of industrial revolution. In the early twentieth century, Henry Ford was the most famous proponent of what's now called vertical integration. He wanted the Ford Motor Company to own as many production elements of a car as possible, including the steel for the chassis and the many parts inside an engine. By the 1920s, Ford controlled the extraction of almost every natural resource required to build a car, other than latex rubber for hoses, valves, and tires. Facing a looming threat of a British monopoly in rubber in 1927, Ford bought a million acres in Brazil and began slash-and-burn clearing to create a rubber plantation, called Fordlandia. But the plantation struggled and had to be abandoned by 1934, mainly because being good at making cars doesn't mean you'll also be good at running a plantation.[1]

Over the past century, the increasing standardization of components has made vertical integration much less attractive. The business school term for this concept is "modularity." As Clayton Christensen explained, "A product is modular when there are no unpredictable elements in the design of its parts. Modularity standardizes the way by which components fit together—physically, mechanically, chemically and so on." In contrast, "A product is interdependent when the way one part is made and delivered depends on the way other parts are made and delivered. Interdependency between parts requires the same organization to develop both components if it hopes to develop either component."[2]

Modularity increases the incentive to partner with outside suppliers that can probably make components more cheaply and quickly through specialization. Michael Dell became a billionaire in the 1980s by realizing that he could order generic, modular computer parts, assemble them in his dorm room, and sell them as Dell branded PCs. The original PC industry exploded largely because it was all modular (with the key exception of Apple, which we'll touch on later). Winning companies like Dell used their inner ears to lean toward partnership.

Similarly, the pioneering business thinker Peter Drucker advocated for focusing on a company's core operations while outsourcing as many non-core functions as possible. In the early 1980s, he gave General Electric CEO Jack Welch this famous advice: "Make sure your back room is someone else's front room. In other words, don't do guard services at your plant. Get someone who specializes in guard services to do them for you. Get rid of in-house printing, in-house conference services, any business that isn't at the core of your focus."[3] Reflecting in 2004 on this approach, Drucker told an interviewer, "Most look at outsourcing from the point of view of cutting costs, which I think is delusional. What outsourcing does is greatly improve the quality of people who still work for you. I believe you should outsource everything for which there is no career track that could lead into senior management."[4]

Yet finding the ideal balance between independence and interdependence still isn't obvious, requiring a well-developed inner ear. Constantly accelerating changes in technology can make it harder to standardize modular components, and even identifying one's core competencies can be trickier than it seems. It's easy to develop leadership vertigo when trying to find the sweet spot between doing too much and outsourcing too much.

Here's another metaphor that has stuck with me since in the early 2000s, when I was the number two executive at a start-up called Pixim. Think of your company as a castle—how much of the surrounding land do you want to claim and defend? If you build a wall in a 40-yard radius around the castle, that will require a lot more construction than building it in a 10-yard radius. So think hard about which markets are truly your core goals and which ones you're willing to leave to others. Perhaps you can make a deal with a neighboring castle to share the land right beyond your wall.

Let's look at several companies that have made very different decisions about where to put their walls.

23andMe: Smart Partnering

Companies with a strong inner ear have a clear sense of high-value versus low-value work. They allocate resources to the functions they can do better than anyone else. And for functions where they have no competitive advantage, they're happy to set up a partnership and collect a share of a more likely reward, instead of 100 percent of a less likely reward.

We saw this phenomenon in Chapter 2, with 23andMe's exclusive joint venture with GlaxoSmithKline. 23andMe's leaders knew that their core competency was acquiring and organizing consumer DNA samples, and doing basic research using their huge database of genetic information. But developing blockbuster drugs would require other competencies that GSK had already mastered, such as designing precision medicines, recruiting the right patients for clinical studies, and navigating the incredibly complicated process of winning government approval.

The joint venture played to both companies' strengths. It might have been theoretically possible for 23andMe to make more profit by going solo. But the joint venture reduced their risk while offering a cash infusion of $300 million, which was necessary because it takes tens of millions of dollars just to get a single new drug to Phase I clinical trials, and typical approval rates at that stage are just 9 to 14 percent. As 23andMe's vice president of business development put it, "We brought this incredible database and some really great genomics science, the ability to find these novel targets that we believe are more likely to be effective as therapies. And GSK brought a 100,000-person organization, with a proven track record of actually going from a target to a therapy."[5]

Daimler: Under-Partnering

There are two ways you can mess up your balancing strategy: by trying to do too much or trying to do too little. For a good example of doing too much, let's again look back to the Daimler example in Chapter 2. By the early 2010s, it was clear that smartphones would be a convenient and desirable way to control and monitor car functions like fuel levels, issue voice commands, and use apps like Spotify, Waze, and Google Maps while driving. Carmakers had the option of developing their own proprietary control and entertainment systems or partnering with outside parties to integrate smartphones into the driving experience.

Apple took an early lead in the car connectivity market with its well-received Apple CarPlay system, which launched in 2014. As one reviewer noted, "CarPlay revolutionized the car infotainment experience, doing away with the often-subpar software created by car manufacturers themselves, and replacing it with an interface run by your iPhone. CarPlay makes it easy to access apps like Phone, Maps and Messages via the car's own touchscreen dashboard display."[6]

But instead of embracing CarPlay or another system, Daimler opted to develop its own proprietary system, Mercedes me, which worked only in Mercedes-Benz cars. By controlling the design of the interface, Daimler believed it could offer a more complete and sophisticated experience, while setting up a platform for premium connected services that would be developed in the future. Mercedes me was well-designed, with software that could locate parking spaces, lock and unlock the car, or visualize fuel and systems data remotely from a smartphone.

But just because you can do something well doesn't mean you should do it yourself. There's no evidence that any consumers chose a Mercedes-Benz because they liked Mercedes Me. In fact, I bet some were disappointed that they couldn't simply plug their iPhones into CarPlay, as their friends who owned other models could. What might Daimler have done instead with the millions it invested in developing Mercedes Me? A partnership could have freed up considerable resources, including the brainpower of Daimler's engineers.

Borders: Over-Partnering

For an example in the opposite direction of outsourcing too much, consider Borders, the second largest national bookstore chain during the 1990s and 2000s.

When Amazon launched in 1994 with the tagline "The World's Largest Bookstore," many traditional booksellers ignored it. The commercial web was still so primitive that almost no one was shopping online. Who would want the hassle, delay, and shipping costs of ordering a book from Amazon when you could enjoy the atmosphere of browsing at a real bookstore and discovering books that you weren't even looking for? But it soon became clear that ecommerce offered some unique advantages in the bookselling industry. With hundreds of thousands of new books published every year, the total count of potential items was so massive that no brick-and-mortar store could possibly hold the entire long tail of demand, not even a Borders or Barnes & Noble superstore. Realizing this, many booksellers started their own e-commerce operations, even though the raw numbers were still small in the mid-1990s.

Yet as late as the spring of 2001, Borders decided that the way to solve its lack of an e-commerce option was by outsourcing the job to its most dangerous competitor. According to the deal announcement, Amazon would handle inventory, shipment, site content, and customer service, while Borders would "leverage its brand name to drive sales" and "offer content unique to Borders, such as store location information and in-store event calendars." As Borders CEO Greg Josefowicz put it, "While our customers' needs are met online by the people who do it better than anyone else, we will provide them with what we do best—the books, music and movies they love to explore in an engaging shopping atmosphere."[7]

Over the next seven years, e-commerce recovered from the dotcom bust and online sales of books soared, with Amazon steadily increasing its market share. Along the way, Amazon gathered big data on the preferences of Borders customers, which it could use to improve its own offerings. In 2008, Borders finally accepted that it needed to build its own competencies in a booming market segment, so it terminated the Amazon partnership and transitioned to its own new e-commerce site.

But by that point it was too late to reverse course from its failure to recognize e-commerce as an existential threat to traditional bookselling. Over the next three years, Borders' financial results would continue to slide, until the company was forced into bankruptcy and liquidation in 2011. While Borders had significant other problems that contributed to its demise, the Amazon partnership played a major part in destroying the company's ability to compete.

I often refer to this kind of blunder as "dropping the baby." Parenting experts disagree widely on nearly every point of advice, but at least they all agree that you should never drop the baby. Borders lost its balance and lost its grip on its core relationship with its own customers.

Tesla: Going It Alone

There's one more category of partnership strategy worth considering, even though it's rare: going it alone. Some entrepreneurs still try to apply Henry Ford's approach to controlling every aspect of a new product or service. Most of them fail, but occasionally one succeeds with a vertical integration strategy—and that success can be truly spectacular. From the early 1980s until 2011, the world's most famous vertical integrator was Steve Jobs, who insisted that every Apple product (from the first Mac to the latest iPhone) should have a "closed architecture" with all components designed by Apple itself. Today, his mantle has passed to Tesla's Elon Musk.

Like Jobs, Musk is a contrarian who ignores conventional wisdom. As he told an interviewer, "Through most of our lives we reason by analogy, which essentially means copying what other people do with slight variations. And you have to do that, otherwise mentally you wouldn't be able to get through the day. But when you want to do something new, you have to apply the physics approach. Physics has really figured out how to discover new things that are counterintuitive, like quantum mechanics."[8]

Musk brought this attitude to Tesla as one of its cofounders in 2003. The electric vehicle start-up had no interest in copying the best practices of the auto industry, including the outsourcing of modular parts. Musk saw no reason to cede negotiating leverage to outside suppliers if it wasn't necessary. As Tesla grew, he aspired to make production more and more of a closed system, with ever fewer outside components. This was especially important for the high-tech batteries and computing technology (hardware and software) that would make or break Tesla's electric vehicles (EVs). As Musk put it, "I do think it's worth thinking about whether what you're doing is going to result in disruptive change or not. If it's just incremental, it's unlikely to be something major. It's got to be something that's substantially better than what's gone on before."[9]

Tesla's vertical integration gives it many advantages, including the ability to gather usage data remotely from every car it produces, enabling constant improvement to every component. The wireless connection runs both ways, allowing Tesla to push software upgrades directly to every vehicle, without requiring a driver to visit a garage.

As one car blogger noted, "Once it started building Models S and X, Tesla found that outside suppliers weren't able to keep up with its rapid innovations, and it gradually brought more and more operations under its own roof. Tesla is said to be the only auto firm that makes its own seats; it dropped Mobileye as a supplier of the computer that powers Autopilot, and now makes the necessary computers in-house."[10] Perhaps most significantly, Tesla produces its own lithium-ion batteries at scale, breaking ground in 2014 on a "Gigafactory" in Nevada that became the highest-volume battery plant in the world. As the company notes, "With the Gigafactory ramping up production, Tesla's cost of battery cells will significantly decline through economies of scale, innovative manufacturing, reduction of waste, and the simple optimization of locating most manufacturing processes under one roof."[11]

By 2016, a Goldman Sachs analyst concluded that Tesla was already about 80 percent vertically integrated.[12] *Forbes* observed in 2020 that, "while traditional companies rely on complex supply chains, Tesla is far more self-sufficient. . . . Anybody who thinks that by dismantling a Tesla and looking at its parts they'd be able to copy it would be seriously mistaken: all they would find is evidence that it's many years ahead of its competitors."[13]

Musk and Jobs are extreme outliers. Most leaders face strategic choices that are similar to those of 23andMe, Daimler, and Borders—the need to find an optimal balancing point between over-partnering and under-partnering. This skill can be learned and improved, as we'll see now with a deeper dive into a fascinating start-up that has turned balancing into a core competency.

Instacart: Balancing Four Core Constituencies

The online grocery space is haunted by the ghosts of start-ups that didn't survive the dotcom bust of 2000–2001, including Webvan (which went bankrupt and had to liquidate) and Peapod (which was sold for a fraction of its peak value). All found that the economics of home delivery of groceries were unsustainable, because there was no way to bring costs down enough to entice a large customer base to cover those costs.

But that history didn't deter Apoorva Mehta, a former supply chain engineer at Amazon who founded Instacart in 2012. In between Amazon and Instacart, Mehta failed at 20 other ideas for start-ups, including an ad network for social gaming companies and a social network just for lawyers. As he told the *Los Angeles Times*, "I knew nothing about these topics, but I liked putting myself in a position where I had to learn about an industry and try to solve problems they may or may not have had. After going through all these failures, releasing feature after feature, I realized it wasn't that I couldn't find a product that worked; I just didn't care about the product."[14]

But Mehta did care about solving the grocery challenge. "It was 2012, people were ordering everything online, meeting people online, watching movies online, yet the one thing everyone has to do every single week—buying groceries—we still do in an archaic way," he said. He couldn't stop thinking about an on-demand grocery delivery platform. In less than a month, he coded a crude version of an app that could order groceries, and another app for gig workers who would do the shopping and delivering.[15]

Unlike Webvan and other 1990s start-ups, Instacart had great timing. Smartphones were everywhere, and Uber had already proven the viability of playing matchmaker between customers seeking a service and gig workers willing to provide it. Mehta knew that there would be plenty of demand if Instacart could solve its technical and logistical challenges. As he reflected in 2015, "People did not want to go grocery shopping and lug all their groceries back to their homes [in the 1990s] and that's still the case today. But this is the first time in history where a company like Instacart is actually possible, because of smartphone penetration."[16]

Mehta promised customers a unique combination of convenience, low prices, and broad selection. As he predicted, demand began to build quickly in Instacart's original market of San Francisco, which drew enthusiasm from leading venture capital firms. The company expanded into 5,500 markets in the United States and Canada in just eight years. As of its funding round in June 2020, Instacart was valued at a whopping $13.7 billion.[17]

I met Mehta in early 2019, when he spoke to my The Industrialist's Dilemma class. He was smart and thoughtful about all aspects of his company, but the theme that stood out was Instacart's sophisticated approach to balancing its partnerships. Mehta described its ever-evolving relationships with four core groups: the customers who needed groceries, the shoppers who fulfilled their orders, the grocery retailers that worked with Instacart, and the consumer packaged goods (CPG) companies that made the products. It's worth exploring how all four of those relationships have contributed to the start-up's rapid ascent to unicorn status.

Customers: Benefiting from the COVID Market Boost

As of 2018, e-commerce still represented less than 5 percent of US grocery sales, but that share was growing quickly. Forrester Analytics predicted that by 2022, the US online grocery market would total $36.5 billion, up from $26.7 billion in 2018. As the *Wall Street Journal* observed, "After years of inertia, U.S. supermarket chains are racing to add online options, such as home delivery and in-store and curbside pickup, to keep shoppers from shifting more of the $800 billion in annual food and beverage spending to e-commerce firms such as Amazon.com Inc. The process is spurring retailers and major food brands to change fundamental aspects of their operations—from staffing and supply networks to the way they organize their parking lots and stores."[18]

Part of Instacart's appeal was that many grocery stores covered part or all of its service charges rather than passing those costs on to consumers. Instacart left pricing up to its individual retail partners, which gave customers an incentive to comparison shop on the app between local supermarkets. As Mehta said when asked about price differences between store shelves and the app, "The retailers tell us exactly what the prices should be, and those are the prices we reflect for the customers. Around 50 percent of the grocers have the same price in the store as they reflect on Instacart."[19] But there was still a delivery fee to the consumer, which led *Harvard Business Review* to describe Instacart's service in early 2020 as "far from mainstream—a luxury for those willing to pay for convenience, skewing towards young professionals in major cities." [20]

But then almost overnight, the coronavirus pandemic changed the online delivery market. Instacart and its competitors saw dramatic growth from customers stuck at home who tried a delivery service for the first time. Suddenly the challenge of recruiting enough gig workers to pull products off supermarket shelves exceeded the challenge of boosting demand. Instacart sold $700 million worth of groceries per week in the first two weeks of April 2020, an increase of 450 percent over December 2019 that drove its first-ever profitable month.[21] That May, Mehta announced that Instacart had already delivered more groceries in 2020 ($35 billion worth) than it had projected for *all* of 2022. A few months later, one survey found that demand for online delivery industrywide had tripled between August 2019 and August 2020.[22]

All that extra demand is unlikely to vanish after the pandemic. While some customers who discovered Instacart in 2020 will return to going to supermarkets in person, I predict that many more will keep using the service because it saves them enough time and effort to be well worth the marginal cost. It's human nature that if you get used to a new and appealing service, and if you can afford to keep using it, it will become hard to give it up. New habits die hard.

Shoppers: Redefining the Worker Relationship

The vast majority of Instacart shoppers are contract workers, free to set their own schedules and responsible for managing their own time. Their ranks grew steadily, hitting a milestone of 50,000 in 2018 and quadrupling again to 200,000 by early 2020. Then the coronavirus demand surge turned that upward slope into a vertical line. The company recruited another 300,000 contract workers in mid-2020, raising its total to more than 500,000. Instacart was hiring even faster than Amazon during the peak months of the pandemic. Some shoppers reported that they were making more money than ever, $100 to $125 per day for three or four deliveries.[23]

But while the influx of new shoppers made it possible for Instacart to scale up its operations, veteran shoppers claimed that working conditions worsened as a result. Many complained about inadequate training and safety practices. One shopper told Bloomberg News that a lot of the new hires "are people who are economically vulnerable and have been laid off. Now they're wandering aimlessly through grocery stores in the worst shopping conditions I've ever worked in."[24]

The debate about gig workers ramped up in 2020 with California's Proposition 22, a controversial ballot initiative that determined whether companies like Instacart and Uber would have to reclassify all of their contract workers as employees. While many Californians were sympathetic to gig workers who didn't get benefits like paid sick leave, overtime, or health insurance, 59 percent of voters chose to keep the status quo. They believed threats by Instacart and its peers to leave California completely if forced to provide benefits (such as healthcare insurance), which would make future profitability impossible. Some gig workers also stated that they were against this legislation as they desired the monetary and time flexibility offered by these positions.

Other states like Massachusetts, New York, and New Jersey have also considered legislation to restrict gig work. And Instacart can't be sure if lawsuits and legislation will spread to the federal level. But for now, at least, the basic structure of the gig economy remains intact.

Grocers, Part 1: Becoming the Retailer's Best Friend

In its earliest days, Instacart's shoppers went into stores without any special status and waited on checkout lines just like regular customers. As Mehta told an interviewer in 2015, "It was a two-party marketplace where we would connect the customer with the personal shopper who would pick and deliver the groceries. But we were doing so much volume from the stores that we were hitting the threshold of how much we could deliver."[25]

Mehta and his team realized that they couldn't offer a compelling service by continuing to send shoppers into supermarkets unannounced and unanticipated. They set out to partner with as many supermarkets as possible, to make the logistics as smooth as possible. For instance, if supermarkets knew when shoppers were on the way, they could make the groceries on their lists available in the back room, greatly reducing the time needed to grab everything off the shelves and check out.

The pitch to grocers was simple: partnering with Instacart would seamlessly provide a home-delivery solution that would be too hard for them to build on their own. The company could also help stores change their physical setups to more effectively service these home-delivery customers. As Mehta put it, "When we started talking to them, we realized that there were more and more ways to partner with them. Today, Instacart builds enterprise software for the retailers so that they can use analytics to better find [scarce products] on their own shelves. And we saw Instacart becoming more and more the retailer's best friend."[26]

As Instacart grew, the vast amounts of information that it could gather and share with its retail partners became more valuable. Instacart knew which products were being purchased at various times by different demographic groups, which was much more detail than a supermarket could spot from its raw sales numbers. Instacart could also help grocers use their distribution centers more effectively to match consumer behaviors, based on its deeper understanding of how sales trends were changing. For some grocers, these value-added services from Instacart could even replace some of the IT and data analytics services they were already buying from companies like IBM. That made an Instacart partnership even more attractive.

By March 2017, more than 130 grocery retailers had signed up as Instacart partners, including major chains like Whole Foods, Costco, and Publix. A new round of $400 million in VC investment, led by Sequoia Capital, had just valued the start-up at $3.4 billion as it set out to double its footprint from 35 to 70-plus markets.[27] But despite all that great news, Mehta's biggest challenge was right around the corner.

Grocers, Part 2: The Benefits of *Not* Being Amazon

In June 2017, Amazon announced that it had acquired Whole Foods for $13.7 billion. The 1,000-pound gorilla of online retail and home delivery had entered the grocery business in a dramatic way. Although Whole Foods was a relatively small player in groceries, with about 2 percent of the overall market, the deal put one of Instacart's partners into the hands of a fierce competitor that never stopped expanding. Whole Foods announced an end to Instacart deliveries after its current contract expired.

But as Mehta told my class, as bad as he felt when the Whole Foods acquisition was announced, the next day was much better. Being Amazon is great, but there are also distinct advantages to *not* being Amazon. The rest of the grocery industry woke up to a new world where Amazon's bottomless resources might turn Whole Foods, over the next few years, into a relentlessly growing and ruthlessly competitive threat, by constantly lowering prices

while raising the bar on customer service. The incumbent supermarkets realized that they needed help to serve customers better, run their companies
more efficiently, and stay relevant in a world of increasing online shopping.

Albertsons, the nation's second-largest grocer, soon announced a new deal
with Instacart that would give it access to another 1,800 US supermarkets
by mid-2018. Other major new partners included Kroger, Ahold, Publix, and
H-E-B. Instacart also expanded its partnership with Costco and announced a
deal with Canada's largest grocer, Loblaw, its first international foray. As Mehta
told CNBC in November 2017, "Ever since the Amazon–Whole Foods deal
happened, things are very different. We were every major retailer's first call."[28]

Mehta's response to the Whole Foods deal won him praise as "Grocery
Executive of the Year" from the trade publication *Grocery Dive*. It noted that
rather than panic about Amazon's entry into groceries, Instacart focused on
partnering with dozens of other companies that now had a bigger incentive
to offer online shopping. It had expanded from 30 markets that January
to 150 by December, proving that it was strong enough to compete with
Amazon. "Speed, agility and vision have vaulted the company ahead of
smaller upstarts that are trying to muscle their way into the market."[29]

By October 2018, Instacart was being described by *Recode* as "the chief
ally to brick-and-mortar retailers in a $1 trillion industry where e-commerce
sales are growing 29 percent year-over-year, but still account for no more
than 5 percent of total sales."[30] The investing community was convinced that
grocery delivery was becoming so mainstream that there was plenty of room
in the market for players other than Amazon.

By the end of 2018, as Instacart passed the milestones of 300 retail partners and service in 15,000 stores, it seemed clear that its success would not
require Amazon's failure. Since then it has even added the last major unaffili-
ated chain, which happened to be the biggest player in groceries: Walmart. In
August 2020, Walmart announced that it was partnering with Instacart to offer
same-day delivery starting in four test markets (Los Angeles, San Diego, San
Francisco, and Tulsa). CNBC concluded that "the move cements Instacart's
hold over the online grocery delivery market."[31] Walmart had been testing its
own two-hour online delivery option called Express Delivery, which it planned
to expand eventually from 100 stores to 3,000.[32] But with demand for delivery
surging during the pandemic, Walmart wasn't taking chances on rushing its
new service. Like most of its grocery competitors, it turned to Instacart.

Consumer Packaged Goods: Leveraging Big Data

The fourth and perhaps most innovative set of Instacart's relationships is
with the consumer-packaged goods (CPG) companies. This is another

data-driven aspect of its business, a way to capitalize on the massive information it gathers about customer behavior. By early 2017, Instacart had 160 CPG partners, including major companies like Nestlé, Procter & Gamble, Unilever, and General Mills that produce thousands of branded products. Instacart could offer them detailed trend analysis across every retailer and region where their goods are sold, for a single investment in data services. It also offered promotional opportunities that could be more effective than advertising—even better than data-driven Google and Facebook ads.

For instance, imagine that you're a brand manager for Cheerios at General Mills. You get weekly and monthly sales data from the major supermarket chains, so you'll know when Honey Nut Cheerios are outperforming original Cheerios and Blueberry Cheerios. But aggregate sales data from supermarkets aren't nearly as valuable as the more detailed data you can get from Instacart's hundreds of thousands of weekly deliveries. What demographic groups are buying more of each flavor? In what size boxes? How price sensitive are they? Are there other hidden patterns in the data that might help you make product decisions to improve sales? And when it's time to launch a new Cheerios flavor, what could be more effective than a discount coupon targeted to Instacart customers who already buy a lot of breakfast cereal?

Amazon may collect and process the same kind of data, but not for as wide a variety of contexts and customer bases. And Amazon has a reputation for keeping to itself granular consumer data rather than sharing it with its suppliers, even for a price.

This kind of marketing might be especially valuable for brands that had always relied on spontaneous purchases that weren't on a customer's shopping list. For instance, Hershey told the *Wall Street Journal* in 2018 that it was paying for promotions to encourage online shoppers to add its candies and snacks to their online baskets, using data to target those promotions based on past purchases. According to Doug Straton, Hershey's chief digital commerce officer, "You cannot think about impulse purchases the same way as in the physical world."[33]

Instacart's power as a data-integrator with the ability to sell insights to CPGs will only grow in the years ahead. While this trove of big data is a by-product of its main business model, it may become a significant source of profit.

Instacart's Future

Instacart was perfectly positioned to capitalize on the pandemic of 2020 with fivefold growth in its existing markets, just from March through June. Meanwhile, it continued to expand into all 50 states, improving its service coverage to more than 85 percent of all US households and more than 70 percent of Canadian households. After achieving its first profitable month, Wall Street began eagerly awaiting a potential IPO, with the company appearing on several lists of "the hottest upcoming IPOs to watch."[34]

But while its model is based on win-win solutions for everyone in its ecosystem, not everyone was happy about the trends of 2020. Some supermarkets complained about the extra costs of filling all those Instacart orders, which were less profitable than traditional supermarket visits. The *Wall Street Journal* reported that California grocer Bristol Farms' doubled its delivery business during the pandemic, yet viewed delivery as a convenience rather than a replacement for in-store shopping. "It's more expensive and not as profitable. It's a two-edged sword," said Kevin Davis, a special advisor and a former chief executive at the grocer. Other chains, including Midwest grocer Hy-Vee Inc., were trying to expand pickup rather than delivery. Delivery "is not something we discourage, but it's nothing we're pushing to grow," said CEO Randy Edeker.[35]

Meanwhile, Instacart is still facing challenges on the labor side after nearly doubling its army of shoppers in a single year. The continued national debate about the rights of gig workers, with various lawsuits and legislation pending, could still throw the entire gig economy into turmoil.

And Instacart's biggest long-term threat remains Amazon. While Whole Foods is still the 10th largest supermarket chain in the United States, with just $16 billion in grocery revenue in 2019 compared to Walmart's $288 billion, who knows how far Amazon will go to expand Whole Foods over the next decade? "Amazon only enters categories and makes acquisitions that it can scale," said Brittain Ladd, a former Amazon executive turned supply-chain consultant. "Amazon didn't enter the grocery category to control only a small percentage of the $840 billion grocery industry. Amazon wants to become the leader in meeting customer demand for food. Based on my research, Amazon can reach 2,150 stores by 2023 to 2025, depending on the strategy they pursue."[36]

Despite all these challenges ahead, I believe Instacart will continue to dominate its market, thanks in large part to the strength of its inner ear.

Getting Balance Right

In a world where market boundaries blur and technologies enable unexpected entrants to scale quickly with capital and big data, the question of ownership versus partnership can truly be life or death.

In the early days of most new companies, it might make sense to do as much as possible yourself, to deliver the best possible customer experiences and grow your market share. But the bigger you get, the more you will probably have to rely on partners—with very rare exceptions like Apple and Tesla. You may be tempted to hang onto too many functions internally. If so, think hard about how you're going to stay balanced as your scale expands. In almost all cases, as we've seen, partnerships with other organizations can lead to mutual benefit and growth.

Systems Leaders evaluate potential partnership opportunities by asking one key question: Will this partnership help us capitalize on new skills that we don't already have, or can't develop quickly enough into a core competency? If yes, as with 23andMe and GSK, the partnership might be hugely beneficial. If not, as with Borders handing over its e-commerce to Amazon, the partnership might sow the seeds of a long-term crisis in exchange for a short-term revenue bump.

Benefiting from the Systems Leadership skills of Apoorva Mehta, Instacart has found a wide variety of co-travelers that benefit from its services. The company's ability to understand the needs of others in its ecosystem, and willingness to be flexible enough to create space for them to thrive, is a delicate balancing act. Instacart proves that when attempted with a strong inner ear, this balancing act can yield disproportionate success for a company, its employees, and its shareholders.

THE SYSTEMS LEADER'S NOTEBOOK

Balancing Ownership and Partnership

- Analyze your industry's changing landscape to decide on partners who are not just appropriate for the present but can help you expand in the future. Consider the possibility that your industry doesn't have to be "zero sum" and multiple parties can win. Always create space where others can win in their efforts, too.

- Focus on the best interests of your real customers, the ones actually paying for goods and services. This is especially important when you might be tempted to share information entrusted to you with partners who don't have a right to it. Never betray the trust of your customers to benefit your partners.

- Whenever possible, think of your suppliers as partners to be helped on a win-win basis, not as costs to be minimized.

PART III
THE BRAWN COMPETENCIES

It's usually not exciting. It's not as sexy as inventing a new AI technology. And it's hard. But being good at brawny capabilities is increasingly becoming a required competency for all organizations, whether they have a digitally native DNA or not.

In this section we will look at the importance of logistics (the spine), how making things is changing from the past but is still a crucial attribute (hands), operating at scale in a global world (muscles), driving and managing an ecosystem (hand-eye coordination), and sustaining a reputation and brand over time (stamina). Once again, in each chapter we will look at companies that have wrestled with, and often excelled at, each of these physical attributes.

As with our exploration of the brainy capabilities, by the time you finish Chapter 12 you will be able to evaluate how your company deals with these five skill sets and give your organization an overall brawn score.

CHAPTER 8

THE SPINE: LOGISTICS

I think from a consumer standpoint, people have lost sight of whether they're shopping in a physical environment or digital environment. In most cases, their shopping starts with that mobile phone in their hands, and it's how they decide where they're going to shop. . . . They get the best of both.

—Brian Cornell, CEO of Target

L ogistics is the spine of any company, holding the rest of the body upright, enabling the limbs to work together and take direction from the brain. Because it's not flashy, it's easy to forget how essential your spine is . . . until an injury leaves you completely incapacitated.

Logistics can be defined as the art and science of producing and moving goods and components, getting the right things to the right places at the right times. It includes sourcing raw materials and equipment, often from around the world. It also comprises creating and managing inventories, warehousing them, and shipping them wherever they need to go, whether that's across town or around the world. Conventional wisdom holds that being an expert in logistics and supply chains will never get you on the cover of *Fortune* (again, unless you're Tim Cook). But these skills are essential to delivering great experiences to customers no matter which industry or sector you're in.

In this chapter, I'll focus on retail because it's an industry where logistical excellence is especially important, and where there's a huge gap between companies that have healthy spines and those that don't. It's also the industry where the myth of start-up/digital superiority is especially strong: specifically, the idea of the so-called retail apocalypse. In Silicon Valley and other brainy outposts, you're likely to hear that the retail apocalypse is inevitable—that it's only a matter of time before e-commerce completely obliterates physical retail. It's true that thousands of physical stores have shuttered in the past few years, after losing huge chunks of their business to Amazon and other e-commerce options. Several famous national retail chains have either gone into bankruptcy or have lost most of their value, including Sears, J.C. Penney, Macy's, Circuit City, and K-Mart.

But as ESPN football analyst Lee Corso often says, "Not so fast, my friend." Those out-of-business or financially crippled retailers didn't fail merely because they operated physical stores in a digital age. They failed because they didn't adapt to changing consumer trends, and because they focused on cost cutting rather than on growth. Reducing expenses is a good way to maintain short-term profits when revenue begins to decline. But in the longer run, you can optimize yourself into starvation. If you can't persuade more customers to buy more stuff, all the efficiencies in the world won't save you. Nor will the pure brawn of having hundreds or thousands of stores and a sophisticated logistics operation.

The retail chains that are defying the apocalypse focus on adding brains to their brawn, applying innovative new strategies to appeal to customers. Instead of counting on their already-strong spines to save them, they're giving their spines greater fortitude by blending the best aspects of physical retail with new approaches to delivering great online experiences. Instead of slashing costs in a desperate attempt to maintain profitability, they're investing heavily in upgrading their logistics, as part of an overall strategy to improve their offerings.

After a brief look at Warby Parker, a brainy start-up that has been growing a surprisingly strong spine, this chapter focuses on three brawny retail giants: Best Buy, Home Depot, and Target. I chose these three (unlike the other chapters that have a single featured case study) because they're taking different approaches to beating the conventional wisdom about the retail apocalypse. What they share are far-sighted leadership teams that have leveraged superior logistics to deliver flexible and deeply satisfying customer experiences, differentiated by Amazon and other rivals.

Warby Parker: A Digital
Start-up Grows Its Spine

Large incumbents have a natural advantage over start-ups in logistics, because of economies of scale. But that's not to say small disruptors can't make logistics a competitive advantage. Warby Parker upended the market for eyeglasses by solving the logistical challenges of e-commerce for a product that people need to try on before buying and then need to customize with prescriptions after buying.

Founded in 2010, Warby Parker was designed to disrupt an industry dominated by one monopolistic conglomerate (Luxottica) that maintained artificially high prices across multiple branded chains (LensCrafters, Pearle Vision, Sunglass Hut, and others). Warby's business model was simple, in theory: win customer loyalty through a combination of low prices and great service, and slash overhead costs by selling online instead of paying all the expenses of Luxottica's brick-and-mortar chains.

Warby offered to ship five frames at once, for free, so a customer could try them on at home, without any sales pressure, for up to five days. The customer then mails back the box of frames with a prepaid shipping label and a prescription for the lenses to be put into the chosen pair. (There are also options if the customer needs a prescription from an optometrist.) Before long, new glasses with the prescribed lenses arrive, for a base price of $95 instead of three or four times that much at a typical eyewear store.[1] No aspect of this model would have worked if Warby hadn't solved the logistical challenge of making it easy and affordable to ship all those frames back and forth.

What's especially interesting is how Warby has gone beyond its original process to adopt a hybrid strategy. It opened its first brick-and-mortar showroom in 2013, barely three years after launching its online business model, and now operates more than 120 physical stores across North America. In 2015 it also established its first national retail partnership with Nordstrom, setting up six pop-up shops inside Nordstrom's locations.[2]

Customers immediately loved the stores, in part because glasses are a significant enough purchase as to be worth the time and effort to leave home. Customers also like getting expert opinions about what looks good on them; they just hate paying vastly inflated prices for an in-store experience. As cofounder Dave Gilboa told *Inc.* in 2017, "When we launched, we said that e-commerce would by now be 10 or 20 percent of the eyeglasses market. It's grown a lot since then, but it's not as big as we anticipated, and that is one of the things compelling us to do more stores."[3]

Physical stores soon became the company's biggest source of growth, without cannibalizing its online sales. Gilboa added, "Once we open a store, we see a short-term slowdown in our e-commerce business in that market. But after 9 or 12 months, we see e-commerce sales accelerate and grow faster than they had been before the store opened. We've seen that pattern in virtually every market."[4]

Getting good at physical retail required an increasingly sophisticated reliance on big data and high-tech inventory management. Warby Parker built its own point-of-sale system, so salespeople with iPad minis could quickly see customers' favorite frames from the website; past purchases, if any; and shipping, payment, and prescription information—and use that information to deliver better service. For instance, if a customer liked a pair of frames in the store, a salesperson could snap a picture on the iPad and send the shopper a personal email, making it easy to order those glasses later on. According to Gilboa, more than 70 percent of customers who got that email would open it, and more than 30 percent would end up buying.[5]

This kind of Brains-and-Brawn integration is as powerful as anything developed by the major retail chains, despite their deeper pockets and vastly larger number of locations. Now let's look at how three of those much bigger and brawnier chains are driving their own innovations.

Best Buy: Redefining Value and Service

Best Buy CEO Hubert Joly spoke to my Stanford class in March 2019 about his company's impressive turnaround. Over the previous decade, e-commerce in the electronics/TV/computer market had driven the bankruptcies of CompUSA, RadioShack, Circuit City, and others. When Joly took over in August 2012, things looked almost as dire for Best Buy. But he saw hidden opportunity in his rapidly shifting market.

While the company was being discussed, both internally and externally, exclusively in terms of the headwinds it faced, Joly reframed each of those headwinds as a tailwind. He recognized that the overall consumer electronics market was booming, with the Great Recession subsiding by 2012 and a slew of new product categories catching on. People were loving smart speakers like Alexa and smart thermostats like Nest. Smartphones were trending toward near-universal consumer adoption, in both their iPhone and Android flavors. But to take advantage of these and other trends, Best Buy had to do a lot more than put products on shelves and wait for customers to show up. It had to redefine its value and service propositions.

Joly's team came up with two major strategies to shift Best Buy's mindset and apply the company's scale and logistical strengths to harness those tailwinds. The first was reinventing the physical stores, accepting that customers were already using them in part as showrooms. The second was redefining customer service as a broader and more intimate relationship that could enhance long-term customer loyalty.

Reinventing the Store Floor

One headwind facing Best Buy was the rise of "showrooming"—the consumer practice of looking at products in a physical store before ordering online to get a cheaper price. If Best Buy could improve the in-store shopping experience, and get closer to matching other people's online prices, maybe shoppers would complete a purchase right in the store instead of redirecting it online.

One idea to improve the experience was to section off stores-within-stores where customers could explore items from various manufacturers, including major brands like Apple, Samsung, Sony, and even Amazon. Best Buy's in-store experts helped customers compare features and mix-and-match components to meet their goals, such as a home entertainment system or a desktop computer plus printer, a tablet, or smart speakers. As these and other categories became more complex, the need for sophisticated, brand-neutral help would continue to increase.

Although many of Best Buy's suppliers were starting to operate their own stores, Joly realized that none of them, not even Apple, could completely satisfy customers with just their own branded merchandise. Technology had gotten too sprawling for any single brand to fill every niche. And people increasingly needed expert help to choose the ideal components for their unique needs and to make everything work together. Joly made a convincing case to his major suppliers, including Apple, that allowing Best Buy to create branded sections of the store for their products was a win-win that would increase sales of their products. Within each mini-store on the floor, the brand's products were merchandised to look as appealing as possible.

Companies like Apple benefited from investing in a mini-store display, even though Best Buy was directly competing with their own stores. Unlike many retailers that responded to disruption through the development of private label brands, Best Buy decided to become extra helpful to their suppliers, even playing a critical role in orchestrating product launches and setting product standards. Treating suppliers like customers and ensuring that they receive value out of every exchange suddenly made Best Buy more relevant.

Joly and Best Buy even helped suppliers that competed directly with them, such as Amazon. He explained that if he excluded any key suppliers from his stores, his own consumers would be the ones to suffer. So Best Buy had to feature products like Amazon's Alexa-based Echo smart speakers and work to make the Amazon mini-stores as desirable as possible, to encourage his rival to build part of its distribution strategy around Best Buy.

As Joly put it, "So many of us buy the easy stuff online. If we're going to take the trouble of going to the store, it has to be worthwhile. What does the store within the store uniquely do? If you're not sure what you want, to be able to touch, feel, experience the new technology and then talk to a human being is incredibly valuable. We also provide a unique service to the vendors, which need a place to showcase their stuff."[6]

The mini-store strategy depended heavily on logistical and supply chain excellence, to make sure all these products from all these brands were in the right places at the right time. Joly also noted that half of the orders being placed at BestBuy.com were being picked up at the store, usually within an hour of the online order being placed, by buyers who didn't want to wait a few days for delivery. That's another essential skill for retailers that want to avoid the apocalypse.

Wing-to-Wing Service

Joly's second major initiative was turning a headwind of increasingly complex technology into a tailwind of a more advanced approach to customer service. Most businesses have IT departments that are responsible for choosing components, installing them, connecting them to other products, troubleshooting problems, and fixing anything that breaks. But individual consumers were on their own with their connected products, and many were floundering with home technology. If Best Buy could become the trusted provider of that kind of wing-to-wing service, the potential was enormous.

He summarized the goal as, "I want to help you figure out how technology can help you live a better life and then help you make sure that things keep going. If Netflix is not working tonight, is it because of Netflix? Is it the piping to the home? Is it the Wi-Fi, the TV, the streaming device? Irrespective of where you bought your products, we have this wonderful offering that will support everything you have in your home."[7]

To implement this strategy, Joly ramped up Geek Squad, a previously underutilized asset that Best Buy had acquired a decade before he became CEO. Founded as an independent company in 1994, Geek Squad originally offered computer-related services and accessories. But now it does far more.

A service contract will get you unlimited diagnosis and repairs not just for your desktop or laptop computer, but for your smartphone, tablet, internet-enabled TV, Wi-Fi router, smart speaker, and pretty much any other kind of electronics or appliances. And if you don't want to schedule a visit at home, you can get 24-hour assistance online or by telephone. That peace of mind might be well worth $199.99 for an annual "Total Tech Support" service contract.

Joly noted that Best Buy is constantly expanding its service offerings. "We've launched a number of initiatives like the in-home advisor program, where we go to your home to see what you need and create a solution for you. We support everything you have in your home, irrespective of where you bought it. And we have a number of initiatives around aging seniors which will help monitor their health, so we can help them live longer in their home independently with the help of technology. We're combining the human touch and the use of technology."[8]

I saw firsthand how this works, and how much it depends on great logistics, when I purchased two televisions from Best Buy. A team brought them into my house, set up the wall mounts exactly where I wanted them, and installed the TVs. Then they stayed long enough to set up my web-based TV services (Netflix, Hulu etc.) and to make sure everything was working perfectly with my remote controls. Delegating those challenges to experts was well worth the extra $100 fee. I also signed up for a one-year contract for Total Tech Support, which came branded with the names of both Best Buy and Geek Squad. The TV installation process reassured me that these people know what they're doing and have the logistical skills to deliver what they promise.

Focus on Customers, Not Competitors

Joly pointed out to our class that if Best Buy had focused on its competitors, it would have probably missed the opportunity to leverage its logistical resources toward becoming more service-driven. But by relentlessly zeroing in on customer needs, it was easier to spot ways to simplify customers' lives.

Joly retired as CEO in June 2019, and the new CEO, Corie Barry, continued the company's successful strategies. Despite the added costs of hiring skilled employees for Geek Squad who were good at both tech support and customer interaction, the service contracts seemed to reinforce product sales. The happier customers were with their tech support contracts, the more likely they were to buy future products from Best Buy.

Even more encouraging, online and offline sales continued growing in tandem, not cannibalizing each other. Despite the pandemic and recession,

Best Buy reported 4 percent overall sales growth in the second quarter of 2020, exceeding analyst estimates. As the *Wall Street Journal* reported, "As Best Buy started reopening stores, heftier categories such as large appliances and home-theater components sold better, highlighting the importance of in-person shopping for such products. That doesn't mean e-commerce slowed down, though. Domestic online revenue grew 242 percent last quarter from a year earlier, reaching over half of all revenue—the highest it has ever been in a single quarter. Online sales didn't falter much after stores reopened, staying 180 percent higher than year-earlier levels."[9]

As Barry shared when she visited our class in January 2021, a company cannot fall in love with how it does business today. It needs to continue to reevaluate how it will change its way of engaging with customers if it will succeed in the future.

Home Depot: Don't Fight the Inevitable

Home Depot faced a different set of challenges from Best Buy, but likewise used strategic innovation to leverage its existing advantages in supply chains and logistics.

Craig Menear was a 16-year Home Depot veteran before becoming CEO in 2014. He had spent the majority of his career dealing with complex logistics, the expectations of builders and home renovation professionals, and the details of running large retail operations. But just a few years into his tenure as CEO, he told an interviewer, "The thing that keeps me up right now is the amount of change that's happening in our business and being able to continue to make the changes we need to have happen to stay ahead of where the customer is taking us."[10]

While many other major retailers resisted e-commerce or tiptoed into it, Home Depot embraced it wholeheartedly. Menear stressed to his leadership team that there was no upside in fighting the inevitable—doing so would only waste time and give the competition the opportunity to get ahead. Instead, he emphasized, you have to meet customers where they are now, not where they used to be. That means reevaluating your business's core strengths to see what unique abilities you can apply toward filling customer needs.

One goal for Menear was continuing to make the Home Depot in-store experience as good as possible, by frequently upgrading the selection of products and investing in training and development for service employees. As he told my class, "We're in the business of delivering great product. That means we need to care deeply about and invest in innovation in our product." He explained that customers go to a Home Depot store for quality products, great advice, and a satisfying experience. But if a retail company offers a crummy in-store experience or bad products on its shelves, no amount of digital innovation will differentiate it.

Having cleared that fundamental bar, Home Depot was able to go after a more ambitious goal: mastering a hybrid model to give customers the best of both online and offline shopping, making the most of its strong spine.

It's Hard to Ship a Kitchen Sink

One fundamental truth about e-commerce is that the bigger and bulkier a product is, the harder and more expensive it is to ship. That's partly why Amazon started out by selling books and CDs, two categories that were small and light. But imagine ordering a supply of lumber for a construction project, or a set of lighting fixtures, or even a kitchen sink. An Amazon van probably can't leave those on your doorstep. But you can swing by your local Home Depot at a specific time and let their workers load up your pickup truck or SUV.

A few months after Menear became CEO, Home Depot began to restructure its supply chain to integrate the experiences of online and in-store shopping. This included developing and deploying a network of distribution centers for store replenishment and direct-to-customer fulfillment. It was a huge logistical challenge to make sure that every Home Depot store could be replenished quickly, without disappointing any customer who would be promised a specific time for pickup.

As Scott Spata, vice president of supply chain direct fulfillment, told a trade publication in 2015, "We prefer to take the 'e' out of e-commerce and just call it commerce. A high number of in-store transactions start online, where we can drive customers to the store armed with all the information they could need. Alternatively, they might want to see and touch a product in a showroom before ordering a specific size or color online. However the customer wants to transact, we'll make it happen on the back end."[11]

The company began building its first direct fulfillment centers (DFCs), designed to support "omni-channel" capabilities like direct-to-consumer fulfillment and store pickup for online orders. The first three DFCs (in California, Georgia, and Ohio) had advanced warehouse control systems to synchronize order fulfillment activities. As the trade publication noted, "Although the DFCs are the spearhead of Home Depot's response to the omni-channel revolution, they would not be possible without a massive remodeling of the company's supply chain."[12]

Spata described the DFCs as the third key phase in a supply chain evolution that had begun in 2007. Phase one was creating centralized replenishment.

Phase two was building Home Depot's rapid deployment center (RDC) distribution network for store replenishment. Now, in phase three the company was adding greater flexibility for a future with more online orders resulting in pickups at stores. Said Spata, "We knew what we had for e-commerce volume at that time, but we also knew we would double, triple or quadruple that in coming years. This is not just growth, but hypergrowth."[13]

As Menear put it in December 2017, "It's what we call interconnected retail. The front door of our store is no longer at the front door of our store. It's truly in the customer's pocket. It's on the job site. It's when they're sitting on their couch. The shopping experience in most categories starts in the digital world, even if it finishes in the physical world. People go and browse and then they swing by the store. . . . 45 percent of the orders that customers generate on HomeDepot.com, they actually choose to pick up in our stores. . . . Over the past several years, we've built a supply chain that moves goods very efficiently from our suppliers to our DCs and stores."[14]

A Hybrid Model Breeds Flexibility

By June 2018, Home Depot had announced plans to spend $1.2 billion over five years to continue to speed up delivery of goods to homes and job sites. It planned to add another 170 distribution facilities so it could reach 90 percent of the US population in one day or less, according to Mark Holifield, EVP of supply chain and product development. The new sites would include dozens of DFCs for next-day or same-day delivery of popular products, as well as 100 local hubs where bulky items like patio furniture and appliances would be consolidated for direct shipment to customers. As Holifield told a logistics industry conference, customers "expect delivery to be free, they expect it to be timely. Sometimes they want it fast and are willing to pay for that. Sometimes they want it free, and they're willing to wait for it. We need to have the right options there. This is part of an $11 billion overall plan to reengineer our company to ensure that we are prepared for the future in retail."[15]

Like Best Buy, Home Depot found that its hybrid model helped it weather the pandemic of 2020. It reported sales of $38.1 billion for its second quarter, a 23.4 percent increase from the second quarter of fiscal 2019. Same store sales in the United States were up 25 percent. Menear noted in his earnings announcement that "the investments we have made across the business have significantly increased our agility, allowing us to respond quickly to changes while continuing to promote a safe operating environment. This enhanced our team's ability to work cross-functionally to better serve our customers and deliver record-breaking sales in the quarter."[16]

Target: Running Toward the Disruption

Our third major retailer, Target, has had one of the most interesting comebacks of recent years. After thriving during the 1990s and early 2000s—the "Tarzhay" era, when stylish private brands made Target much cooler than Walmart or Kmart—the company struggled during and after the Great Recession. Sales dropped, many stores fell into disrepair, and the leadership struggled to recapture market share from Amazon and other competitors. The board went outside the company to hire a new CEO, Brian Cornell, in August 2014. He spoke to my Stanford classes in April 2019 and again in January 2020 about the company's multifaceted resurgence.

Cornell told us that the key elements were improving Target's use of big data, improving its in-store value proposition, and building a hybrid model for blending traditional sales and e-commerce. Like Best Buy and Home Depot, Target leveraged its core competencies, especially logistics, in ways that its competitors didn't. Cornell described how he threw down the gauntlet: "In February 2017, we laid out a vision for the company. We said we're going to spend $7 billion over three years to reimagine our stores, build new, smaller stores in urban centers and on college campuses, reinvest in our brands, invest in technology and fulfillment capabilities, and make a big investment in our people. The success we're seeing now is really a combination of all those elements starting to mature. We're executing at scale and they're all starting to work together. That's driving great top line growth, market share gains, and more traffic in our stores and visits to our site."[17]

Wall Street slammed Target initially when it committed to invest that $7 billion on in-store upgrades, supply chain improvement, and other elements of Cornell's plan. But he was right that you can't save your way out of a downturn. As my former boss Jeff Immelt often says, "You have to run towards the disruption, not away from it."

Using Big Data to Strengthen Target's Spine

Big data was the foundation for all the other aspects of Target's turnaround. Surprisingly, prior to 2013 the company had no centralized data governance and no department dedicated to overall data strategy. As online sales continued to grow, Target needed to ramp up data science and analytics to further drive its online business. It formed a new dedicated team to build an increasingly data-rich capability. Tech veteran Paritosh Desai was recruited to lead the new group, Enterprise Data, Analytics and Business Intelligence (EDABI). As Desai recalled, "The company had a tremendous opportunity to gather data to improve decision making and how the business was run.

And I figured if I could start with helping the e-commerce activities, longer term there would be an opportunity to impact the whole organization—in stores, across the supply chain—everywhere." [18]

Cornell stressed the importance of EDABI to Target's turnaround, calling it "an investment in understanding the consumer and what they were looking for. . . . While I can talk a lot about strategy, the other thing we've recognized is how important it is to have the right capabilities in place, whether that's technology or supply chain capabilities, or product design, or our focus on execution at store level. Data and analytics have been important guideposts for us as we've gone through this journey. On an average week we get 30 million consumers shopping our stores, a similar number going to Target.com. So we have all this rich data, and now we understand where consumers are shopping, what they're looking for."[19]

Improving the Stores

Cornell put a priority on combining EDABI's big data analysis with Target's logistical excellence to reconfigure the stores, while still keeping prices competitive with both Amazon and Walmart. Over the last several years, Target has also broadened its offerings by adding groceries, adult beverages, an increased selection of toys, and other products that are staples for young families. It got better at adjusting inventory from store to store based on what local customers really want, even keeping toilet paper in stock when people started hoarding it during the coronavirus pandemic. Target also reinvented its private label brand portfolio, adding more than two dozen new brands (like Cat & Jack and Good & Gather), a quarter of which are now generating more than $1 billion in annual sales, according to Cornell.

As the *Wall Street Journal* noted in October 2018, after Target posted its best results in more than a decade, "The company has been shedding some of its stalwart brands and launching new ones. Stocking exclusive merchandise is part of [Cornell's] strategy to fend off competition from Amazon and other chains. Private-label brands also tend to be more profitable for retailers."[20]

The company has added a wide variety of smaller footprint stores in lucrative urban markets like New York and Los Angeles, as well as on college campuses. These stores cater to millennials and Gen Z, different demographics than the young suburban families who were company's traditional core customers. These new stores not only broadened Target's customer base but have been hugely successful, with sales per square foot up to four times greater than Target's older, larger stores.

Meanwhile, Target is being more innovative about partnerships, and not merely with major consumer brands like Disney and Levi's. The company is creating showrooms for rising direct-to-consumer brands such as Harry's (shaving supplies), Casper (mattresses), and Quip (toothbrushes). And Target's acquisitions of delivery services Grand Junction and Shipt have enabled it to offer the same-day delivery options that many online shoppers are beginning to expect.

"There's a Blurring and Blending"

Like Best Buy and Home Depot, Target has embraced a different kind of e-commerce that makes the most of its unique spine—the back-end strengths that its competitors can't match. The logistical challenges of seamlessly blending digital purchasing with in-store fulfillment are harder than you might assume.

For instance, imagine that you're browsing Target.com, planning to get a curbside pickup at your local store in a couple of hours. What if the store doesn't have enough staff to gather and pack your items in the time allowed? What if the inventory software is slightly off, and instead of having two in stock of the lamp you had your eye on, the last one just went to an in-store shopper? What if the cash registers are too backed up for any staffers to have time to run outside with your curbside order?

Solving those and other challenges wasn't easy, but tackling them gave Target a strong competitive advantage. As one analyst noted, "Known as ship-to-store, Target's e-commerce platform turns physical stores into mini-warehouses for online customers. That makes it possible for customers to order a product online and then pick it up in a store on the same day. Ship-to-store reduces Target's shipping and handling costs and takes advantage of already existing space in physical stores. And if a customer decides to do some shopping while already there at Target, the benefit is two-fold."[21]

Cornell thinks that asking customers to choose between online and in-person shopping is increasingly a false choice. "I think from a consumer standpoint, people have lost sight of whether they're shopping in a physical environment or digital environment. In most cases, their shopping starts with that mobile phone in their hands, and it's how they decide where they're going to shop, what they're looking for. They're looking at their latest Pinterest, or they have their shopping list there. I think more and more there's a blurring and blending that's taking place. And I think the consumer today is enjoying the fact that shopping has become really easy. They get the best of both. They get a physical experience when they want it. When they don't have time, they can shop from their desk or from their classroom. And we've made it really easy now for them to interface with our brand on their own terms."[22]

Getting Logistics Right

Let's face it: logistics isn't sexy. But just as plumbers and electricians quietly keep our water running and our lights on, logistics experts are critical for delivering great customer experiences. Any company that excels at logistics will have a competitive advantage in a world where customers demand the right products in the right places at the right times. Great operational excellence is a priceless asset, especially when combined with strong digital capabilities.

Pundits repeatedly predicted the demise of Best Buy, Home Depot, and Target in the age of e-commerce. But all three were fortunate to have Systems Leaders who invested resources intelligently to blend the best aspects of digital and physical. All three used their access to capital to enhance and expand their logistics and supply chain infrastructure, as well as their websites and other points of consumer contact. All three doubled down on shoring up their brawny capabilities, while adding brainy new capabilities. As a result, all three have been able to defy the pundits, using their healthy spines to pull away from their competition.

THE SYSTEMS LEADER'S NOTEBOOK

Logistics

- Don't fight the inevitable: customers increasingly want to shop online, and e-commerce activity is accelerating. If you have physical locations, focus on combining digital capabilities with logistical excellence to deliver great customer experiences.

- Use software to add service opportunities in combination with physical products.

- Not every product can be easily shipped and delivered via e-commerce. Look for ways in which the nature of your products and solutions can serve as a barrier to entry to other companies (especially Amazon, which can't sell and deliver *everything*).

CHAPTER 9

HANDS: THE CRAFT OF MAKING THINGS

*Analog is sometimes better than digital. Great craftsmanship
happens in analog. In music we hear better sound when it is analog,
and we see it in the engineering and design philosophies within
a company. We need to have appreciation for analog and what it
brings to the world.*

—Young Sohn, President of Samsung Electronics

ands are my metaphor for the craft of making physical products, whether as simple as a paper clip or as sophisticated as a Steinway grand piano. This competency includes understanding the trade-offs in your specific industry involving quality, cost, scale, and speed. It requires being smart about how you prioritize those variables, while treating manufacturing as just one aspect of your overall business strategy.

This represents a mindset shift from the industrial revolution, when the best hands were those that could make the most stuff at the lowest costs. The original titans of early twentieth-century production, such as Henry Ford, focused on never-ending improvements in efficiency and economies of scale. Throughout the post–World War II boom years, the companies that sold the most washing machines and televisions were generally those that could produce them quickly enough. The bigger your manufacturing capacity, the lower your unit costs, and the more revenue you could pour into advertising to drive demand for your products.

That classic model began to change in the 1970s, when globalization brought more foreign goods to the United States—many of them appealing to consumers with higher quality, lower prices, or both. This new competition drove many US manufacturers to relocate their factories to lower-cost parts of the world, especially Southeast Asia and Mexico. If your biggest expense was labor, why pay $20 per hour for a unionized worker in Ohio if you could pay $2 per day to someone in Bangladesh or China? Tragically for millions of Americans, job migration toward the cheapest available labor devastated various industries over the past half century. Improvements in global shipping made it easy and cost-effective to build just about anything on the other side of the world.

There are still plenty of companies that make things this way, producing commodities or near commodities very cheaply by maximizing their economies of scale. For instance, while you can buy fancy pens for $5 or more each, Bic still sells basic ballpoint pens in multipacks for a unit price of about $0.20. Bic can afford to sell pens for pennies because it produces them at massive scale. In turn, the super-cheap price boosts demand among cost-conscious pen shoppers. A low-cost/high-volume commodity business model can still work—but it's no longer the only path to manufacturing excellence.

More and more companies over the past decade, both start-ups and incumbents, have been bringing dramatic innovation to their manufacturing processes and business models, working toward high-quality products at prices perceived to be fair. Perhaps the most significant new manufacturing technology is additive manufacturing (AM), which can be defined as "technologies that build 3D objects by adding layer-upon-layer of material, whether the material is plastic, metal, [or] concrete. . . . Once a [computer aided design] sketch is produced, the AM equipment reads in data from the CAD file and lays downs or adds successive layers of liquid, powder, sheet material or other, in a layer-upon-layer fashion to fabricate a 3D object."[1]

Additive manufacturing seems poised to explode in the decade ahead, making it possible to design and to build things cost-effectively in a higher-wage country like the United States. Companies with great hands can now afford to hire and train skilled workers locally, because factories with advanced robotics need far fewer workers. Yet those workers now have much more responsibility for using and maintaining sophisticated machines. When you combine local hiring with local sourcing of advanced materials, this new model of manufacturing can be both high-quality and high-volume, yet still affordable relative to global competition.

A good way to understand this trend is via a type of production possibilities curve designed by my Stanford colleague Robert Burgelman, which plots "delivered cost" (DC) against "perceived value" (PV).[2] (See Figure 9.1.)

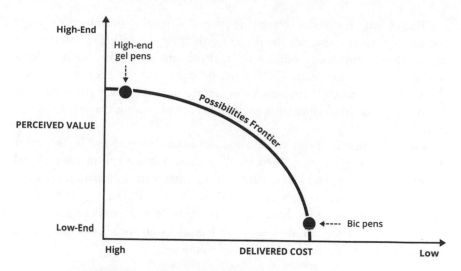

FIGURE 9.1   The Perceived Value/Delivered Cost Curve

On the lower right end of the possibilities frontier, you can profit by selling a product with low PV for a low DC, like Bic's cheapest disposable pens. You can also profit on the upper left end of the frontier, by selling a product with high PV for a high DC, such as gel pens that cost 20 times more. But the best option of all is to leverage new technology to shift the frontier curve outward, enabling higher perceived value for the same or even lower delivered costs. (See Figure 9.2.)

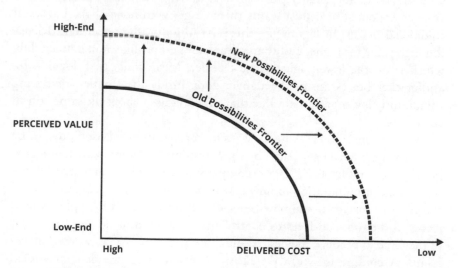

FIGURE 9.2   When An Innovation Moves Out the Possibilities Frontier

This chapter focuses on companies that are figuring out how to change the game in their respective industries by shifting their PV/DC curves outward. They're increasing quality by making products with fewer defects and less need for maintenance, repairs, or replacements. They're also driving down costs to their customers—often not just monetary costs but also by saving production time from previous types of manufacturing. (Time is money!)

First we'll briefly revisit two companies from earlier in the book: smart Align and strong Daimler. Then we'll see how Samsung, a massive global conglomerate, is applying its expertise in manufacturing electronics toward new markets like cars and pharmaceuticals. Then we'll do a deeper dive into Desktop Metal, a start-up that's riding the trend of additive manufacturing, aiming to upend the world of industrial production with its cutting-edge, high-quality, yet affordable 3D printing solutions.

Align: Never Stop Improving Production Processes

As we saw in Chapter 4, Align Technology has been a tech innovator since it launched in 1997. Its Invisalign dental aligners had to be high quality with extremely limited defects if they were going to compete with traditional wire-and-bracket braces. That became even more true later, with the rise of cheap competitors like the SmileDirectClub. Invisalign's brand message stresses its top-quality performance, moving your teeth exactly where your orthodontist or dentist wants them to go, with none of the hassles of traditional braces. In Figure 9.3, this puts Align on the upper left, delivering high value for higher cost than cheap competitors like SmileDirectClub, which is on the lower right of the frontier. Meanwhile, traditional wire-and-bracket braces are in the danger zone inside the frontier, delivering significantly lower perceived value than Invisaligns at about the same cost to customers.

Align is constantly looking for ways to improve its production process, by studying the big data generated by the 9 million Invisalign patients to date. For instance, in October 2020 the company announced "SmartForce Aligner Activation," an innovation in how it would produce aligners. Select areas of the aligner's surface would now be "specifically contoured to apply optimal forces to the tooth surfaces to control the location, direction and intensity of the force to produce the desired outcome and minimize unwanted movement." According to Mitra Derakhshan, Align's vice president of Global Clinical, "The additional activation is now automatically determined by the

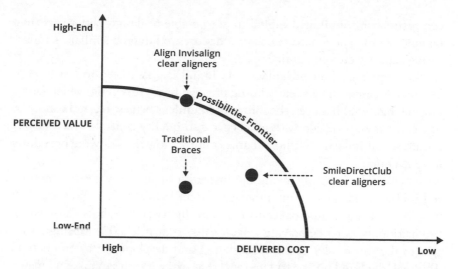

FIGURE 9.3   The competitive space for orthodontia solutions

software and fabricated into the aligner as SmartForce Aligner Activation, thereby reducing doctors' inclination to overcorrect certain movements in their treatment plans."[3]

Even companies like Align that essentially invented a completely new production process can never stop improving that process, if they want to stay on their industry's evolving value/cost frontier. And every Align innovation pushes the frontier a little further outward, making it harder for competitors to keep up.

Daimler: Smart Factories with a Human Touch

Another company we previously looked at, Daimler, has been a manufacturing pioneer since the nineteenth century. Mercedes cars set the global benchmark for high-quality craftsmanship, with a workforce of 300,000 committed to maintaining those high standards as a moat against competitors. Like Align, Daimler has consistently reevaluated and refined its manufacturing processes to take advantage of the latest innovations in its industry. It also built up a network of global manufacturing facilities far beyond its home in Germany, which required considerable political maneuvering in countries as diverse as Brazil, France, Hungary, India, Indonesia, Malaysia, South Africa, Thailand, the United States, and Vietnam.[4] A competitor with unlimited capital might be able to design better cars than Daimler, but it would need years if not decades to build up similar manufacturing capacity on four continents.

Yet despite all those advantages, no brand is guaranteed to last forever. Daimler's vehicles are currently losing prestige relative to Tesla, which (as we saw in Chapter 2) has been the source of Daimler's biggest recent headaches. The company's obsession with excellence and quality control, which helped it lead the car industry for more than a century, now risks slowing or stalling its reinvention.

But Daimler is hardly giving up; instead it's constantly getting smarter, rethinking its manufacturing processes for an increasingly digital world. It was the first major automaker to integrate lightweight robots into vehicle production. Now it's embracing what it calls "Industrie 4.0"—the digitalization of the entire value chain, from design and development to production. This includes building "smart factories" that make it easier to mix and match elements for various car models, such as gasoline, diesel, hybrid, and fully electric engines. Daimler predicts that "automobile production will change from large-scale to one-off production, where every car is built to individual customer requirements."[5]

In a smart factory, the products, machines, and entire environment are networked with each other and with the rest of the global enterprise. As one Mercedes executive noted, "Digitalization enables us to make our products more individual, and production more efficient and flexible. The challenge is to plan for the long term while remaining able to respond rapidly to customer wishes and market fluctuations."[6] New processes that are already or will soon be in use include:

- ▶ 3D printing/additive manufacturing: for rapid prototyping of parts and tools.
- ▶ Human augmentation: new ways of controlling robots inside vehicles, with workers instructing the robots via Wi-Fi.
- ▶ Machine learning: lightweight robots can improve their movements by observing and copying human workers.
- ▶ The production data cloud: all production data worldwide is being made available to every plant in the network, enabling faster sharing of useful information.

Does this mean that robots are taking over? Not according to Daimler: "The direct cooperation between people and robots means the cognitive superiority of people is ideally combined with the power, endurance and reliability of robots. . . . It is not aimed at the maximum mechanization or full automation of activities."[7]

I was somewhat critical of Daimler's efforts to improve its innovation and other brainy competencies, so it's worth stressing that its hands are still world-class, the envy of any company that makes physical products. Daimler lives on the top left of the frontier curve, reliably delivering high-value vehicles for a relatively high cost. But its archrival, Tesla, is aggressively pushing the industry's curve outward, while Daimler struggles to keep up. A decade ago, Americans who could afford to spend $50,000 on a car might be torn between Mercedes, BMW, or Porsche. Today, a rapidly growing share are choosing Tesla.

Samsung: Applying a Mastery of Manufacturing to New Markets

Samsung Electronics is the most prominent division within Samsung, a global conglomerate based in South Korea. In addition to making a wide array of computers, televisions, household appliances, and telecommunications equipment, Samsung Electronics is the world's largest producer of mobile phones and the second largest producer of semiconductors. In short, this company excels at manufacturing. And as former President and Chief Strategy Officer Young Sohn told my classes in April 2019 and January 2020, Samsung never stops innovating to improve its competitive advantages in manufacturing and apply its expertise to new fields, such as automotive and pharmaceutical production.

During his eight years with Samsung, Sohn was instrumental in helping expand a company that already enjoyed incredible size and scale. He guided its corporate venture business and led its $8 billion acquisition of auto parts supplier Harman International in 2016. As the *Wall Street Journal* reported, "The transaction, the largest in Samsung's history, comes as the smartphone market is maturing. It is a bet that automobiles, which have looked roughly similar for decades, will be the next place to fit in more chips and screens. Around 65% of Harman's revenue came from supplying chips, audio systems or other parts to vehicles."[8]

Sohn, who became chairman of Harman as a wholly owned subsidiary, spoke about how Samsung sees automobiles becoming more like "smartphones on wheels." With increased computing power, communication capabilities, and entertainment systems, vehicles will soon not merely connect directly with people's smartphones; they will act like actual smartphones themselves. Samsung's expertise at making all those sophisticated components is boosting Harman's existing advantages.

The company also realized that making pharmaceuticals at scale depends on having disciplined process manufacturing, another of its core strengths. After launching a drug manufacturing division in 2011, Samsung partnered with some of the world's biggest pharmaceutical companies, including Bristol-Myers-Squibb and Roche, which needed additional high-quality production capacity. Samsung Biologics turned a profit in 2015 and is already one of the world's largest contract-drug makers. With demand for increasingly complex medicines skyrocketing, Samsung began building a fourth facility in South Korea that will become the largest biologic drug production site in the world in 2022, with nearly 2.5 million square feet of floor space (slightly more than the Louvre).[9]

Samsung has a reputation as a digital leader, but Sohn urged my students not to downplay the ongoing importance of analog. "Analog is sometimes better than digital. Great craftsmanship happens in analog. In music we hear better sound when it is analog, and we see it in the engineering and design philosophies within a company. We need to have appreciation for analog and what it brings to the world."[10]

A big share of Samsung's revenue comes from supplying semiconductor and display components to other companies that compete directly with its own consumer products, especially smartphones. Sohn explained that Samsung's ability to do this stems from its reputation for best-in-class quality and reliability at the component level, to such a degree that some of Samsung's customers have no real choice but to incorporate Samsung parts.

How did the company get so good at manufacturing? By forcing the component-making units of Samsung Electronics to compete for inclusion in the company's own smartphones and other products. The teams that make displays and semiconductors are driven to outperform non-Samsung suppliers. This high bar for quality within the company creates a virtuous circle; the component groups have to outperform their competition just to stay in use at Samsung, and the process of becoming best-in-class leads to component sales far beyond Samsung.

From Sohn's perspective, Samsung's size and reach don't guarantee future success, but they offer a great opportunity to keep improving its production capabilities and spreading them into new geographic markets and new product markets.[11] The company's hands are likely to become even stronger in the years ahead.

Now let's turn to one of today's most interesting innovators in additive manufacturing.

Desktop Metal: The Start-up Leading a 3D Revolution

Desktop Metal (DM) was founded in 2015 by a team of pioneers in advanced metallurgy and robotics, with the goal of revolutionizing 3D printing as a faster, cheaper, higher quality, higher volume option for additive manufacturing. As the company's vision statement puts it: "Desktop Metal exists to make 3D printing accessible to all engineers, designers, and manufacturers. We are reinventing the way engineering and manufacturing teams produce parts—from prototyping through mass production."[12]

Prior to launching Desktop Metal in Massachusetts, Argentine-born Ric Fulop had been an entrepreneur for 15 years with six previous start-ups. He then spent five years as a partner with North Bridge Venture Partners, leading successful investments in companies like Dyn, a web application security company; Onshape, a CAD company; and Markforged, a carbon 3D printing company.[13] He could have stayed in venture capital, but by 2013 he was itching to get back to running a company. As he later told *Forbes*, "Investing is very slow. It's molasses. It's not very operational, and I'm an operator. It's kind of boring, honestly. This is more fun."[14]

Fulop explained his decision to go all in on 3D printing when he spoke to my Stanford class in April 2019. Although the core idea of additive manufacturing had been around for decades, he saw that recent technological improvements were creating opportunities to make the entire field vastly bigger. Some kinds of parts would become easier and cheaper to produce via additive manufacturing; others would become possible to produce for the first time. Fulop saw an opportunity to compete against large incumbents such as HP, by developing new capabilities that older manufacturers would be unable to match. With the right blend of technology and capital, a disruptive start-up in additive manufacturing could zoom to major player status in just a few years.

He told us that 3D printing in 2019 was roughly where the semiconductor industry had been in 1979: the basic technology had been around for a while, but people were just barely beginning to tap into its potential. Fulop predicted that the total market for additive manufacturing would grow at least 10 times over the next decade, as the process expanded from a narrow range of niche customers to a mass market with a wide range of applications. He made a persuasive case that everyone from small machine shops to high-volume producers would soon be ready to invest in high-quality, reliable, cost-effective 3D printing machines that could handle new alloys and materials.

The Technology

Videos of Desktop Metal machines in action look almost like science fiction. Layer after thin layer, a 3D printer can build almost anything made out of metal, from airplane parts to industrial equipment to medical products to toys. Imagine a future when your car repair shop never has to wait a few days to get the specific part you need, because a mechanic can simply print one in less than an hour. The opportunities for flexible, customizable manufacturing seem limitless.[15]

Desktop Metal's first 3D metal printing system, the Studio System, was pitched as compact and office-friendly, not requiring the personal protective equipment or separate facilities that other 3D printers required. Debuting in December 2017 for $120,000, it eliminated the previously typical dangerous powders and high costs per use. The Studio System could do high-quality prototyping, tooling, and production, giving customers an accessible way to print parts on the fly at low volumes. As of August 2020, it was DM's biggest seller and the source of a majority of its revenue.[16]

In March 2019, DM introduced a second, industrial-sized product called the Production System. This one was driven by a new printing process called single pass jetting (SPJ), a faster version of the typical binder jetting process found in powder-based ceramic and metal printers. SPJ uses more than 32,000 jets in conjunction with powder spreaders to jet millions of droplets per second. Desktop Metal claimed that SPJ and other innovations made the Production System up to 100 times faster than the most common method for metal 3D printing, and up to 20 times cheaper.[17]

That October, DM also introduced a machine called Fiber for customers who wanted to print high-resolution parts using a composite like fiberglass rather than metal. Fulop's pitch was that Fiber would "deliver very high-resolution parts . . . using materials stronger than steel yet lighter than aluminum—all starting at a subscription price just under $3,500 per year."[18] It would be especially useful for consumer electronics.

For its fourth major product, DM launched the Shop System in November 2019, calling it the world's first metal binder jetting system designed specifically for machine shops and metal job shops. It was a midsized offering for customers who needed something bigger than the Studio System but not as massive as the Production System.[19] It would be ideal for industrial companies like Caterpillar, which might need to print replacement parts for large equipment in remote locations.

All of these sophisticated printers showed the power of DM's research and development team. The company had more than 120 patents issued or pending by August 2020.[20]

The Business Strategy

Desktop Metal's business model depends on close, long-term relationships with demanding B2B customers, many of whom need customized solutions. Buying one or more of these printers and adapting your production system to it requires a leap of faith, beyond the capital investment. Customers need to feel comfortable trusting Desktop Metal as a long-term partner. The purchase decision isn't about saving some money on the margins; it's about whether DM can be a reliable partner, even at premium prices.

Different market segments have very different needs, which requires DM to stay flexible. Some of its prototyping customers want a complete wing-to-wing solution: machines, ink, metal powders, and support on demand. Others, like Lockheed-Martin or Owens Corning, are large enough to have their own relationships with metal suppliers, so they need fewer products and services from Desktop Metal.

Consider a start-up like Lumenium, one of DM's early customers, which needed 3D printing at volume to produce a new type of internal combustion engine with a complex design. When Lumenium CEO Bill Anderson saw Desktop Metal's machines at a Pittsburgh trade show in 2017, he was blown away. "We were pretty stunned by the booth," he told *Forbes* in 2018. "We never thought those parts could be produced in quantity at low cost." Working closely with DM, Lumenium found that 3D printing could cut both time and cost. One tricky engine component that had previously taken a week to produce at a cost of $980 could now be done in four days for just $148.[21]

Fulop stressed to my class that while a long sales lifecycle can be frustrating and challenging for DM employees, once validation is achieved the company can become embedded into its customers' manufacturing processes. When Fulop and his team win the confidence of a customer—whether as big as Caterpillar or as small as Lumenium—they earn the right to sell into that company for years to come. Strengthening the *customer's* hands is where DM's real potential lies for outsized profits over time.

(This trade-off has a lot in common with Instacart's, as we saw in Chapter 7. The more time and effort Instacart invested in nurturing its partnerships with the supermarket chains, the greater the long-term payoff. Convincing supermarkets of the value Instacart could provide might be hard, but once it became clear that trusting Instacart for home delivery paid off, those partners would have little incentive to break away.)

Desktop Metal had to develop deep domain knowledge for customers in a wide range of industries, including robotics, industrial parts, the military, aviation, green energy, and perhaps most important, automotive. By 2020 it was partnering with some of the world's leading automakers, including Ford,

BMW, Renault, Toyota, Volkswagen, GM, and Nissan. DM also received strategic investments from Ford and BMW.[22]

As Fulop told *Forbes* in 2018, "This is the reason that Ford and others have supported us. In the time it takes the [traditional] process to produce 12 propellers, Desktop Metal would produce over 560."[23] The magazine noted that his office desk displayed dozens of small metal parts that DM had 3D printed. One was a miniaturized steel prototype of a water pump for a BMW car; it cost $80 to make previously, but barely $5 via 3D printing.[24]

These improvements would mean big cost savings in material as well as fuel costs. Desktop Metal was moving the frontier of additive manufacturing's PV/DC curve, offering its customers the same or in some cases better perceived value at lower delivered costs, including the cost of time.

The Financial Gamble

Desktop Metal drew considerable interest from venture capitalists early on, thanks to its disruptive technology and potentially massive future market. By 2018, it was valued at more than $1 billion, with $277 million in funding from firms like New Enterprise Associates and Kleiner Perkins.[25] Ford, already a blue-chip customer, kicked in a $65 million strategic investment and put its chief technology officer on DM's board. Not bad for a three-year-old company with 225 employees.

Rather than gradually move toward an IPO, Desktop Metal suddenly went public in August 2020 via a merger with Trine Acquisition Corp. Trine CEO Leo Hindery Jr. gushed during an investor conference call that "Desktop Metal will be the only pure-play opportunity available to public market investors in the additive manufacturing 2.0 space, and we believe the Company is in the process of revolutionizing the industry. Desktop Metal's technology will be a significant first step in replacing a mass manufacturing base which has become antiquated."[26]

After analyzing hundreds of potential acquisitions, Hindery said, Trine chose Desktop Metal as its most compelling investment opportunity, because it combined:

- ▶ An exceptionally robust portfolio of products and intellectual property.
- ▶ A business model capable of generating high margins and powerful, recurring revenue streams. He praised DM's "proprietary distribution network of over 80 partners across more than 60 countries."
- ▶ A booming market. "Industry experts forecast that the additive manufacturing industry will realize explosive growth over the next

decade, reaching over 10X the 2019 market size. We believe Desktop Metal's go-forward plan is eminently reasonable and achievable viewed alongside these strong, secular tailwinds." [27]

During the same investor call, Fulop projected that the overall industry would grow from $12 billion to $146 billion by 2030. He expected DM's revenue to triple from $26.4 million in 2019 to $77.5 million in 2021, and then to grow even faster, approaching $1 billion in 2025.[28] "We believe Desktop Metal is uniquely situated to lead the industry into this new era. Whereas prior additive technologies have been primarily focused on prototyping, our portfolio is . . . capturing value at every stage from R&D to high-volume mass production."[29] Fulop added that Desktop Metal would ramp up shipping its four products by the end of 2021, and that it would also generate revenue from "recurring consumables" (the "razor & blades" business model) and providing services to its growing customer base.

Not surprisingly, many investors were eager to buy shares, with one calling DM "the next $10+ billion company" despite its post-merger valuation of $2.5 billion.[30] It now had plenty of capital, including $300 million from Trine and $275 million from other pre-merger investors. It had an experienced management team and R&D team. It had disruptive technology, protected by those 120+ patents. And it had first mover advantage in an industry projected to grow by 10 times in a decade. What could go wrong?

As always when we try to predict the future, *anything* could go wrong. Desktop Metal is already smart and getting stronger by the day. In five years, it might dominate the market for additive manufacturing. Or it might still be a niche player, quietly earning profits in a low-volume industry that never explodes to the extent that observers are projecting. Or it might be out of business, replaced by some other upstart not on anyone's radar yet. Nothing is certain, except the principle that being both smart and strong is the best possible protection in an unpredictable world.

Whatever its future, Desktop Metal has already developed amazingly strong hands in just its first five years. It proved that manufacturing is far from a boring or trivial competency. Being great at making things still matters—and making things in innovative ways that move the curve of an entire industry can matter even more.

Getting Manufacturing Right

Even though economic value is increasingly shifting to digital companies that don't make anything tangible, organizations that can master advanced manufacturing capabilities can also thrive. While the late twentieth century saw manufacturing scale up through low-cost labor and high-volume production, today it's all about the smart application of technology and data. Virtually any company that makes anything needs to commit serious resources to automation, robotics, mass customization, and (when appropriate) additive manufacturing.

In addition, as products become increasingly connected via the internet of things (IoT), manufacturers have to do more to understand at a deep level how their customers' customers use their products. Like Align, they can apply new manufacturing capabilities to deliver mass customization in ways that were previously impossible. Like Samsung and Desktop Metal, they can develop intimate relationships with their customers that deliver unique solutions through the combined power of technology, big data, and a commitment to service.

The next wave of manufacturing leaders won't be those who merely slash costs via cheap labor. They will be companies that can simultaneously deliver high value, high volumes, and high touch service at the same time.

THE SYSTEMS LEADER'S NOTEBOOK

Manufacturing

- Lean into platform transitions with the goal of moving the frontier of your industry's perceived value/delivered cost curve. If possible, don't wait for your competitors to drive change first and force you to play catch-up.

- Know the impact of your products on the income statement and balance sheet of each major customer or market segment. Think about how you can customize your products accordingly, based on your deep understanding of those customers or markets.

- Be flexible in your business model, if you serve multiple market segments. Just as Desktop Metal realized that it needed to develop both office-sized *and* industrial-sized machines, think about different solutions you can offer at different price points.

CHAPTER 10

MUSCLES: LEVERAGING SIZE AND SCALE

I always hate to talk about size, because of the idea that big, dumb, and stupid go together. But we have this incumbent advantage that we really have to use to our advantage. If all we do is ride the incumbent advantage, it will be a disaster, but having that gives us a fair amount of lead time to pivot in different directions.

—Charlie Scharf, CEO of Wells Fargo
and former CEO of Visa

Among the people I see every day in Silicon Valley and San Francisco, it's a fundamental article of faith that physical size and scale don't determine success. People in my world frequently use the metaphor that large physical incumbents are lumbering dinosaurs, seemingly powerful but vulnerable to the next meteor that will wipe them off the earth.

I think the dinosaur metaphor has gotten out of hand. After six years of teaching my The Industrialist's Dilemma class, I can confirm that many leaders of established companies are neither old, slow, nor prehistoric in their thinking. Instead, they are making the most of their size and scale, while never assuming that size and scale alone guarantee future success. They tend toward paranoia rather than complacency, knowing that at any moment some unknown catastrophe might come hurtling at them. Their risk awareness and lack of hubris help them leverage their muscles as a true advantage, even in situations when being big might seem like more of a burden than a blessing.

There's an inherent tension between the day-to-day management of a sprawling global enterprise and the innovation needed to keep such an enterprise on top for an extended period. As with many of the challenges that Systems Leaders face, this requires seemingly contradictory skills. You have to make sure the right things are happening this week/quarter/year to hit your financial targets, while simultaneously building in flexibility, helping your company develop new strengths, and laying the groundwork for new sources of revenue that might not come to fruition for years.

While maintaining their size and scale, these organizations are simultaneously developing *new* muscles that will enable them to compete when the game changes. They may not transform from football players to ballet dancers, but they can become more flexible and pivot quickly to confront new challenges, while retaining the power to protect their existing markets.

In this chapter, we'll look at several incumbents in highly competitive industries that are facing pressure from innovative upstarts as well as rapidly changing customer trends. All are trying to leverage their enormous size and strength, on a global scale, to stay relevant, to thrive, and to survive whatever meteors might be approaching.

First we'll briefly revisit AB InBev, which (as we've seen) became the global giant of beer production and distribution, just when it started to seem like the world's beer drinkers cared more about obscure microbrews than about the ability to order a Bud anywhere from South Korea to Costa Rica. Then we'll look at CNN's struggle to remain one of the world's most respected news sources, at a time when millions of Americans are drawn to cheaply produced talk shows and punditry rather than expensively produced traditional journalism. Next, we'll see how Visa, the dominant powerhouse of the credit card industry, is confronting massive changes in the payment space.

Finally, our featured example is Michelin, the 130-year-old tire manufacturer that operates in 175 countries with 130,000 employees. Michelin is skilled at leveraging the global scale of its design and manufacturing expertise, while empowering its local managers to customize offerings for their regions. But it faces serious long-term challenges that go to the heart of its self-image, forcing the management team to question just what kind of company it will be in the future.

AB InBev: Making Size a Source of Innovation

In Chapter 6 we explored the challenges facing AB InBev, which had spent decades growing into the world's largest producer of alcoholic beverages. By the 2010s, the size and scale that had once seemed like an unbeatable competitive advantage began to feel as bulky and immobilizing as a lumbering brontosaurus. The global beer industry became increasingly diverse and fragmented, while other trends made it hard to manage the company's many regional markets.

Once it became clear that a small team with minimal capital could launch a profitable craft beer for a niche market, was it still a big deal that AB InBev could produce and distribute massive quantities of Budweiser and Coors Light? Especially if traditional mass-market advertising was becoming less and less effective, and even the power of Super Bowl commercials was diminishing? Meanwhile, after one final mega-deal with SABMiller in 2016, AB InBev faced the reality that future growth via acquisitions would be impossible.

CEO Carlos Brito confronted this existential threat with appropriate seriousness. For starters, AB InBev flexed its financial muscles to buy eight of the fastest-growing craft brands in the early 2010s and worked on upgrading and rebranding some of its core brands. More important, it allocated major resources to build a dedicated, independent business unit with a mandate to innovate and shake up the whole company. Pedro Earp, the new chief disruptive growth officer, pursued a wide range of experiments to drive future growth.

One key example of leveraging AB InBev's scale was how Brito and Earp fixed the decentralization of data across the company's many regions and units. Not surprisingly for a company that had scaled up through M&A, AB InBev had never fully integrated the data systems of all the brands it had acquired over the years, nor of all its global geographic units. ZX, AB InBev's internal innovation group, found this to be a significant constraint, since many of its initiatives depended on the smart use of big data. For instance, the e-commerce group needed sophisticated sales analysis for its craft beer platforms, but the relevant data was scattered and often hard to access. The company was also missing opportunities to transfer insights and strategies from developed markets to emerging markets, and vice versa. By hiring more data experts with a mandate to integrate and analyze global data, AB InBev added muscles that its smaller, more local competitors couldn't match.

All of these moves paid off in 2020, when the global beer market was badly hurt by the coronavirus pandemic. Despite a 17 percent decline in revenue in the second quarter, both AB InBev's top-line and bottom-line results exceeded analyst expectations. As one analyst noted, "The company's investments behind B2B platforms, e-commerce channels and digital marketing have accelerated in the past few months, which is likely to aid growth."[1] The company didn't wait around to be disrupted by more agile competitors. It diverted precious resources to initiatives that trained its existing muscles to become more flexible. It added agility while maintaining the advantage of its unique size and reach.

CNN: Using Scale as a Shield

CNN, now part of the Warner Media division of AT&T, launched in 1980 as the first 24-hour cable news channel. Forty years later, it has grown to massive scale as a global news organization. You can find CNN International playing in hotels in more than 200 countries, available in English, Spanish, and Arabic versions. CNN has nearly 4,000 journalists working from nine news bureaus in the United States and another 28 news bureaus around the world. This massive news operation updates CNN.com and the company's other websites 24/7. It also generates content for every social media platform and every digital format, from brief email alerts and smartphone app notifications to longform documentary videos.[2]

This global scale creates significant management challenges, as Warner Media's News and Sports Chairman Jeff Zucker told my class in April 2020. CNN's news bureaus are expensive to staff, but they're the only way to have reporters on the ground almost instantly, anywhere in the world when a hurricane, war, terrorist attack, or other big moment makes people turn to CNN. Unlike an American-focused news channel such as Fox News, which has a much smaller international staff and limited visibility outside the United States, CNN doesn't have the luxury of focusing its content on the preferences of its home country. Perhaps not coincidentally, CNN has consistently trailed conservative-leaning Fox News in US ratings over the past decade, sometimes averaging just two million viewers in primetime compared to Fox's four million. More recently, CNN has also trailed liberal-leaning MSNBC—another network that focuses on the US market—in total viewers.[3]

On the other hand, CNN's global scale offers some protection against domestic adversity, such as a US president who denounced the network as "fake news" and "the enemy of the people." CNN's multinational, multiplatform revenue streams also offer a cushion against the steady decline in television advertising revenue for all US cable channels, a trend that has grown with the rise of "cord cutters" who abandon cable to get all of their television via streaming services. Advertising revenue dropped even more in 2020, when big companies slashed their marketing budgets in response to the pandemic and recession.

Zucker told my class that he sees no real tension between pursuing credible reporting as a public service while simultaneously chasing profit in competitive markets. On the contrary, he thinks CNN's global reputation for solid journalism is the ultimate driver of its $1 billion plus annual profit.[4] That reputation, built up over 40 years, helps it weather downturns in the crucial US market.

CNN can't assume that its business model will continue to thrive as the worldwide consumption of news and information continues to evolve, and as advertising continues to shift away from television. But CNN's ability to leverage its powerful global brand—to flex its muscles on the world stage— leaves it in a strong position relative to competitors who get all their revenue from a narrower audience in a single country. For instance, in a few years we might see CNN transitioning to a subscription model to make up for the collapse of traditional advertising, much as other premium journalism brands like the *New York Times* and the *Wall Street Journal* have done.

Scale can give you backup options in case your main business plan falters.

Visa: Riding the Incumbent Advantage

Few people appreciate the scale of Visa, the global credit card giant that has been an industry pioneer since 1958. Its 19,500 employees generate $23 billion in revenue and $15 billion in operating income by processing nearly $9 *trillion* in payments in 200-plus countries. Visa's market cap is closing in on $500 billion as I write this, after five years of steady growth in its stock price. Perhaps most impressive are the 3.4 billion Visa cards in circulation—one for every two humans on the planet.[5]

Then-CEO Charlie Scharf (now the CEO of Wells Fargo) spoke to my class in 2016 about how Visa was responding to numerous threats from digital innovators in the payments space. His comments are still relevant because his successor, Al Kelly, has generally continued Scharf's strategy, with great success.

His theme was finding new ways to leverage Visa's size and strength against new payment methods like Square, PayPal, Stripe, Apple Pay, and others. Rather than assuming that no start-up could overcome Visa's competitive advantages, especially its network effect of near-universal acceptance, Scharf pushed for constant innovation. He drove the organization to keep finding new ways to serve partners and customers, creating digital tools that would add value for anyone who issued or carried a Visa card.

As he told us, "I always hate to talk about size, because of the idea that big, dumb, and stupid go together. But we have this incumbent advantage that we really have to use to our advantage. If all we do is ride the incumbent advantage, it will be a disaster, but having that gives us a fair amount of lead time to pivot in different directions."[6]

For instance, Apple had the power to set up Apple Pay, but it didn't have Visa's relationships with 15,000 banks and the ability to process 138 billion transactions a year. Nor could any of the payment start-ups approach Visa's reach, especially given the tight government regulation of the banking industry, which Visa was very good at navigating.

Scharf explained that Visa has three distinct priorities. First is continuing to thrive in traditional credit cards, competing with the likes of MasterCard, American Express, and UnionPay in China. Second is penetrating aggressively into the developing world, where electronic transactions are lagging. Third is digital innovation, going wherever transactions are taking place by following the lead of innovators like PayPal and Square. He added, "Honestly, I think everyone who is in the flow of transactions should be scared to death. Whether it's the bank, the network, the acquirer, or their equivalents in the e-commerce world, theoretically they can all be replaced."[7]

One example of leveraging scale to drive innovation is in fraud prevention. While new entrants might build lower-cost transactional systems, they lack the big data and powerful risk algorithms that Visa uses to protect consumers and merchants. As Scharf put it, "When that card is swiped or dipped or tapped across the world, we know who you are, we know where you are. We know if you've been there before. We help people quickly determine whether there's fraud—that's why fraud is so low."[8]

Scharf noted that Visa needs to be exceedingly cautious when considering the impact of any potential new innovation on its legacy relationships. When it developed a new service that appealed directly to consumers, called Visa Checkout, Visa was careful to also promote its value to card issuers. By making it faster and easier to use a Visa card on participating retail websites, Visa Checkout would drive more transactions and fees to the bank issuing the card. No matter how much Visa appeals to end users, it can't maintain its growth without continuing to support its banking partners.[9]

While doing everything in his power to encourage innovation and remove internal roadblocks, Scharf never lost sight of Visa's essence. "Everywhere I go, every town hall, every conversation, I always talk about the importance of the existing business. We've increased our ability to process transactions up to 56,000 transactions a second, and it's flawless. Because we've got huge swaths of people inside the company that work their butts off to do that."[10] Those in the core business deserve appreciation and respect because they give Visa the muscles to expand into innovative new services.

Michelin: Confronting an Identity Crisis

When I researched Michelin and interviewed some of its senior executives in 2018, I was struck by the consistency of its 130-year history of innovation and leadership in the tire industry. From its modest beginnings in 1889 in Clermont-Ferrand, France, Michelin grew to become the world's second-largest tire manufacturer. More than 60 percent of its net sales are generated outside Europe, under a wide range of brand names including BFGoodrich, Uniroyal, Kleber, Warrior, Kormoran, Riken, Siamtyre, Taurus, and Tigar. Its workforce of 130,000 spans the world, with 68 production sites in 17 countries delivering tires to 175 countries.[11]

In short, the company's existing muscles were very impressive. Yet its leaders, including then-COO and current CEO Florent Menegaux, told me that Michelin urgently needed to build up new and different muscles.

By 2018, the tire industry was rapidly fragmenting with the rise of smaller, cheaper tire manufacturers that made it harder to sell premium tires at premium prices. The rise of electric vehicles (which cause tires to wear differently) and ride-sharing (which changes the life cycle of tire purchases) made traditional business plans outdated. Various cost pressures were also coming to bear in different countries, especially the complex but huge market of China.

As Menegaux told my Systems Leadership class in April 2019, Michelin couldn't think of itself as a tire company anymore. It needed to excel at additional products and services, or risk becoming increasingly commoditized as a component supplier. His leadership team was redefining the company's core competencies and reorganizing its workforce to maximize the growth of its non-tire businesses.

In June 2017, Michelin had announced its first global reorganization in more than 20 years, aiming to "improve the company's reactivity and maintain competitiveness, enabling it to smoothly meet future challenges."[12] It set aggressive goals for three non-tire units that would have to become more entrepreneurial and experimental:

> ▶ Services & Solutions—which referred to "telematics" services for owners of car and truck fleets, such as digital tracking of vehicle locations, gas milage, tire conditions, idle time, and other metrics.
> ▶ High-Tech Materials—which was responsible for monetizing Michelin's materials technology and innovations outside of the tire industry.
> ▶ Experiences—which included the company's famous travel-related Maps and Guides, mobile apps, and lifestyle branded products.

The goal was to grow the revenue contribution of these non-tire businesses from about 10 percent to about 25 percent within five to seven years.[13]

Many employees felt challenged by the pace and extent of the changes underway, as the culture became less hierarchical and more collaborative. They were expected to shift from a product-driven mindset to one focused on the customer experience. As President of Michelin North America Scott Clark observed, "It is an interesting challenge for us because our history is as a very capital-intensive, industrial company, with a focus on ROI. However, applying that mindset to a start-up mentality is not always healthy and productive."[14] Global Marketing Director for Services & Solutions Eric Duverger added, "In tires it is the life of consumers at stake. But in services you can take more risk and move faster. Michelin has built its brand equity on safety and quality. [But in] the service world you need a new set of skills and a new mindset."[15]

In addition to rethinking its identity as a tire company, Michelin was also reconsidering its identity as a French company. Despite its global workforce, the company's French roots were deeply embedded. To rise to senior leadership positions, employees were expected to be fluent in French and to have lived in France, which put those from other countries at a disadvantage. Some were concerned that the French culture of risk aversion and respect for tradition might slow the pace of change.

Duverger, who is French but works at Michelin's US headquarters in South Carolina, characterized Americans as generally more optimistic and open to risk, compared to the more cautious French culture.[16] But Menegaux viewed these kinds of differences as healthy: "Michelin originated from France but we are not a French company per se. We spend a lot of time exchanging cultures, and the French education is very conceptual. The American, on the contrary, is very programmed to action."[17]

Let's look at how Michelin attempted to leverage its muscles in its core tire business, while making those three other units an increasingly big part of its identity.

Tires, Part 1: Confronting the Innovator's Dilemma and the Amazon Effect

Michelin's tradition of innovation goes back to its founding. In 1891, the company developed the first detachable tire for bicycles; four years later, it introduced the first pneumatic automobile tire. One of its greatest inventions was the 1949 introduction of radial tire technology, which made driving safer, smoother, and more fuel efficient for all kinds of vehicles, from the smallest cars to the heaviest trucks.

Michelin's priority had always been to sell the safest and highest-quality tires, which required an abundance of investment in R&D and product testing. The organization preached zero risk tolerance or room for error on safety issues, driving the widespread conviction among employees that "the quality of the tire was sacred above all else," as Duverger put it.[18] But those high standards became harder to maintain as the tire market fragmented over the past two decades, with many new players emerging in developing countries such as China and India. Back in 2000, the world's top three tire manufacturers—Bridgestone, Michelin, and Goodyear—represented 60 percent of the global market. But by 2016, the Big Three's share was down to 37.6 percent, including Michelin's 14 percent. Midsized tire makers had grabbed 28.2 percent, and the remaining 34.1 percent went to small tire makers, each with less than 2 percent.[19]

Meanwhile, electric cars such as Tesla's had higher torque than gasoline-fueled automobiles, which led to heavy wear on tires and more frequent replacements. The boom in ride-sharing companies like Uber and Lyft eliminated many rider preferences regarding tire brands. And consumers who still bought their own tires were increasingly influenced by cost and fuel efficiency rather than brand name and perceived quality. All of these trends started to make tires more of a commodity than a differentiated product. This was an example of Clay Christensen's "innovator's dilemma," in which a high-priced/high-quality brand finds (to its horror) that most of its customers are OK with an inferior but cheaper substitute, if it continues to improve over time.

Another source of pressure: e-commerce giants like Amazon and Alibaba posed a threat to Michelin's value chain by getting in between the tire-maker and its customers. People were increasingly saving money by shopping online rather than at car dealerships or car supply stores, both of which had an incentive to push more expensive tire brands. As EVP of Automotive Business Lines Yves Chapot told me, "The big threat with these companies is if they know the customers better than Michelin, and they tell us, 'Okay, just provide us the tires. We'll take care of the rest.' "[20] This was an example of the so-called Amazon effect, in which a producer loses contact with its own customers and is increasingly at the mercy of a powerful intermediary.

All of these forces pressured Michelin to cut prices, just when raw materials for tires were becoming more costly. Most of the industry's newer entrants and disruptors did not have an existing brand to protect, which gave them the flexibility to compete on price. Michelin seemed to be playing catch-up, and there was some internal concern whether the company could maintain its product leadership position.

This was compounded by a cultural attitude that sounded like a tyrannosaurus lording it over small mammals. As Clark put it, "Our weakness is that historically we had enormous product performance gaps relative to our competition. I think that bred a little bit of complacency and arrogance."[21] That's why Menegaux was relentless about persuading his workforce to embrace a new mindset and vision for the company, not merely new products and services.

Tires, Part 2: The Power of Going Glocal

Some of Michelin's competitors enjoy significant support from their national governments, such as the Chinese tire-makers that get subsidies to undercut foreign manufacturers in the world's largest tire market. To remain effective, Michelin needs a strong presence in each country where it does business and has a reputation as a trustworthy partner. This blending of both global muscle power and local knowledge—nicknamed "glocal" competence—is increasingly a requirement of success for any organization that competes on a worldwide level.

As Menegaux told my class, "I frequently use a very nice word, which is 'glocal.' As a corporation, we have to act in a global manner to get synergies and efficiencies. However, to meet customer expectations everywhere we are, we have to be extremely local. In the U.S., believe it or not, a lot of people think that Michelin is American. And in China, a lot of people think Michelin is Chinese. We grow by being as local as possible when it makes sense, and as global as possible when it makes sense."[22]

The company had to find ways to keep cutting production costs and consumer prices on its Chinese tires, or else Michelin would be completely priced out of the Chinese market. Glocal competence made it possible to produce Chinese tires that looked and drove differently than European or American tires. Still, there was no easy answer to declining tire revenue, making growth in the non-tire units all the more important.

Services & Solutions: Applying Historical Scale to the Digital Leading Edge

During the 2010s, Michelin's corporate customers began to seek advanced services along with their tires, including maintenance and scheduling alerts and detailed information about performance and durability. The Services & Solutions group offered customer support, fleet management for businesses with lots of vehicles, a worldwide network of distribution centers, and alternative billing models (such as charging per ton transported or by number of aircraft landings). It also offered telematics for trucking fleets, which included gathering, storing, and transmitting vehicle information, and analyzing vehicle performance and conditions.

Menegaux described Services & Solutions as "absolutely essential" and the key to staying connected with fleets and preventing third parties from coming between them. As he explained, "Fleets need somebody to manage information for them and to provide turnkey solutions, so they know they are protected and that somebody is managing the asset properly."[23] His mandate to the group was to create unique, custom-tailored products and services that would justify premium pricing to these corporate customers.

Michelin had already made several deals to expand Services & Solutions. In 2014 it acquired Sascar, a digital fleet management company in Brazil; this was another example of glocal strategy, giving Michelin the expertise of Brazilians who understood the nuances of their country. Another acquisition in 2017 was NexTraq, a telematics solution provider to utility vehicles in North America. Both added new muscles: high-tech processes to improve driver safety, fuel management, and fleet productivity. In addition to those and other acquisitions, the S&S group also launched its own new digital services for fleet management: MyBestRoute helped drivers choose the optimal routing; MyInspection digitized and standardized vehicle inspections; MyTraining facilitated driver training; and MyRoadChallenge motivated drivers to drive safely.

One example of technical innovation was connecting tires to the internet of things, using radio frequency identification (RFID) sensors that could capture data about tire conditions and vehicle performance. An example of business model innovation was offering "tires as a service"—instead of buying tires à la carte, fleets using this option could smooth out their expenses with a flat fee for every mile they drove.[24] These and other new offerings were only possible because of Michelin's scale, especially its massive database of information on tire usage, arguably the best in the industry.

Nevertheless, the group's growth was just 10 to 15 percent in its first few years, not enough to reach Menegaux's targets. The head of Services

& Solutions, EVP Sonia Artinian-Fredou, was concerned that the problem was finding the right talent for a high-tech, service-oriented unit. Michelin had long emphasized promoting from within, but now it needed to recruit outsiders with fresh perspectives. EVP of Research and Development Terry Gettys agreed: "We are trying to operate like Silicon Valley technology companies, [but we are] emerging from within an existing corporation that has a long culture and history. So you have to continually push people to take more risks, to go faster, to listen to the customer directly."[25]

Unfortunately, some potential new hires still perceived Michelin as an old-school, industrial tire company. As Artinian-Fredou put it, "The new generation, they are not so excited to join a large company like Michelin."[26] Menegaux agreed that hiring remained a big challenge for the higher-tech units. He told my class, "We have more than 350 different types of skills required just in research, and hundreds required in marketing. We now have to recruit a new type of marketer that understands how to use data. My take is that in five years, 50 percent of the jobs in Michelin are not even defined today. So there will be a lot of opportunities for people to join and develop those skills."[27] He remained optimistic that hiring would become easier as Michelin's brand evolved.

High-Tech Materials: Spreading Innovation to Other Industries

Most people have no idea that Michelin has long been a world leader in materials science and its applications. With the 2017 reorganization, the company recognized that this competency has the potential to become a significant source of revenue beyond the tire industry, rather than just an internal R&D function. Menegaux explained the crucial role of this group: "High-Tech Materials exists because we need to continue investing massively to have the best tires in the world, because that is our signature. But our capacity to extract value from all the innovation in the market will become more and more difficult. There are many other businesses that are truly benefitting from our know-how [in materials technology] if we apply it to other sectors."[28]

For example, Michelin developed the capability to make mold components via 3D metallic printing. It enjoyed a first-mover advantage since the industry was focused on plastics at the time and recognized the opportunity to take that technology to market for components other than tire molds.

To add extra muscles to the High-Tech Materials group, Michelin entered into numerous partnerships with smaller companies. For instance, a 2015 joint venture with French machine manufacturer Fives Group led to Fives Michelin Additive Solutions, which offered industrial customers a complete 3D printing solution. FMAS could handle everything from the design and manufacture of machines, to complete production lines, to related services such as redesign of parts, installation, production support, and training.[29] A 2019 joint venture with French energy company Faurecia—called Symbio— would develop hydrogen fuel cell systems for light vehicles, trucks, and other applications of "hydrogen mobility." A 2020 joint development agreement with the Canadian firm Pyrowave would industrialize an innovative plastic waste recycling technology by combining Michelin's expertise in materials science with Pyrowave's research in recycling. And another 2020 partnership, with the Swedish firm Enviro, would develop an innovative process to transform used tires into raw materials.[30]

Experiences: New Polish for an Old "Jewel"

I was surprised that Menegaux considered the Experiences group, especially its world-famous Michelin Guides, to be the "jewel" of Michelin's brand and an emotional boost to the entire company. The first Michelin Guide, which rated restaurants and hotels on a three-star scale, was published in 1900 as a giveaway item to encourage the new fad of driving in France. The Michelin brothers never imagined that this little side project would evolve into the world's most prestigious rating organization, with a three-star Michelin rating becoming the Holy Grail for chefs around the world. The company published its first Tourist Guide for travelers in 1929 and continued to expand the range of its guides in the decades after World War II.

Menegaux believes that even in the age of infinite information on the web, there's still tremendous value in authoritative guides, especially for high-end dining and travel services. "We are going to be their trusted partner for the selection of their accommodations, their food, and what is nice to see. And we will have them organized and we will connect them. We will be a partner to our customers on very important social stuff, just like Michelin is in the tire."[31]

By the mid-2010s, Michelin was selling 13 million maps and guides per year, plus 20 million licensed lifestyle products. ViaMichelin, a trip-mapping service, calculated over 200 billion kilometers of trips for customers. In 2016, diners booked 39 million tables through Bookatable, the company's restaurant reservation application. Michelin expanded its Experiences group in 2017 by acquiring a 40 percent stake in Robert Parker's Wine Advocate, an international reference for wine reviews. With this acquisition, the company hoped to establish a firm position within the fine food and wine market. Several months later, it added a 40 percent stake in Guide du Fooding, an annual restaurant guide and event marketing company.[32]

Putting resources into the Experiences group made sense because it was another way for Michelin to leverage its worldwide reputation. Not only were the Michelin Guides the oldest and most prestigious brand in restaurant and hotel reviews, but they were the first to be truly global. A guidebook about a single country can't match the impact of a worldwide series. An American executive making her first trip to Tokyo or Buenos Aires probably won't have time to research all the guides for those cities, but she can trust that a Michelin guide is reliable.

Michelin's Murky Future

The jury is still out on Michelin's efforts to strengthen and retrain its muscles so it can continue to thrive during the most competitive global climate in its long history. The company's many investments within Experiences, High-Tech Materials, and especially Services & Solutions have been a big bet, but *not* making those moves would have meant taking an even bigger risk. The key question is how long it will take for Michelin's non-tire initiatives to pay off, and if they will pay off at scale all over the world. For instance, by 2019, Services & Solutions was bringing in more than $600 million in global revenue, but that was still only 2 percent of Michelin's total revenue of $28.6 billion.[33]

In the summer of 2018, the senior executive team stressed the severity of the challenges ahead. Duverger cautioned, "I think in four years we will not be there, it is going to take more time. . . . We have a big hill to climb when going to market on services."[34] And Terry Gettys, the EVP of Research and Development, predicted, "If we derail in four years, my best guess would be that we were too slow to react to change . . . that we did not adapt our processes and our people and our culture and our whole business approach for those domains differently than the domain of tires."[35]

I lean more toward the optimism of Florent Menegaux, a Systems Leader who balances short-term challenges with a clear and compelling long-term vision, which he communicates clearly and relentlessly at every opportunity. He knows that transforming a global behemoth is daunting, but he's convinced that the eventual payoff will be a new set of competitive advantages that make the most of Michelin's size and scale. Menegaux is convinced that Michelin can continue to take pride in its history and traditional French culture, while getting better and better at recruiting the global, high-tech, non-French, entrepreneurial talent it needs to thrive in the decades ahead.

As he told my class in the spring of 2019, "Right now, we are undertaking a massive transformation in many, many directions—technology, people, management, business [models]. You cannot imagine the number of transformations we've had. It's getting so massive and so complex. But people understand why we're doing it, and we're going to win."[36]

Getting Scale Right

One of the biggest advantages of blending digital and physical is the ability to quickly communicate with customers on a global basis and then incorporate their needs into your products and services. The hard part is mastering the skills required to operate at scale while also delivering customized solutions for unique customer segments.

Many industries now have global incumbents—such as AB InBev, CNN, Visa, and Michelin—that face daunting challenges from new competitors. In addition to facing start-ups that have the advantage of new technologies and business models, some also face unfair competition from China who get protection and support from the government. It would be easy for these incumbents to feel like lumbering dinosaurs surrounded by faster, leaner, more agile newcomers. But the key lesson of this chapter is that incumbents can also become faster, leaner, and more agile while simultaneously operating at scale.

Michelin, in particular, has embraced its situation by developing a materials science platform that serves multiple market segments and geographies, by placing employees in local areas to customize solutions, and by expanding globally into new markets that complement its core businesses. Despite its ongoing challenges, Michelin is a role model for leveraging scale to build new competitive advantages through the use of data, efficient global supply chains, and distribution excellence.

Companies are increasingly expected to deliver solutions across wide geographies, with customizable features, and with the speed that both corporate and individual customers have come to expect. New disruptors usually don't begin with these capabilities in their early days, and old incumbents may never have had them. But all must quickly build up these muscles if they want to be successful in the future.

THE SYSTEMS LEADER'S NOTEBOOK

Leveraging Size and Scale

- Redefine your core competency around technologies and products that enable widespread reach, whether via data, product distribution, or manufacturing.

- Put your employees as close as possible to your customers. Even in a world that increasingly depends on digital communication and collaboration, understanding local markets requires humans to live and work among the people who use what you sell.

- Overcommunicate when your teams are operating at scale. Making a new strategy or vision stick requires extremely clear messaging, repeated frequently, customized for different factions of a large organization. You can't change an entrenched culture with just a few emails.

CHAPTER 11

HAND-EYE COORDINATION: ORGANIZING ECOSYSTEMS

The challenge is maintaining a strong relationship with all of your stakeholders. Making sure you thoroughly understand what's driving them and motivating them, and trying to work productively with them. Finding a way forward that helps the company grow, thrive, prosper, and better serve our mission.

—Mark Laret, President and CEO, UCSF Health

Every company is at once its own ecosystem and part of a larger ecosystem, an interconnected web of organizations that align for their mutual interests. Within a single company, entities such as departments, business units, and unions usually have clearly defined relationships and pecking orders. In contrast, in an external ecosystem of suppliers, channel partners, investors, regulators, and competing firms, the relationships and relative strengths tend to be in constant flux. Dealing with the competing needs of an ecosystem's members is a constant juggling act—and like any juggling act, doing it well requires great hand-eye coordination.

Whether you lead a small department or a global organization, you'll face some tough questions regarding your ecosystem. When should you be tough and assertive in attempting to shape it? When should you hang back and let others take the lead in how your industry evolves? What can you do if you have a very different vision for the future of your market compared to your channel partners or key competitors?

Systems Leaders address these questions by seeking clarity about which members of the ecosystem are true friends, which are clearly enemies, and which might be both in different situations—that is, *frenemies*, a valuable coinage. A similarly useful concept is *coopetition*, which is credited to Ray Noorda in the early 1990s, when he was the CEO of Novell. Noorda described puzzling situations in which fierce competitors sometimes need to cooperate with each other, knowing that after a short-term problem is resolved, they will once again fight each other for the same customers.[1]

You may be wondering why this chapter puts hand-eye coordination with the brawny competencies, while I previously defined the inner ear (balancing ownership and partnership) as a brainy competency. Balancing is fundamentally internal, a way to make strategic decisions about which functions an organization should control directly and which it should assign to partners or other allies. But hand-eye coordination is a much more physical skill, because it's about imposing one company's vision on an entire ecosystem, which may include everyone from suppliers to government regulators. It's about using your strength to influence the behavior of others who are beyond your immediate control.

Often, it's not easy to tell who or what is really driving the direction of an industry or market. One useful tool for leaders in these situations is an "influence map" of an ecosystem. This visualization allows you to sketch which entities are pressuring others and the magnitude of these influences.[2] Varying the sizes of the circles and the thickness of the arrows will help you grasp the various sizes of the stakeholders, the nature of their relationships, and the amount of influence they have over each other. An influence map can help you sort out your friends, enemies, and frenemies, and decide where to apply your resources to influence the decisions of all three groups.

Among other benefits, the map can capture which relationships are relatively balanced (requiring skillful diplomacy) and which are unequal (giving you the option of imposing your will if diplomacy fails). It can help you understand stress points within the ecosystem and anticipate actions by various players that will put new stresses on each other. It can also help you track the results of your strategic moves and changes in your overall market. Figure 11.1 is an example.[3]

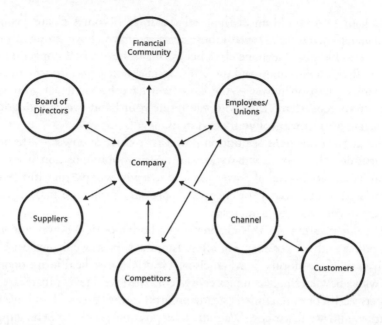

FIGURE 11.1 A Sample Influence Map of a Company and Its Ecosystem

For any circle that connects to your organization on the influence map, you can draw a 2-by-2 grid (developed by my colleague Robert A. Burgelman) to categorize your relationship with that entity, in terms of how dependent you are on each other as well as how much you can influence each other's behavior.[1] See Table 11.1.

		DEPENDENCE	
		Low	High
INFLUENCE	**Low**	You and the other entity are basically **strategically indifferent** to each other. You can partner as equals or walk away with little or no consequence.	You are **strategically subordinate** to the other entity, stuck in a position of defensiveness. Since you really need them, you have to find ways to accommodate their needs.
	High	You are **strategically dominant** over the other entity, with the power to impose your will if you choose to exercise that power.	You and the other entity are **strategically interdependent,** with the potential to become great partners in a stable, long-term ecosystem. You might also wage an evenly matched battle for control of the ecosystem.

TABLE 11.1 The Relation of Influence and Dependence Between Two Parties

Adapted from Robert A. Burgelman, Stanford Graduate School of Business

As your understanding of these relationships becomes clearer, you can begin to deploy resources toward those areas where you have strong influence and where changing someone else's behavior can have a real impact on your results. The influence map and the 2-by-2 grid can help you understand your company's "position power"—the clout you have by virtue of your status within your ecosystem. They will help refine your hand-eye coordination as you juggle the elements of your ecosystem.

But just as important as position power is "influence power"—the ability to persuade others to do what you want, even if your position is equal or subordinate. Either kind of power can lead to a win-win partnership, but you might need to outsmart your enemies or pressure them into making moves that are in your own best interests.

The organizations in this chapter apply both position power and influence power to their ecosystems in interesting ways. First, we'll consider UCSF (University of California San Francisco) Health, a vast healthcare organization with a bewilderingly complex ecosystem. Then we'll revisit Instacart from the perspective of evaluating its steady progress toward greater hand-eye coordination, and we'll see how Walmart uses position power to bend suppliers to its will. Finally, we'll do a deep dive into Google's Android division, which makes the operating systems that power about four out of five of the world's smartphones. While Android is a unique business within a unique industry, its approach to managing its ecosystem offers powerful lessons for the rest of us.

UCSF Health: Juggling Myriad Stakeholders

UCSF Health is consistently acclaimed (by *U.S. News & World Report*, among others) as one of the 10 best medical institutions in the country. President and CEO Mark Laret is responsible for more than 950 hospital beds, nearly two million annual outpatient visits, and a P&L with revenue of more than $4 billion. In his two decades with the organization, Laret has led initiatives to improve patient experiences, to improve the quality and safety of care, and to establish a regional network of hospitals and physicians. He oversaw construction of UCSF Health's newest hospital complex, UCSF Medical Center at Mission Bay, which opened in 2015 and includes specialized hospitals for children, women's services, and cancer treatment.[5]

As part of the University of California at San Francisco, with numerous hospitals and clinics around the Bay Area, UCSF Health trains 3,300 students, 1,600 medical residents, and 1,100 postdoctoral scholars in the life sciences and health professions. Its providers are leaders in virtually all specialties, including cancer, cardiology, children's health, neurology, and transplant. They also do advanced biomedical research and direct more than 1,500 clinical trials each year.[6] Those numbers represent a dramatic turnaround since 2000, when Laret was hired to save a deeply troubled nonprofit that was losing $1.5 million per week, following a failed merger attempt with Stanford Medical Centers.[7]

The size and scale of UCSF Health are impressive, but when Laret spoke to my class in May 2018, I was struck even more by the complexity of its ecosystem. He explained how he juggles the competing needs of patients, doctors, nurses, students, insurance companies, suppliers, labor unions, technology companies, the philanthropists who support UCSF Health, and the politicians and bureaucrats who regulate it on behalf of San Francisco, the state of California, and the federal government. And as part of the University of California, the largest public university system in the country, UCSF Health also faces the challenges of academia, from competing for internal resources to pursuing federal and private research grants. All of these entities are constantly trying to influence the decisions of Laret and his management team. Figure 11.2 shows the UCSF influence map.

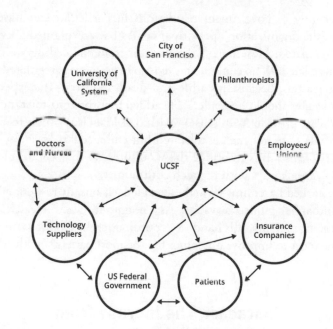

FIGURE 11.2   An Influence Map of UCSF and Its Key Constituencies

He described a big part of his job as trying to influence all the entities on that map that are themselves trying to influence UCSF Health. He disciplines his calendar to be proactive toward all these groups, asking himself first thing every morning, "Who do I need to influence today?" He can't merely fill his calendar by addressing other people's requests for meetings or by solving the problems that land in his inbox. He has to allocate his time as well as the hospital's resources toward whichever actions will have the greatest impact on the ecosystem.

In any given week, Laret might be trying to resolve a nurses' strike at one of his hospitals, listening to a pitch from a medical technology start-up, calling philanthropists to raise hundreds of millions for a new building, working with lobbyists to support a regulatory bill at the state legislature, and meeting with his boss, the chancellor of UCSF, about a budget shortfall. While that range of challenges would overwhelm many leaders, Laret sees them all as part of organizing his ecosystem to improve outcomes for patients. "The challenge is maintaining a strong relationship with all of your stakeholders. Making sure you thoroughly understand what's driving them and motivating them, and trying to work productively with them. Finding a way forward that helps the company grow, thrive, prosper, and better serve our mission."[8]

Conforming to government regulations in particular can have a huge impact on the organization's performance. As Laret explained, "Everything we do is regulated. How far off the floor or from the ceiling we can stack things is regulated. Who can put an eyedrop in your eye is regulated. And for legitimate reasons, because it's a life-and-death industry. The expectation is that no mistakes should be made."[9] He added that the zero-tolerance culture of a healthcare provider is in tension with San Francisco's high-tech culture, where mistakes are not merely tolerated but embraced as learning opportunities. Part of his job is to bridge those cultures, so that UCSF Health can partner in various ways with the tech community.

When I asked Laret how he makes tough decisions, he responded without hesitation that he's guided by values. As a nonprofit, UCSF Health's first priority is serving patients. His hand-eye coordination has to focus on whatever will do the most to improve outcomes for the most patients, within financial limitations.

Instacart: The Journey from Low to High Influence

In Chapter 7 we used Instacart as our primary case study for the brainy competency of balancing ownership and partnership. You'll recall that in its first few years, Instacart didn't have any leverage to influence its ecosystem of supermarkets and grocery suppliers. It was a small fish in a big ocean, trying to avoid being eaten by larger predators. Its short-term goal was simply to establish a stable, sustainable position within the industry, in part by convincing supermarket chains that Instacart could help them by providing a convenient and easy way to offer their customers a home delivery option.

But as Instacart grew, and especially with the home delivery boom during the COVID pandemic of 2020, it gained significant clout within its ecosystem. The balance of power shifted, as more supermarkets needed Instacart's army of professional shoppers to get food to customers who couldn't or wouldn't leave home. When lacking a delivery option became devastating for supermarkets, the leading delivery service suddenly had far more position power. Instacart also built up the clout to lobby politicians and make its case to voters. For instance, it spent an astonishing $27 million in the fight over California's Proposition 22 ballot initiative, arguing that gig workers should continue to be treated as independent contractors, not employees.[10]

Instacart's market-shaping power might not be as literally physical as running a manufacturing plant, but it has a real-world impact on every player in its ecosystem, from home-delivery customers to shoppers to supermarkets to consumer goods producers. Instacart still has to balance the demands of all those groups, but now it's doing so with the scale and clout to organize its ecosystem, instead of merely adapting to it. Figures 11.3 and 11.4 show two influence maps that visualize the company's journey from a start-up begging for favors within its ecosystem to a major player able to influence its partners:

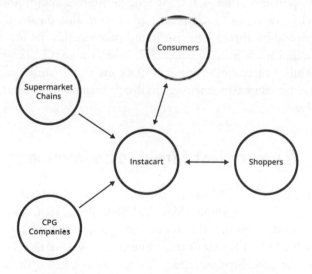

FIGURE 11.3   A Simple Influence Map of Instacart
and Its Industry in the Start-up Phase

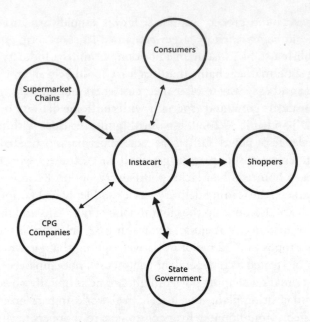

FIGURE 11.4   A Simple Influence Map of Instacart
and Its Industry in Its Mature Phase

In terms of the 2-by-2 grid, Instacart migrated from the upper right quadrant of subordination to the lower right quadrant of interdependence with several of its partners. These days, many supermarket chains and consumer brands need Instacart as much as it needs them. This means that its challenges go beyond balancing ownership and partnership, the brainy, internal competence that we covered in Chapter 7. Now Instacart has brawny market clout, the ability to make a serious impact on the fortunes of its friends, enemies, and frenemies. Its ongoing challenge is to use that clout wisely and benevolently.

Walmart: Not Afraid to Be Dominant

Speaking of using clout within an ecosystem, benevolently or otherwise, it's hard to find a clearer example than Walmart. From its founding by Sam Walton as a single store in Arkansas in 1962, to its current status as a retail behemoth with 11,500 locations in 27 countries, Walmart's ecosystem strategy has been remarkably consistent. Walton believed that the key to retail success was driving prices as low as possible for his customers, in part by getting goods as cheaply as possible from his suppliers. His motto, drilled into generations of Walmart executives, was "Buy it low, stack it high, sell it cheap."[11] To that end, Walmart has always tried to push aside middlemen and haggle directly with manufacturers to bring costs down.

As Walmart grew over the decades, its position relative to manufacturers evolved from subordinate to interdependent to dominant. As more and more Americans shopped at Walmart consistently, its clout within the retail ecosystem grew exponentially. By the 1990s, if your company made any kind of consumer product and you wanted to be seen as a national brand, you needed to be on Walmart's shelves more than Walmart needed your product. Which meant that what the haggling Sam Walton had done in the old days could be replaced by a far more aggressive and one-sided process. As journalist Charles Fishman wrote in a classic 2003 exposé:

> By selling a gallon of kosher dills for less than most grocers sell a quart, Wal-Mart may have provided a service for its customers. But what did it do for Vlasic? The pickle maker had spent decades convincing customers that they should pay a premium for its brand. Now Wal-Mart was practically giving them away. And the fevered buying spree that resulted distorted every aspect of Vlasic's operations, from farm to factory to financial statement. . . . The real story of Wal-Mart, the story that never gets told, is the story of the pressure the biggest retailer relentlessly applies to its suppliers in the name of bringing us "everyday low prices". . . .
>
> On basic products that don't change, the price Wal-Mart will pay, and will charge shoppers, must drop year after year. But what almost no one outside the world of Wal-Mart and its 21,000 suppliers knows is the high cost of those low prices. Wal-Mart has the power to squeeze profit-killing concessions from vendors. To survive in the face of its pricing demands, makers of everything from bras to bicycles to blue jeans have had to lay off employees and close U.S. plants in favor of outsourcing products from overseas.[12]

Walmart retained a very aggressive negotiating approach as it became increasingly dominant in American retail. Its executives weren't afraid to be seen as the bad guys, imposing strict rules on sales reps who were granted a mere 30 minutes to pitch a Walmart buyer. A meeting, by the way, that often required two connecting flights to reach Walmart's remote headquarters in Bentonville, Arkansas. Walmart could get away with being so demanding because the vast majority of its suppliers were stuck in the "high dependence/low influence" quadrant.

In the last few years, facing price competition from Amazon and other e-tailers, Walmart has continued to ramp up pressure on manufacturers. A trade publication reported in 2017 that Walmart was asking suppliers to "make logistics improvements that would help them get $1 billion more in sales by working harder on shipping orders in full and on-time, which would trim delivery costs, reduce re-orders, and reduce out-of-stock problems."[13] One consultant observed that brands that agreed to play ball with Walmart could expect better distribution and more strategic help, while those that chose not to would see their distribution limited: "Once every three or four years, Walmart tells you to take the money you're spending on marketing initiatives and invest it in lower prices. They sweep all the chips off the table and drill you down on price."[14]

Of course, some Walmart suppliers have a lot more clout than Vlasic Pickles. Apple, for instance, can negotiate the terms for distributing iPhones via Walmart on a much more equal footing; they're in the interdependent quadrant. While Walmart can credibly threaten to replace Vlasic with generic pickles, customers who really want an iPhone would rather shop elsewhere than accept a substitute. To keep those customers loyal to Walmart, the company will grant Apple exceptions to its strict rules. That's just another aspect of its skillful ecosystem management, with an eye on its stated goal: "Everyday low prices on a broad assortment—anytime, anywhere."[15]

Android: Mastering a Truly Global and Often Hostile Ecosystem

When Google commercially released the Android operating system (OS) for smartphones in 2008, it took the opposite strategic approach from Apple's closed iOS for its new iPhone. Google's leadership believed that rather than jealously guarding a proprietary smartphone OS, the company could best thrive by giving the operating system away to anyone who wanted to build smartphones. As their website puts it, "By being an open-source platform, Android's source code is available for anyone to view, download, modify, enhance, and redistribute without requiring any sort of fees, royalties, or other costs. This is the opposite of closed source/proprietary software which never makes its source code public and strictly prohibits any modification."[16]

From the perspective of 13 years later, that decision looks like a resounding success. Android is now the operating system for 2.5 *billion* smartphones, tablets, and other mobile devices around the world, made by about 1,300 third-party original equipment manufacturers (OEMs), with a combined market share north of 80 percent.[17] Google invests several billion dollars each year in constantly improving Android and expanding it into new uses, such as smart watches, smart speakers, and automobile operating systems. In return, it generated an estimated $18.8 billion in revenue from Android in 2019, including:

▶ $9.1 billion from the Google Play app store, which wouldn't exist without Android.
▶ $7.5 billion from search advertising on Android devices.
▶ $2.2 from Google Maps and Google Pay, both of which derive much of their revenue by being used on Android devices.[18]

It sounds like a happy ending—a foundational decision that paid off better than former CEO Eric Schmidt probably dared to hope in 2005, when Google acquired a tiny start-up called Android Inc. for a reported $50 million.[19]

But even with a dominant share of mobile operating systems, 2.5 billion devices in circulation, and $19 billion in annual revenue, Android still faces enormous challenges because of the mind-bending complexity of its ecosystem. Just think about the entities on its influence map whose decisions can make or break Android's ongoing success:

▶ About 1,300 smartphone OEMs worldwide, who have the option to drop Android at any time if they discover a better alternative or become disgruntled with the strings attached to Android's free OS.
▶ Thousands of app developers, whose efforts are essential to stocking the Google Play app store and making it the world's biggest, with even more choices on offer than Apple's App Store.
▶ Hundreds of cellular carriers around the world, who have the power to disrupt the entire mobile market with a change in their policies.
▶ Government regulators in every country in the world, some of whom are on high alert for any predatory, monopolistic abuses of Android's massive market share.

The result is a complex ecosystem that Figure 11.5 can only approximate.

I interviewed many Android executives in 2013, 2015, and again in 2018, while developing three case studies for the Stanford GSB. Let's dig into some of the deep, long-term challenges they continue to face.[20]

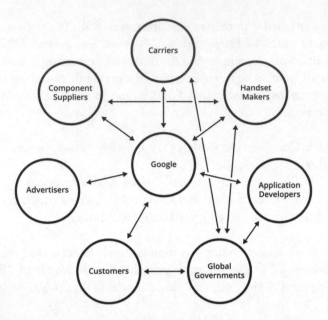

FIGURE 11.5   An Influence Map of Google and the Android Ecosystem

How Do You Brand Something That's Invisible and Free?

With OEMs and wireless carriers taking advantage of the freedom to customize Android to fit their goals, the consumer experience on an Android
phone can vary significantly from device to device. So how can Android
even talk to consumers about its user experience, rather than hundreds of
different user experiences? If branding is about defining a market position,
what do you do if you don't control a single position?

Bob Borchers, a former Apple exec who became vice president of marketing for Google's platforms and ecosystems, was acutely aware of this
challenge. At Apple, he noted, every element of the consumer's interaction with the brand is controlled. But with Android, the image of Google's
software is at the mercy of somebody else's hardware. Android didn't even
own its own brand logo, a green robot that was open source via a Creative
Commons license.[21]

This was intentional; an open-source mascot and logo would encourage
wide promotion of the Android platform. Google's direct marketing costs for
Android were significantly lower than those at Apple, because its partners
were launching devices and Android benefitted from the billions spent on
marketing by OEMs like Xiaomi and carriers like AT&T. Google's goal was
to ensure the right degree of consistency across the devices. While devices

would be positioned differently in each market, the underlying promise of Android had to be the same.

Nevertheless, as Borchers noted, "Only 50 percent of people know Android is affiliated with Google, and of those that do, less than half know that Google employees do the work to write the software."[22] His job was to try to create a clean, consistent message for Android, despite the distributed nature of the marketing across ecosystem partners. But in Borchers' consumer brand-checking reports, characteristics associated with the device were often mistakenly attributed by users to the operating system (OS) and vice versa. "A lot of that comes from not having a unified story. Brands are based on consumer experiences, and there are just so many different Android experiences that it's not clear what we're about."[23]

Recognizing that it needed a vehicle to show off Google's ideal vision for the Android experience, Google created Android One, a version designed to give users a streamlined, Google-centric experience on OEM-branded devices. OEMs like Nokia could create distinct product lines, like the Nokia 8 Sirocco, with Android One already built in. That way, purchasers of the Sirocco could experience Android as Google intended—with Google Play, Google Assistant, Photos, Maps, Lens, Gmail, Drive, Docs, and Chrome all integrated.

Sagar Kamdar, a director of product management for Android, noted that Android One provided two major benefits. First, it allowed OEMs to spend time and resources building hardware elements that consumers cared about, such as better cameras, while leaving certain software platform innovations to Google. Second, it gave Google a way to show users what was possible with a Google-focused experience. As he put it, "For Android One, success is a consumer saying: *I bought this phone because I know exactly what an Android device is, and I sought it out.*"[24]

How Do You Keep Driving Innovation Against Deep-Pocketed Competitors?

Android's leaders put a high priority on consistently wowing customers by relentlessly improving the operating system. They believed that technology should not simply be "bearable," but should deliver excitement and joy. The team worked to build artificial intelligence into the Android OS, supporting Google Assistant as a new way to drive innovative experiences to speakers, televisions, and cars, along with smartphones. Despite having more than 80 percent market share, the Android team knew that serious competition could emerge at any moment, from a tiny start-up, a tech giant, or anywhere in between. In particular, they worried about:

▶ Samsung, which sold the most Android phones of any OEM—296 million in 2019.[25] This relationship, a key part of Android's ecosystem, had been strong for years, until Samsung announced its own "Tizen" OS in 2012. The first Tizen smartphone didn't appear until 2014, and the Tizen App Store didn't go live (with only 25 apps) until 2015.[26] Even though Tizen was a bust, Samsung was clearly looking for ways to reduce its dependence on Android.

▶ Amazon, which chose to "fork" (modify) the Android OS to create the Fire OS, which was installed on its Fire Phone and Kindle Fire tablet starting in 2014. But because the Fire OS didn't allow access to the Google Play Store or the use of Google apps, the Fire Phone failed to catch on.[27] Since then, Amazon has doubled down on becoming not merely a great retailer but a cutting-edge tech company, via Alexa's artificial intelligence, Echo Dot speakers, Amazon Web Services, and other innovations. If it chooses to, it can develop its own mobile OS for all sorts of connected devices, far beyond smartphones and tablets.

▶ Facebook, which launched an ill-fated, branded smartphone (partnering with HTC) in 2013, but then declared that it wasn't planning to build a competitive OS. Facebook's goal was to gain mobile advertising market share, and in theory it was indifferent to which OS hosted the Facebook app. But if it ever changes its mobile strategy, Facebook could certainly afford to challenge Android.

While these and other potential threats might keep the Android management team up at night, they believed that continuing to drive innovation was the key to staying ahead.

How Do You Serve Emerging Markets, Where Every Penny Counts?

As the smartphone market exploded in the early 2010s, it became clear that there were at least two distinct submarkets. Middle-class and wealthy consumers in Europe and North America were willing to pay premium prices for cutting-edge phones, upgrading every two years or so. And in the developing world, millions would be thrilled to get cheaper smartphones, without all the latest bells and whistles. But how different would the ecosystem in the developing world look? As Jamie Rosenberg, vice president of Android, told me in 2015, "Markets like India, Brazil, and Indonesia could develop in the same way that developed markets have, or they could be very different. Maybe apps will monetize very differently in these markets. There may be models in these markets that we have to make sure our platform is friendly to, whether it's how people consume data and think about data charges, whether media and content are more typically ad-supported than premium, or how games are distributed and monetized."[28]

To take India as an example, the migration to smartphones accelerated in 2014, a year that saw 186 percent market growth. As prices decreased and Indians embraced phones with mobile advertising, the Android team knew they had to focus on this huge population. They developed a slimmed-down version of Android that would work with less-powerful but more-affordable smartphones. Then Google partnered with local OEMs, giving them new hardware specs that would make these phones easier and cheaper to produce. Google's assistance enabled the OEMs to sell basic smartphones running Android for as little as $100. Google also designed variations to meet local preferences, such as FM radio or dual SIM cards that let users operate multiple accounts on a single device. By the end of 2019, India crossed 500 million smartphone users out of its total population of 1.38 billion, a blistering rate of growth over six years. 74 percent owned affordable phones from one of the country's top four OEMs (Samsung, Xiaomi, Vivo, and OPPO), which all ran versions of Android.[29]

Another key product for the developing world was the Android Oreo Go Edition, a version of the operating system for lower-end devices. Rosenberg noted that the Android team set a high bar for customizations to its software, but once a feature had high demand, the team would invest heavily. "Over the years, we saw a tension develop between the need to innovate in the OS to take advantage of advanced hardware capabilities, and the need for that same OS to run well on the lowest cost Android smartphones. And at a certain point we decided we couldn't leave that segment behind, even if it meant creating a new variant of the OS for less advanced hardware configurations. We're giving up some efficiency by maintaining this additional variant with Android Oreo Go Edition, but we're able to reach a new segment of users."[30]

Paul Gennai, director of product management for Android, explained some of the changes necessary in emerging markets: "In the past, our platform and apps were expanding year on year, which made it hard for lower-end hardware devices to run them. With Android Oreo Go Edition, we rewrote many of Google's own apps, not only to make them smaller and more data efficient, but also to make them better suited to users of these devices—things like more visual user interfaces and better interaction with voice. Maybe more importantly, we set thresholds for the app ecosystem more generally to keep performance high. These changes don't just benefit the consumer—they benefit the OEMs and the carriers too."[31]

As Gennai summarized Google's goal: "One-size-fits-all just doesn't work anymore. Having less money doesn't mean you should have a lesser experience."[32]

How Do You Build Your Own Hardware Without Alienating Your Hardware Partners?

Despite Android's steady growth, Google's management knew that software alone would not keep them atop the mobile industry. "To push forward on computing, you need to do it at the intersection of hardware and software," said CEO Sundar Pichai—summing up the critical truth that value in most industries now lies at the convergence of brains and brawn.[33]

Back in 2010, Google had introduced the Nexus line of smartphones, which were designed by Google but manufactured by partnering OEMs. The purpose of Nexus wasn't to enter the hardware industry at scale, but to create an environment conducive to cutting-edge innovation. As Pichai explained, "Suppose we want to make a better photography experience for the user. We have to look at the whole stack, from image sensors to processors to software and user interface. Nexus allows us to do this."[34] Although Nexus never gained much market share, that didn't bother Google. Its goal with Nexus wasn't to take share from the OEM partners, but rather to show the OEMs how Android *should* and *could* work with cutting-edge hardware.

In late 2016, Google discontinued the Nexus and launched two versions of the Pixel, a high-end, Google-branded phone that would directly compete with the smartphone manufacturers that drove Android's growth. The Android team realized that they would have to work doubly hard to manage their partnerships with OEMs, while also partnering with the new Pixel team. On the internal org chart, Android and Pixel were separate business units with separate managements—but to the rest of the smartphone ecosystem they would both be perceived and treated as simply "Google." As Kamdar put it, "We of course want Pixel to be differentiated, but now that we're our own OEM, our OEM partners are asking: *How do you think about us relative to your own hardware products?* So it's a balancing act for sure."[35]

Unlike the Nexus, which had put Android software into third-party devices, Pixel gave Google control of the end-to-end user experience, including a pure version of Android with no customizations. It would give Google a way to reshape consumer perceptions of the company. Sabrina Ellis, vice president of product management for Android, noted, "For Google, being such a data-driven company, it was difficult not having the ability to quickly experiment on our search experiences and have the data on-hand to see how it's working. Now we can beta test and give consumers the designs and the phone specifications we feel they really want. With Pixel, we're showing the ecosystem what can be done with Android. We're trying to lift the bar."[36]

Google established a firewall between the Android and Pixel teams, aiming to eliminate any perception of favoritism or collusion by OEMs like Samsung, which partnered with Android while competing with Pixel. No government commission or antitrust watchdog required the firewall, which made collaboration between the two units unwieldy. But so far, the firewall has helped keep the OEMs from abandoning Android in protest. As part of the give-and-take of their interdependent relationship, they would just have to live with competing against Pixel in terms of quality, features, and pricing.

I have used many generations of Pixel phones and love them, but so far it has turned out to be a high-end, low-market share product, not the category killer that the OEMs might have feared in 2016. As of the end of 2019, just 0.4 percent of smartphones sold worldwide were Pixels.[37] Even for a company as powerful as Google, it's hard to sway customers from a smartphone brand that they're already comfortable with. It's not just about customer loyalty or inertia, as Ellis observed: "The stakes are high because the switching costs—the hundreds of dollars it takes to go from an Apple or Samsung to the Google phone—are much higher."[38]

How Do You Keep Growing Without Drawing the Wrath of Regulators?

On July 17, 2018, the European Union's antitrust commission announced that it was fining Google $5.1 billion for alleged anticompetitive practices related to Android. The ruling claimed that by requiring its own set of apps as preloads on Android-enabled devices, Google was giving its apps and search engine an unfair advantage. The EU demanded that Google decouple certain apps that it provided to its Android partners from Chrome and Search.[39] This was a serious threat to Android's partnership-based business model, not only in Europe, but potentially all over the world. What would happen if regulators in other countries followed suit?

As it had after similar rulings in the past (including a $2.7 billion EU fine in June 2017), Google pushed back both in courts of law and the court of public opinion. CEO Sundar Pichai stressed that Google did not require any OEMs to include, promote, or favor its services; it was up to each OEM. For example, the Amazon Fire tablet runs on an Android operating system, yet ships with no Google apps preinstalled. While most Android devices came preloaded with a number of apps (some of them Google's, some not), they could easily be disabled or deleted by the consumer. Pichai also argued that Android had not hurt competition, but rather had expanded it via its free distribution, which expanded the options for software developers, phone manufacturers, and consumers alike. He claimed that the EU ruling would limit the choices available to everyone in the smartphone ecosystem, concluding that the decision "sends a troubling signal in favor of proprietary systems over open platforms."[40]

Google's chief legal counsel, Kent Walker, further argued that Android's business model enabled developers to create apps without having to code hundreds of different versions and allowed manufacturers to make hardware customizations, as proven by the thousands of different phone options available to customers. Sanctioning Android would make it harder for app developers to create new content—the opposite of the European Union's goal of increasing consumer choice and competition.

Since that huge fine, Google has continued to fight accusations of anticompetitive practices with a combination of legal defenses, government lobbying, and public relations initiatives. On the Android website, for instance, you'll find a detailed, carefully crafted list of "Android facts" about how the operating system supports fair competition and innovation across the entire mobile industry.[41] Despite Google's roots as an antiregulatory Silicon Valley start-up, its leadership team understands that the world's governments now loom large on the company's influence map. They are applying the hand-eye coordination necessary to confront those influences.

In its relations with governments—as with its relations with OEMs, cellular carriers, app developers, and other entities—Android is a role model for skillfully adjusting its strategies as the ecosystem evolves and new challenges continue to emerge. Its reward is holding an astonishing 80 to 85 percent global market share and all the billions that flow from it.

Getting Ecosystems Right

Shaping an ecosystem to meet your objectives requires the thoughtful deployment of capital and personnel into those areas that will ultimately determine the long-term competitive landscape of an industry. Unlike the design, production, and distribution of products, organizing an ecosystem requires a keen understanding of the players involved, their motivations, and their unique strengths and dependencies.

This kind of juggling sometimes requires direct confrontation, such as when negotiating with suppliers. Other times it requires an indirect approach, such as by helping others in your ecosystem develop products and services that complement your own. Leaders may be called upon to collaborate with other companies of varying sizes and capabilities, from dangerously large and successful organizations to brand new, unproven start-ups.

UCSF Health, Instacart, Walmart, and Google are very different organizations that share outstanding hand-eye coordination. They know that actively guiding and organizing the other members of their ecosystems is a mission-critical competency. In an increasingly interconnected world, the ability to shape an ecosystem will continue to rise in importance, from a competitive advantage to an existential imperative.

THE SYSTEMS LEADER'S NOTEBOOK

Organizing an Ecosystem

- Develop an industry influence map and dependence/influence tables to help your team understand how various constituents interact with each other in your industry, and who really has power over others.

- Be very clear about distinguishing when your company is essentially dabbling in a space (like Google's Pixel) and when something is critical to your success (like Walmart's low prices). This distinction will affect how much pressure you may need to put on your ecosystem partners.

- Be mindful of any governmental regulations that may restrict your strategic and tactical options, especially as you grow big enough to attract the scrutiny of regulators. Like it or not, government agendas may shape your competitive landscape—stay in front of government regulation

CHAPTER 12

STAMINA: SURVIVING FOR THE LONG RUN

One of the things I have become a student of is how institutions outlast the generations who created them. How they live up to the ideals that first made them successful but also question the status quo.

—Satya Nadella, CEO of Microsoft

Longevity is the ultimate challenge for any business. Countless start-ups fly high for a few years on the strength of a breakthrough innovation, only to crash when competitors catch up or their industry takes an unexpected turn. Despite the start-up world's faith in "failing fast" and then pivoting to new business models, that kind of strategic nimbleness is much more easily said than done.

But some companies do figure out how to adapt and evolve, decade after decade. They steadily build a reputation and brand image through both good times and bad, long after their founders have retired or died. As times change, these companies make a sharp distinction between the products or services that originally put them on the map but may need to be left behind, as opposed to the fundamental values and mission that can and should remain consistent as the core of their identity.

I call this skill stamina, and I've grouped it with the brawny competencies because it often requires driving change on a massive scale. It's one thing when the founders of a start-up like Instagram or Slack explain a strategic pivot to 20 or 30 staffers in a single location. It's quite another when an executive team tries to transform products, business models, and especially mindsets across an organization of tens of thousands (or hundreds of thousands) of employees, many of whom have grown comfortable with the old ways of doing things and will resent or oppose innovation. Exercising one's stamina can be especially tough when circumstances require closing decades-old factories or doing mass layoffs.

Consider the companies we've discussed that were born in a very different world, decades or even more than a century ago: Daimler, Michelin, Walmart, John Deere, AB InBev. Or consider some other long-term survivors that Jim Collins and Jerry Porras profiled in their 1994 classic, *Built to Last*: 3M, Walt Disney, Boeing, Sony, Procter & Gamble. For all of their differences, these companies share a clarity about which parts of their history and culture are still relevant and essential, and which can safely be jettisoned. They all had the stamina to survive tough times and regroup to make the most of new opportunities, often by adding products or services that their founders wouldn't recognize. They all took advantage of the fact that you don't have to be perfect once you've established a strong reputation; consumers will have a certain amount of patience while you recover from missteps or reinvent your offerings for a new era.

In this chapter we'll start with three brief examples of the power of stamina. National Geographic proved that an organization that became famous in the nineteenth century could still thrive in the twenty-first. Microsoft, which achieved unprecedented success and market power in the 1980s and 1990s, found the stamina to recover after a series of strategic mistakes in the early 2000s. Even Netflix, a relative newcomer founded in 1997, has been around long enough to survive two major pivots in its business model, despite internal and external skepticism to both transformations.

Then our featured example is Johnson & Johnson, which has evolved continuously for 135 years and counting. J&J draws its stamina in part from its famous Credo, written by chairman Robert Wood Johnson in 1943, to make decisions in line with its values. Its leaders see new technology as a tool, never a panacea, as it fights to stay competitive in a huge range of markets. It's also facing a series of daunting legal and public relations challenges that threaten its brand and reputation.

National Geographic:
New Outlets for Old Values

The National Geographic Society was founded in 1888 in Washington, DC, for "the increase and diffusion of geographical knowledge." Its 33 cofounders were a diverse group of geographers, explorers, teachers, lawyers, cartographers, military officers, and financiers who wanted to encourage Americans to become more curious about the world around them. They launched *National Geographic* magazine nine months later, and circulation boomed to two million in the early 1900s, after it switched from overly technical articles to general interest articles accompanied by photographs. *National Geographic* soon became known for its stunning and pioneering photography, including the first color photos of the sky, the oceans, and the North and South Poles.[1]

The National Geographic Society grew over the decades to become one of the world's largest nonprofit scientific and educational institutions. It still sees itself as a guardian of the planet's resources and focuses on ways to broaden its reach. It has provided more than 14,000 grants since 1890, for work across all seven continents. This includes, as its website notes, "the most comprehensive scientific expedition to Mount Everest, working to better understand human-carnivore conflict in Gorongosa National Park in Mozambique, telling stories that help explain the world and all that's in it, and groundbreaking work that has transformed our understanding of the great apes and what it means to be human."[2]

The Society has stuck to its core mission—"using the power of science, exploration, education and storytelling to illuminate and protect the wonder of our world"[3]—while adapting to a wide range of new outlets, including television channels, books, websites, documentary films, and in-person events around the world. *National Geographic* is still consistently one of the top-selling 10 magazines in the United States, with a circulation of about four million and a total reach of 28 million.[4]

In 2015, the nonprofit Society started National Geographic Partners as a for-profit joint venture with 21st Century Fox to reorganize its many properties and publications. (Disney took over Fox's role in the joint venture after a 2019 deal.) The joint venture returns 27 percent of its proceeds to the nonprofit Society. Thanks to its huge portfolio of media assets, National Geographic now reaches millions of people, with television networks in 172 countries and publications available in 41 languages.[5]

I've loved *National Geographic* magazine for its great writing and stunning pictures since I was nine years old. I had a National Geographic poster of the known universe on my bedroom wall; it's now framed on the wall of my Stanford office. That kind of nostalgia can help drive brand loyalty while an organization builds new generations of fans. For instance, my son only knows National Geographic as a producer of cool videos that he streams on his phone. But the brand's stamina will endure as long as the content it generates is outstanding, in any format.

Microsoft: Finding the Stamina to Recover from Dark Times

Microsoft's origin story is the template for every tech entrepreneur's fantasies. A brilliant geek (Bill Gates) drops out of college, starts a business with his best friend (Paul Allen) on a shoestring budget, commercializes software for the growing personal computer market (MS-DOS), outsmarts one of the world's biggest companies (IBM) in a contract negotiation, leverages each successful new product into the next (Windows and Office), makes a fortune in an IPO, becomes the world's richest and most influential businessperson, then rides into the sunset to save humanity via bold philanthropy. The end. Roll credits.

Of course, the real story of Microsoft's first 25 years is more complicated, but let's focus on what happened after Gates retired as CEO in January 2000, handing the baton to Steve Ballmer. The next 14 years are generally seen as the darkest period in Microsoft history, when it almost completely lost the technological and strategic high ground it had enjoyed in the 1990s. Under Ballmer, the company seemed stuck on a treadmill, producing bloated and uninspiring upgrades of existing products, such as the widely disparaged Windows Vista operating system of 2007. Even when Microsoft tried to innovate, the results were often dismissed as inferior to those of cooler companies like Apple. Remember the iPod versus Zune comparisons of 2006?*

As the stock price stagnated for a decade, Ballmer went through increasingly harsh shareholder criticism and press coverage, including a 2012 *Forbes* column that called him "the worst CEO of a large publicly traded American company" because he had "steered Microsoft out of some of the

---

* Zune was an ill-fated MP3 player that was supposed to challenge the iPod but was widely mocked by tech experts and critics. A typical review by Engadget concluded, "Ever hear the phrase go big or go home? The only thing big about the Zune right now is the marketing campaign." (https://www.engadget.com/2006-11-15-zune-review.html)

fastest-growing and most lucrative tech markets."[6] The board finally nudged Ballmer into retirement in late 2013, replacing him with Satya Nadella, then the head of Microsoft's Cloud and Enterprise Group.

Since 2014, Nadella has been widely praised for reaching back to the values that originally made Microsoft great—not slavish devotion to old products but the aggressive, technology-led spirit that had once driven Gates and Allen. The company's focus on cloud-based software, especially its wildly successful subscription model for Office 365 and other key applications, has helped revive its stock price along with its reputation. Its Surface tablet PCs and other hardware products have drawn great reviews.

Asked by the *Wall Street Journal* in 2019 where he finds inspiration, Nadella replied, "In the hard work that leaders in companies and institutions do to stay relevant. One of the things I have become a student of is how institutions outlast the generations who created them. How they live up to the ideals that first made them successful but also question the status quo."[7] That's a good summary of stamina: surviving tough times by distinguishing the permanent essence of an organization from the unessential details that can and should be challenged.

Netflix: The Courage to Reinvent a Brand, Twice

Compared to the other companies discussed in this chapter, 23-year-old Netflix is still a newbie. But its relative youth makes it a great example of how to build stamina, and why it matters. Even young companies can find it hard to distinguish their core mission from the products and services that should be subordinate to the mission. It takes stamina (as well as insight and courage) to pivot to new business models—ideally *before* adversity forces you to make those pivots.

Reed Hastings and Marc Randolph started Netflix in 1997 in Santa Cruz County, geographically removed from the dotcom frenzy then consuming the San Francisco Bay Area and Silicon Valley. They knew there would be demand for a service that let people skip the hassle of driving to a video store to rent movies and TV shows, and then back again to return them. Netflix users could simply visit the website to create a queue of DVDs they wanted to watch, wait for them to arrive in their mailbox, then easily mail them back in the postage-paid envelopes provided.[8]

It may not sound innovative in retrospect, but Netflix was truly ground-breaking, designing and refining sophisticated warehousing and tracking systems to keep all those DVDs circulating around the country, with minimal glitches or delays. People who tried the service loved its convenience, as well as the fact that there was no extra charge for keeping DVDs indefinitely; you simply wouldn't receive the next items in your queue until you returned the previous ones. By eliminating late fees, logistical hassles, and virtually all out-of-stock frustrations, Netflix created an appealing alternative to Blockbuster, the dominant movie-rental platform. By 1999, with about 100,000 US subscribers, Netflix shifted from pay-per-rental to a monthly subscription model with unlimited rentals.[9] That shift drove word-of-mouth and growth even faster.

By 2006, with more than six million US subscribers, Netflix was riding high, as was its stock price following its 2002 IPO. No competitors were even close to its dominance of the rentals-by-mail market. But Hastings and his team knew that the company wouldn't stay on top if it defined itself around physical DVDs. They started an internal push to innovate video streaming on demand. This new option launched in 2007, just when a critical mass of US homes were getting high-speed internet access.

At first, Netflix's streaming option offered far fewer movies and TV shows than its DVD service, and the user experience wasn't always smooth. Some critics and shareholders questioned why the company was pouring millions into streaming while consumers were still very happy with the DVD service. Criticism intensified in 2011, when Netflix announced a plan to spin off DVD rentals as a separate company, to be called Qwikster. Hastings's blog post announcing the change drew 27,000 mostly harsh comments, including one that said, "Splitting Netflix in two so that you have Netflix and Qwikster is the worst business decision since New Coke."[10] The stock price plunged for two months, until the plan was scrapped.

But despite the Qwikster fiasco, Hastings was right that streaming was the future, even if DVDs at that point still offered users a much broader range of entertainment. The company topped 26 million US subscribers by 2012. Today, of course, the overwhelming majority of US Netflix subscriptions (60.1 out of 62.5 million in 2019) are exclusively for its streaming service.[11] The company made the right strategic pivot at the right time to sustain its core mission of delivering great entertainment.

Netflix's other major shift was producing its own original content, beginning with a $100 million deal in 2011 to acquire *House of Cards*, featuring A-list talent such as director David Fincher and actors Kevin Spacey and Robin Wright. Hollywood was stunned by this move, as the *New York Times* reported: "The deal immediately makes Netflix a player in premium television programming. *House of Cards*, a serialized political drama, will look and feel like a traditional TV show, but it will not be distributed that way. . . .

It will be marketed through Netflix's recommendation engine. And it will probably be released in batches, several episodes at a time, since subscribers like to binge on serialized shows. . . . By licensing *House of Cards*, Netflix is essentially selling itself to Hollywood as an alternative to networks like HBO—and indicating that it is willing to pay high prices for high-quality shows."[12]

As with the shift toward streaming, this huge investment drew skepticism, especially from Hollywood moguls who believed that betting on entertainment properties required specialized experience and intuition that Netflix's data geeks and algorithms lacked. But again, Hastings and his team showed the insight and courage to recognize the need to evolve while still ahead, rather than waiting until they were in trouble. They knew that Netflix couldn't thrive for the long run as a platform for other people's content. As competitors began building their own streaming platforms, they would surely restrict Netflix's access to the movies and TV shows that users really wanted. Long-term survival would require building a library of high-quality content that Netflix fully owned,

Today, as Hastings predicted, virtually every major media company has its own streaming video platform. But Netflix continues to thrive, adding 15.8 million net new global subscribers just in the first quarter of 2020, as the COVID pandemic dramatically increased demand for streaming. As the *Wall Street Journal* reported, "Usage was boosted in the quarter by several popular original efforts, including the third season of the drama *Ozark* and the documentary series *Tiger King: Murder, Mayhem and Madness*. Netflix said *Tiger King* was sampled by 64 million member households."[13]

Netflix is a role model for thinking and training like a marathoner, not a sprinter. Its efforts to build up its stamina should continue to pay off as its industry becomes even more competitive in the years ahead.

Johnson & Johnson: An Old Incumbent Facing New Challenges

Johnson & Johnson was founded in New Jersey in 1886, by three brothers who sold ready-to-use surgical dressings and later first-aid kits, baby powder, and various personal products. It expanded to the United Kingdom in 1924 and later to Mexico, South Africa, Australia, Argentina, Brazil, and the Philippines.[14] In 1959, it acquired McNeil Labs in the United States and Cilag in Europe, becoming a major pharmaceutical producer.[15] Then with its acquisition of Janssen Pharmaceuticals in 1961, J&J solidified its position as one of the world's leading research-based pharma companies. It has continued to grow its consumer, medical, and pharmaceutical businesses around the world.

Today it's hard to grasp the sheer size and breadth of this conglomerate, which generated $82 billion in revenue in 2019. Many of its more than 250 brands are iconic, or at least would be impressive stand-alone businesses. They include:

- ▶ Over-the-counter drugs and consumer products like Tylenol, Motrin, Benadryl, Bengay, Imodium, Pepcid, Sudafed, Listerine, Band-Aid, Stayfree, and Mylanta.
- ▶ Food brands like Splenda and Lactaid.
- ▶ Cosmetics and skin care brands like Clean & Clear, Neutrogena, Aveeno, bebe, Rogaine, and Lubriderm.
- ▶ Vision care products like Acuvue and Visine.
- ▶ Medical device brands like Acclarent, Cerenovus, and Mentor.[16]

But despite all those powerful consumer brands, fully half of J&J's revenue comes from its pharmaceuticals subsidiaries, which make prescription drugs like Remicade (for rheumatoid arthritis), Stelara (for psoriasis), and Zytiga (for prostate cancer), to name just a few. Pharmaceuticals are even more important to the bottom line, with pretax profit margins of about 31 percent, far greater than the 17 percent and 16 percent margins of J&J's consumer and medical device groups.[17]

As we saw in our discussion of 23andMe, the prescription drug industry's business model is high risk, high reward. It takes billions in investment capital to research and test a significant new medication. But a US patent is only valid for 20 years after a drug's invention, which includes however many years are required for testing, for surviving the FDA's notoriously tough approval process, and for winning a patent. In practice, a company like J&J often has just a decade or so to cash in on an innovative new medication, before other companies can produce generic versions that will undercut its power to charge premium prices.[18]

Alex Gorsky, J&J's CEO since 2012, spoke to my The Industrialist's Dilemma class in February 2018. He has a profound awareness of the weight of J&J's past successes, and deep pride in its role in fighting diseases like Alzheimer's, HIV, and cancer. But he's also deeply aware that success is never guaranteed in any of J&J's three industries (pharmaceuticals, medical devices, and consumer products). In addition to competing with disruptive biotech start-ups as well as its traditional Big Pharma rivals, J&J has been working hard to restore its public reputation in the wake of lawsuits, the opioid crisis, and public outcry over prescription drug prices.

The Credo as J&J's Foundation over Time

Gorsky's focus on customer outcomes is in line with J&J's 77-year-old Credo, which serves as the guiding document for what the company will and won't change. It's a key element in the company's stamina. Robert Wood Johnson, chairman from 1932 to 1963 and a member of the founding family, wrote the Credo in 1943, just before J&J went public and long before anyone was discussing "corporate social responsibility." As the company notes, "Our Credo is more than just a moral compass. We believe it's a recipe for business success. The fact that J&J is one of only a handful of companies that have flourished through more than a century of change is proof of that."[19]

The Credo is about priorities, not tactics or products. It intentionally puts stockholders and profits last, behind the people who use J&J's products, the employees who make them, and the public good. R. W. Johnson was essentially advising his future successors on how to balance these obligations in every future decision. As a landmark document of American business, it's worth reading in full:

> We believe our first responsibility is to the patients, doctors and nurses, to mothers and fathers and all others who use our products and services. In meeting their needs everything we do must be of high quality. We must constantly strive to provide value, reduce our costs and maintain reasonable prices. Customers' orders must be serviced promptly and accurately. Our business partners must have an opportunity to make a fair profit.
>
> We are responsible to our employees who work with us throughout the world. We must provide an inclusive work environment where each person must be considered as an individual. We must respect their diversity and dignity and recognize their merit. They must have a sense of security, fulfillment and purpose in their jobs. Compensation must be fair and adequate and working conditions clean, orderly and safe. We must support the health and well-being of our employees and help them fulfill their family and other personal responsibilities. Employees must feel free to make suggestions and complaints. There must be equal opportunity for employment, development and advancement for those qualified. We must provide highly capable leaders and their actions must be just and ethical.
>
> We are responsible to the communities in which we live and work and to the world community as well. We must help people be healthier by supporting better access and care in more places

around the world. We must be good citizens—support good works and charities, better health and education, and bear our fair share of taxes. We must maintain in good order the property we are privileged to use, protecting the environment and natural resources.

Our final responsibility is to our stockholders. Business must make a sound profit. We must experiment with new ideas. Research must be carried on, innovative programs developed, investments made for the future and mistakes paid for. New equipment must be purchased, new facilities provided, and new products launched. Reserves must be created to provide for adverse times. When we operate according to these principles, the stockholders should realize a fair return.[20]

Unlike some companies that write and then ignore similar mission statements, J&J engraved the Credo on a large wall in the entrance of its headquarters. It's also prominently displayed at other locations around the world. Every new hire is taught about it, and every employee is asked to fill out an annual survey about how well the company has lived up to the Credo. Veteran J&J executives swear that it's not just lip service. As one of them told me in a conversation, "The longer you work for the company, the more you see how important it is and how it actually does factor into decision making. It leads to a culture where differences of opinion are valued, and patients truly are put first."

Gorsky knew that public mistrust of large corporations, especially in the pharmaceutical industry, is much greater now than in R. W. Johnson's day. He told my class that the Credo's principles remind everyone at J&J to treat big data, AI, genomics and other new technologies as tools, never as ends in themselves. Gorsky reminds his executives to stay focused on patient outcomes as their top priority. He knows that technology can't save the company if it ever forgets its original purpose.

Business Line Expansion as the Key to Long-Term Growth

Gorsky stressed that another key aspect of J&J's stamina is its massive portfolio of product lines and consumer brands. "When you're in a business for over 130 years, there are going to be cycles when some businesses are up and others are down. We've experienced it across all of our businesses. It's one of the reasons we've had 55 consecutive years of dividend increases and 34 consecutive years of a AAA credit rating."[21] While it's hard to grow an $82 billion conglomerate, Gorsky's growth strategy is to leverage its technology and global resources wherever the best opportunities can be found, whether in pharmaceuticals, medical devices, or consumer products.

He noted that as the CEO overseeing all that diversity, he might spend a single day in various meetings about advanced cancer treatments, about a new approach to robotic surgery, and about whether a forthcoming Neutrogena commercial should star Jennifer Aniston or Kerry Washington. Even far below the CEO level, product diversity helps employees: "You can work in Johnson & Johnson and be part of a start-up, in a small group, and then you can scale it and be running a multi-billion-dollar division."[22]

The late 2000s brought transformational breakthroughs in the understanding of the human genome, diagnostics, biologics, and the underlying cell biology of diseases. Pharma companies began prioritizing the development of specialty medicines, which had far fewer potential patients than primary care therapies but could often be commercialized at a lower cost and command a higher price. Such drugs also didn't require the vast marketing dollars spent on primary care treatments.

Johnson & Johnson was initially unprepared for this change in the market. By 2009, the company was about to see revenue drop by almost $9 billion due to patent expirations, which would reduce its pharmaceutical revenues by a third. Even more alarming, J&J's pipeline lacked major new drugs to replace these expirations, in part because its organizational structure wasn't built to ride the new wave of specialty medicines. It was too focused on potential mass market drugs that might eventually reach millions of patients, rather than allocating resources and talent to niche drugs that might reach only 100,000 patients but could still be highly profitable.

Under Gorsky, J&J shifted its expansion focus from primary care medications to areas such as cardiovascular, metabolism, immunology, infectious diseases, and oncology. The company added pulmonary hypertension with its acquisition of Actelion in 2017. By 2020 it had 12 pharmaceuticals worth more than a billion dollars each, plus a coronavirus vaccine nearly ready for clinical trials.[23]

Embracing and Nurturing Innovation to Build Stamina

Gorsky believed that if R. W. Johnson were still running the company today, he would hire data scientists to find the secrets hidden in huge data sets of genetic information, and AI specialists to work on detecting early warning signs of diseases that doctors might otherwise miss. He would never allow existing products to hinder the research and development of new ones.

One new process that excited Gorsky was CRISPR, which allows medical professionals to "edit" compromised DNA segments that cause genetic diseases. By modifying target cells to "self-destruct," CRISPR can be used to destroy antibiotic-resistant bacteria.[24] Another exciting new technology was a sophisticated cancer treatment called CAR-T therapy, which extracts a patient's immune system T-cells, responsible for determining the specificity of the body's immune response to foreign antigens.[25] The extracted T-cells are then genetically engineered to produce synthetic receptors that can recognize and attach to tumor cells, after being reinfused into the patient's body.

As J&J raced to develop these and other high-tech treatments, it faced a slew of new competition. Venture capitalists had started investing heavily in biotech start-ups, which were better positioned to gamble on unproven technologies, as their leaner structures allowed them to pivot more quickly than Big Pharma. Meanwhile, Amazon began reaching into multiple segments of the healthcare market, acquiring the online pharmacy PillPack in 2018, seeding the nonprofit healthcare entity Haven, investing in AI medical tools, and partnering with the Pittsburgh Health Data Alliance to innovate in cancer diagnosis, medical imaging, and precision medicine. Apple invested in both software and hardware technologies like the Apple Watch, which could store a patient's medical information and perform basic tests like pulse rate and an EKG. Google launched an effort to collect and analyze US health records, collecting tens of millions of patient records by 2020.[26]

While the tech giants don't currently compete with Big Pharma on drug development, their ownership of patient data could pose a future challenge to J&J. But at least for the short term, J&J's deep expertise provides strong protection against all these newcomers. It would be almost impossible for a biotech start-up or even a tech giant like Apple or Google to quickly master the vast complexities of getting new drugs developed, tested, approved, and distributed. J&J's deep relationships with the FDA and other regulators are a huge competitive advantage.

When he spoke to my class, Gorsky's enthusiasm about emerging innovations in genomic analytics was (forgive the pun) contagious. He spoke about J&J's efforts to combine different oncology diagnostics to make it possible to detect cancer earlier than ever. He gushed about the power of cloud computing to link scientists around the world, and the power of the web to deliver useful content directly to consumers.

As he put it, "I've been in this business for almost 30 years and I can't think of a more exciting time to be in this industry, because of the explosion that's taking place in science and technology. We're literally on the cusp of curing things like HIV and hepatitis C. You can have a hip procedure like I did a couple of years ago and be walking with a walker around the recovery floor within a couple of hours. It's pretty remarkable."[27]

Partnering to Avoid "Not Invented Here Syndrome"

Many well-established companies fall prey to an affliction known as "not invented here syndrome" when their history of innovation leads them to disparage outside sources of innovation. But J&J has shown the confidence to make partnerships a bigger part of its business model, recognizing that nothing in the Credo implies that innovation needs to be generated internally. The important thing is for the company to keep learning from any available source, including the biotech start-ups that J&J invests in.

As Gorsky noted, "I am incredibly lucky to work with about 134,000 associates who are very smart, committed, hardworking, values-based. They're the people who make us who we are, and we couldn't do it without them. But we also know that we can't do everything. So if you look across Johnson & Johnson, be it in the pharmaceutical group or the medical device group or the consumer group, about 50% of the time we discover and develop things internally. The other 50% of the time we go external, and that's been the case for the last twenty years. We're agnostic about the source of the best science and technology. Especially in today's world of science, if you're not constantly making connections, building relationships with academic centers, with the venture community, with other start-ups, you're never going to be at the cutting edge."[28]

In its partnerships with biotech start-ups, J&J brings all the benefits of its global manufacturing operations, its clinical development and regulatory expertise, and its distribution muscle to reach millions of potential consumers. These advantages can complement the strengths of new biotech companies, which can pivot more quickly than Big Pharma in pursuing scientific leads. Over the past two decades, J&J set up four different partnership programs to identify the most exciting external discoveries and fold them into its manufacturing machine:

- ▶ JLABS was a network of eight life science incubators that gave start-ups access to lab space, mentorship, and a research community for a monthly fee. While this program was no-strings-attached, J&J formed relationships with the start-ups that used the space, giving it an advantage over other Big Pharma companies seeking to capitalize on their discoveries.
- ▶ Innovation Centers were located in four research hotspots: Boston, South San Francisco, London, and Shanghai. These hubs reached out to local, very early-stage healthcare start-ups.
- ▶ JJDC was J&J's strategic venture arm, tasked with investing in promising start-ups at every stage from the earliest seed-level to second round ("Series B") financing and beyond.

▶ Janssen Business Development (named for the pharma company acquired in 1961) sought partnerships or acquisitions with established pharmaceutical companies or midsized to large biotech companies.

To maximize the impact of these partnerships, J&J committed to killing internal research projects whenever an external alternative was making faster progress. That helped reassure outside companies that J&J wasn't playing favorites with its in-house researchers.

Legal and PR Challenges: Using Stamina to Survive Crises

Despite its progress on all these fronts during Gorsky's tenure as CEO, J&J has faced a series of legal and public relations problems over the same period. It has been sued more than 100,000 times over its product safety and marketing practices, related to products such as talc-based baby powder, the antipsychotic drug Risperdal, and opioids.

The entire pharmaceutical industry has gone through similar problems, losing its formerly great reputation as the source of lifesaving medications. Perhaps the worst example of perceived broken values was demonstrated by "Pharma Bro" Martin Shkreli, who egregiously raised prices on a lifesaving drug and defrauded investors with his activities.[29] It is no exaggeration to say that in some circles Big Pharma is almost as maligned as Big Tobacco—allegedly reckless, greedy giants who care only about profits, not how their products may hurt people. When politicians as far apart as Bernie Sanders and Donald Trump attack the same industry for price gouging, that's a bad sign. By 2018, only 38 percent of Americans trusted pharmaceutical companies, according to the Edelman Trust Barometer.[30]

Even within an unpopular industry, J&J faced a unique set of terrible headlines. For instance, in 2019, it was ordered to pay $572 million to the state of Oklahoma for its alleged role in the opioid crisis; a month later, it had to recall 33,000 bottles of Johnson's Baby Powder over asbestos concerns that had led to thousands of lawsuits. The company also faced tens of thousands of lawsuits over its Pelvic Mesh products and lost an $8 billion jury verdict over allegedly inappropriate marketing of an antipsychotic drug, Risperdal. While J&J contested these allegations, the headlines fueled a precipitous drop in its reputation, from near the top among all pharma companies to 57th out of 58 in 2019.[31]

This reputational collapse was especially troubling because, with privacy laws progressively restricting corporate access to consumer data, J&J depended more than ever on earning consumer trust and consent. It was trying to deepen its direct relationships with customers, via tools like social media and niche websites. But could any of those tactics work if some people were starting to see J&J as basically evil?

Perhaps the most significant factor in the industry's reputation problem stemmed from the public outcry over soaring drug prices. As presidential candidate Bernie Sanders said in 2019, "The United States pays by far the highest prices in the world for prescription drugs. This has created a health care crisis in which one in five American adults cannot afford to get the medicine they need."[32] His proposal to create a single-payer healthcare system is slowly gaining support. Even many Americans who oppose single-payer healthcare tend to support a public insurance option that would have stronger negotiating leverage over Big Pharma.[33] Under the status quo, more than 900 health insurance companies negotiate separately with the drug makers, with little leverage because the top 10 insurers combined account for just over 50 percent of the insurance market.[34] Add in the fact that most Americans are tied to their employer-provided healthcare plans, and it's clear why the drug companies are under little competitive pressure to bring down prices for drugs under patent.

Big Pharma often blames pharmacy benefit managers (PBMs)—companies like Express Scripts, Caremark, and Optum that manage prescription drug benefits on behalf of health insurers—for hiding their culpability in rising drug costs. The PBMs often add a steep but invisible markup to the prices charged by the drug companies. To show the flaws in this system, J&J led a movement toward price transparency. In 2019, it became the first drug company to disclose its list prices in its TV commercials. It also published the groundbreaking Janssen U.S. Transparency Report, which publicly listed prices, rebates, discounts, and net prices for major drugs. Never before had this level of drug pricing detail been disclosed, earning praise from the media. But even with transparency, J&J knew that the debate over drug pricing would only get worse in the years ahead, as more people lived into their eighties and needed more medicines than ever.

Recent signs suggest some positive momentum for the company's reputation. In 2020, a new US government study concluded there was no strong evidence linking baby powder to ovarian cancer.[35] J&J's efforts to combat the verdict in the Risperdal lawsuit also resulted in a public win, with a reduction in its fine from $8 *billion* to $6.8 *million*.[36] And J&J's stock outperformed other large-cap pharmaceuticals in 2019, even as its litigation issues peaked.[37] The stock price has roughly doubled overall since Gorsky took over in 2012. While that's not the hypergrowth of a Silicon Valley unicorn, it's impressive for a behemoth with $82 billion in revenue.

J&J believes that in the long run, most consumers care more about great products than about any headlines regarding litigation, pricing, or government regulation. As the company continues to roll out innovations that improve people's lives, from the simplest over-the-counter products to the most complex cancer treatments, Gorsky believes that most people will again see J&J as a positive force in the world.

Ultimately, he has faith that the company's stamina will carry it through tough times. As he concluded in front of my class, "You've got to be constantly thinking about your strategy, your resources, and your model—as your customers evolve, as they make decisions in different ways, as new capabilities get introduced. If you're not constantly evolving, then there's no way you can be successful."[38]

Getting Stamina Right

It's almost a paradox that stamina and strength, which imply consistency, can only be achieved through relentless change and with a culture that enables ongoing variations. Like an athlete, a great company can't keep doing the exact same exercise routines over time; it has to keep adding mileage on the treadmill or weight on the resistance machines.

Organizational stamina must also be consistent throughout the company. In a firm like J&J, every business unit seeks to stay competitive in discrete areas, and each aspires to be best-in-class against its competition, regardless of sector. In some cases it might make sense to share back-end platforms or best practices, but rigidly enforcing uniformity across a company might damage its stamina.

Finally, a company's culture and values can serve as a North Star that guides employees toward actions that reinforce their dedication to a long-term mission. For National Geographic, that mission is disseminating knowledge. For Microsoft, it's developing software that helps people work and communicate. For Netflix, it's entertaining the world by being the best global media distribution service. And for Johnson & Johnson, it's serving the patients, doctors and nurses, and all others who use their products. This kind of public-spirited mission can inspire employees to keep doing the hard work that builds stamina, leading to an enduring legacy that survives the inevitable ups and downs of any company's life.

THE SYSTEMS LEADER'S NOTEBOOK

Stamina

- Make customer outcomes the primary driver of your company's behavior. By understanding the impact of your products and services on your *customer's* business or personal life, you can deploy resources correctly and effectively.

- Make sure that your company's mission is clear and easily understood throughout the organization, and that it works as a set of guiding principles through good and bad times. If not, change it.

- Drive change deliberately and thoughtfully. Even when dealing with potentially existential threats, show confidence in the company's overall path. Paradoxically, to be seen as an institution that will endure over time, you must constantly act as though change and evolution are the norm, not a reason to panic.

PART IV

THE POWER OF SYSTEMS LEADERSHIP

The Brains and Brawn framework provides a way to evaluate how your company is doing in blending key digital and physical activities. The 10 competencies covered in Parts II and III of this book offer a new way to compare your organization to its competitors, beyond the usual metrics.

Ultimately, however, your goal isn't just measuring these competencies—it's improving them by driving change in your organization. The best business leaders I have met are all Systems Leaders—skilled at blending the best of digital and physical, recognizing emerging patterns, and making key decisions in a rapidly changing landscape.

In our final chapter, we explore the key attributes of Systems Leaders and look closely at two CEOs who demonstrate the power of Systems Leadership.

CHAPTER 13

THE SYSTEMS LEADER: DRIVING CONSTANT PROGRESS ON BRAINS *AND* BRAWN

If you were filling your own job today, would you rehire yourself? Are you the best person for the role now, rather than when you first got the job? If you're no longer the best person, what are you going to do about it?

—Katrina Lake, Executive Chairperson of Stitch Fix

teach the Brains and Brawn framework to audiences all over the world, from huge multinational companies to start-ups on almost every continent. Whenever I finish a presentation about these ideas, the question I hear most often is, "I get it, but where do I start?" People say that the opportunities are exciting, but the challenges of acting on them sometimes seem overwhelming. I respond by urging the audience to start by asking themselves four key questions:

1. What does the trend of combining digital and physical mean for *your customers* and their businesses?
2. How can your company's core technologies and relationships provide an advantage against the competition?
3. What products and services do your customers need that you are not currently delivering?
4. How can you stand out as a leader by widening your perspective, seeing the context, and embracing risk during times of rapid change?

These questions get to the heart of Systems Leadership, a phrase you've seen throughout this book, including in the "notebook" sections of the 10 previous chapters (Parts II and III). It's my term for the art and science of maximizing both the Brains and Brawn of an organization. In this final chapter, let's get more specific about exactly what Systems Leadership means, how you can get better at it, and how it relates to the Brains and Brawn competencies. Then let's look at two outstanding Systems Leaders who demonstrate the need for driving constant progress at two very different companies: Katrina Lake of Stitch Fix and Julie Sweet of Accenture.

The Urgency of Systems Leadership

I define Systems Leadership as the ability to master processes and strategies from different perspectives at the same time: physical and digital, breadth of market and depth of market, short term and long term, what's good for the company and what's good for its ecosystem. Systems Leaders combine the IQ to understand their company's technology and business model with the EQ to build effective teams and inspire them to new heights. They use short-term execution skills to hit their financial targets this year, while also driving changes that may not pay off for five years. They grasp the big picture and essential details simultaneously. They understand how all the elements of an organization affect both internal and external stakeholders, and how interactions internally and externally shape a company's outcomes.

When I described Systems Leadership to one Fortune 500 CEO, his response was, "Wow, that sounds hard." He was right, of course. But Systems Leadership is hard in the same sense that running a marathon, playing guitar, doing calculus, or driving on a highway are hard. For all of those competencies, the baseline of required innate talents isn't exceptionally rare. The key is putting in the consistent effort over time to learn and then master the right skills. It's about practice much more than talent.

If you've read this far into the book, I have no doubt that you have the intellectual and emotional right stuff to become a Systems Leader. But you have to choose to commit to that goal, because it will make a massive difference to your career. It can determine whether you'll rise as far as your talents can take you or get stuck along the way. And whether you work for a large incumbent or a small upstart, your mastery of Systems Leadership and the 10 Brains and Brawn competencies can determine your organization's success or failure. The stakes are that high.

Systems Leadership Versus Traditional Leadership

Traditionally, executives rose to senior management through expertise in one particular function, usually operations, engineering, sales, marketing, or finance. When put in charge of a business unit or a whole company, their backgrounds naturally biased them toward seeing the landscape through one primary perspective. To cover everything else, they tended to rely heavily on colleagues who were experts in other functions, including groups like R&D, human resources, legal, and government relations. Leaders could set broad goals, delegate the details, and assume that things would work out, as long as they had a competent team. There was no need to be immersed in every department's details.

But the complexity of modern business makes that dynamic outdated. Every internal function is more interdependent than ever; for instance, a small shift in the sales department's strategy can wreak havoc on manufacturing and finance, and vice versa. Moreover, every player in a company's external ecosystem of partners, competitors, and customers can shake up carefully laid plans at any moment. As a result, today's leaders need a much broader range of expertise and skills, compared to their predecessors. They need to be good at fitting *all* these pieces together to deliver optimal value to customers and shareholders.

This is not to imply that you need to be omniscient or memorize every detail of every aspect of your business. No one can possibly do that. But you need to learn enough to have meaningful conversations with experts of all stripes. You need to know enough to ask the right questions, not necessarily to answer them. Then you need to consider what you're learning from those experts and how their perspectives fit into the bigger picture of your company's strategic priorities and those of your ecosystem partners. Finally, you'll need the self-confidence and courage to make decisions under extreme uncertainty, because trying to play it safe and stick to the status quo can lead to disaster.

To develop that breadth of knowledge, you'll have to commit to lifelong learning and a constant openness to new experiences. That might mean anything from reading articles about artificial intelligence to buying coffee for colleagues you've never spoken to before to setting up a TikTok account so you can understand Generation Z. Above all, it means breaking out of your information bubbles—resisting the urge to stick with people from the same background as you, who see the world the same way you do.

A Synthesis of Two Kinds of Thinking

Table 13.1 offers a quick-and-dirty way to compare the stereotypes of a Silicon Valley/digital leader (left), a traditional/industrial leader (center), and a Systems Leader. Let's consider each of them in terms of six challenges.

	DIGITAL THINKER	PHYSICAL THINKER	SYSTEMS LEADER
Orientation	Horizontal (platform)	Vertical (domain)	Scalable on both axes
Technology	Software (platform)	Hardware (asset)	Innovative platform with an operating front end
Outcomes	Winner-takes-all	Continuous improvement	Dominant share
Workers	Flexible / gig	Enhance / loyal	Portfolio career
Customers	Single platform	"Units of one"	Customizable COTS
Government	Libertarian	Engaged	Balanced

TABLE 13.1   Duality of the Systems Leader

Digital thinkers are obsessed with building a horizontal platform that can scale to infinity. For instance, Facebook won't be satisfied until every human on the planet is using a Facebook product; the first 2.5 billion don't even represent the halfway point. The next row follows logically; digital thinkers prefer software over hardware because it's so much easier to scale than any physical product. Their ideal outcome is winner take all, because digital markets tend to settle on one dominant player (Google in search, Uber in ride-sharing, etc.). Their ideal workers are flexible—either gig-based or the kind of people who change jobs every year or two, if they start to get restless. Their ideal customers are happy with a single basic offering, which also makes scaling easier. And their ideal government is libertarian, imposing minimal regulations or interference in private markets.

Physical thinkers have very different priorities and values, from top to bottom. They generally have domain expertise in a particular area, so they focus on vertical success—building great products for a narrow but deep market, such as Mercedes owners. Vertical success is often hardware-based, and outcomes are often framed around continuous improvement. For instance, if Burger King's revenue growth outpaces the growth of McDonald's and Wendy's by 2 percent, that's a huge year. Historically, if General Motors made a Chevy 2 percent more fuel efficient or 5 percent faster, that was a victory. Physical thinkers try to inspire employees to stay with an organization for many years, to reap the benefits of institutional memory. They think about customers as "units of one" who prefer customized solutions; the company's goal is to provide distinctive solutions that lock customers in. And they see nothing wrong with government rules and regulations if they can turn their mastery of government relations into a competitive advantage.

Systems Leaders combine both sets of skills and mindsets. They understand and appreciate both hardware and software, both vertical expertise and horizontal scale. They aren't hell-bent on achieving Amazon-like winner-take-all dominance, but they want bigger outcomes than fighting for each fraction of a point of market share. They try to build employee loyalty through various benefits (financial and emotional) but understand that almost no one has decades-long careers at a single company anymore. Their ideal customers seek a "customizable off the shelf" (COTS) solution that can easily be tweaked to individual needs. (Think of the Netflix algorithms that make a sci-fi fan's browsing experience so different from a rom-com fan's.) And Systems Leaders see the ideal government as balanced—regulating products and protecting workers where appropriate, but never overregulating in ways that inhibit innovation or hurt customers.

The Orchestra Conductor Without a Score

It helps to imagine a Systems Leader as an orchestra conductor, surrounded not only by all the functions within the company but also by external forces such as demanding customers, aggressive competitors, and unreliable ecosystem partners. Most conductors come from a background of expertise on a single instrument, but when they move to the podium, they have to widen their perspective. Good conductors retune their ears to take in all the instruments at once and get them all working in harmony. The metaphor breaks down, however, because a conductor has a score that spells out exactly how every instrument should be contributing to the piece. But a Systems Leader operates in a state of constant uncertainty about what will happen next, and while not having a score, knows the basic tune and needs to inspire the team to play the music harmoniously together.

Systems Leaders rely on their ability to recognize patterns and apply past experiences to new situations. They combine the clarity to focus on improving the lives and fortunes of their customers with the courage to lead their people into the unknown. The next five sections will show how these daring conductors get the best performance out of every section of the orchestra, without allowing the overall sound to collapse in cacophony.

Operating at Intersections

Operating at intersections means pursuing two or more goals at the same time, because you know that succeeding at each of them will delivery powerful synergies that you couldn't get from them separately. This skill underpins many of the Brains and Brawn competencies that we've explored.

There can be multiple types of intersections:

- ▶ **An innovative technology meets an innovative business model.** This powerful combination drives some of the most successful companies of our time, including many of the examples in the previous chapters. For instance, think of how Align blended cutting-edge technology (digital scanners and 3D printers) with an innovative business model (making dentists a channel partner to offer orthodonture to adults) to deliver an appealing customer benefit (straight teeth through a convenient, affordable, nearly invisible process). Align might have succeeded with its new technology alone or with its new business model alone, but the synergy was orders of magnitude more valuable.
- ▶ **Short-term results meet long-term change.** In the old days, companies would elevate leaders who were great at running a business unit according to its plan and hitting its quarterly and annual targets. The company might also celebrate visionary thinkers who could plot new strategies for 5 or 10 years out. But operators and innovators were treated as separate groups with very different skill sets. Today, in contrast, Systems Leaders know how to operate at scale *and* know how to manage innovation. In fact, they find their greatest satisfaction at that intersection. Think of Pedro Earp at AB InBev, trying to maximize today's microbrew brands while experimenting with bold new ways to deliver beer to future customers.

> ▶ **Global strength meets local expertise.** To make the most of both assets in a challenging market, think of how Michelin developed its "glocal" strategy in China to compete against low-cost Chinese tire producers. It found a sweet spot of quality and price that neither its fellow global giants nor its local Chinese rivals could match.

Sometimes operating at intersections means spotting connections between disparate businesses that aren't obvious between seemingly disparate businesses. Think of how Samsung realized that its manufacturing process for semiconductors, which requires clean rooms, lots of capital equipment, and strong operational discipline, is similar to the process for manufacturing pharmaceuticals. The company's leaders concluded that their competencies in one industry could be applied to a radically different one. Today, improbably, Samsung is the world's largest manufacturer of generic biologic drugs.

Systems Leaders constantly scan the horizon for potential intersections between "what we're already good at" and "what else we might be able to do with these skills."

Predicting the Future and Preparing for It

You don't need to be a professional futurist to know which technologies are going to continue to impact business and society for at least the next decade, among them robotics, data analytics, artificial intelligence, machine learning, cloud computing, blockchain, and additive manufacturing. The challenge is figuring out how those and other innovations will affect various aspects of your organization, including core functions like administration, R&D, sales, and manufacturing. Like it or not, certain jobs in all of those areas will become obsolete, while new jobs will be created in areas as yet undreamed of.

These unavoidable trends force Systems Leaders to make tough decisions, the sooner the better. Their inner ears help them figure out what a company should produce itself and what should it buy from suppliers. Their muscles help them build scale intelligently, staffing up or retraining employees to replace the ones whose old jobs are going away. Their prefrontal cortexes help them weigh the risk of making too many changes too quickly against the risk of being left behind in the industry in 5 or 10 years.

As you make these tough decisions about the future, be mindful of the biases you've developed over your career. There's nothing shameful about being biased, as long as you're self-aware enough to recognize when you might be wrong. For instance, I was trained as a business unit operator at companies like Intel and GE, and as an executive and CEO at Silicon Valley start-ups, so I look at opportunities from an operating perspective. People who trained as engineers, accountants, sales reps, or lawyers will see the world differently.

Another pitfall to avoid when predicting the future is groupthink. One of my favorite aphorisms comes from Carl Ice, the recently retired CEO of BNSF Railway: "You're never wrong in your own conference room." Systems Leaders seek outside opinions from trusted sources beyond their direct reports. They get out of the office regularly to visit remote facilities or meet with informal advisors, or ideally both. Ice told my class that every year he rode at least 12,000 miles on his railroad, so he could see firsthand the condition of its operations.[1] Anyone insightful enough to understand the industry and honest enough to challenge the leader's conclusions can become a valuable sounding board or devil's advocate.

Managing Context

Context is defined as "the circumstances that form the setting for an event, statement, or idea, in terms of which it can be fully understood and assessed."[2] Facts in isolation are not truth; they can lead you badly astray if you misunderstand their context. To emphasize this point, I often show my classes a slide with a simple equation that I learned from my co-teacher at Stanford and former GE CEO, Jeff Immelt:

Truth = Facts + Context

Here's an example of what happens when context changes. During the 1980s, most American business leaders saw globalization as a virtually unambiguous good, a way to sell more stuff around the world while reducing supply costs and (via offshoring) labor costs. But over the last decade, while the fundamentals of global free trade have remained basically the same, the context is now different. China has become a rising global superpower, not just a place to make sneakers or cell phones cheaply. Offshoring has devastated large parts of the industrial Midwest in the United States, leading to the opioid crisis and extreme populist politics, among other consequences. Even Germany, whose largest trading partner is China, is now seeing unexpected competition from Chinese companies.[3] Rather than rushing into new avenues for globalization that seem beneficial on the surface, Systems Leaders take time to consider the wider context.

Another example of managing context came up when I was teaching a case study about social media. I asked the room why Facebook has become widely hated in recent years, while its fellow tech giant Google—which also tracks and monetizes the actions of its users—has avoided that kind of visceral negative reaction. My students were stumped, until a guest speaker noted that Google's declared mission is organizing the world's information to help you find whatever you want. If a Google search helps you find something, Google doesn't care whether the information lives on its own site or somewhere else. Their goal is to be helpful enough that you'll want to return, *not* to lure you into a walled garden of content for hours every day. In other words, the facts of Facebook's business model sound great for Facebook: users get addicted to consuming and sharing content, which makes the platform more effective for highly targeted advertising. It's only when you consider the context of user resentment and feelings of exploitation that the long-term dangers of that model become clear.

Systems Leaders think about the context of every message they share with staff, via any medium. They never forget that risk and uncertainty can scare the hell out of their people. Asking them to change the way they've been operating for years is much more effective when done with a tone of quiet determination, not panic. A context of reassurance and calm can go a long way, even if you feel the opposite of calm inside. Trying to explain something by saying, "We have to make this change for these reasons, we know how to do it, let's get started," is a powerful way to drive change.

The Product Manager Mindset

Systems Leaders who start from a background in finance, sales, marketing, or other nontechnical functions often need to put in extra effort to become well-versed in their company's technology. It's worth the time to do extra reading and other research to be able to have well-informed, peer-to-peer discussions with the people who actually sling code and design machines. Former Nokia Chairman Risto Siilasmaa wrote about why he took courses on AI and machine learning: "As a long-term CEO, I'd gotten used to having things explained to me. Somebody else does the hard work and I can focus on figuring out the right questions. Sometimes CEOs and Chairmen may feel that understanding the nuts and bolts of technology is in some way beneath their role, that it's enough for them to focus on 'creating shareholder value.' Alternatively, they may feel that they can't learn something seemingly complicated and therefore don't consider trying. Neither one is the entrepreneurial way."[4]

The combination of learning, listening, and showing empathy to experts adds up to what I call the product manager mindset. In many companies, the product manager is at the hub of a wheel-shaped org chart, constantly interacting with engineering, customers, manufacturing, sales, finance, research, and other departments. It sounds like a fun, interdisciplinary job, but (at least in Silicon Valley) it's actually very tough. You're responsible for everything related to your product, but you have no direct control over the people who can make or break its success. The key skills are interpersonal: learning how to get along with different personality types in all those functions. Systems Leaders listen closely to what those experts need and whatever problems they may spot before the rest of the organization. The goal is to become a polymorph who can fit into any internal subculture, winning the respect of the natives.[5] A great product manager will have everyone supporting her, saying things like, "She understands what we need and fights to get it for us."

Systems Leaders usually have more operational authority than product managers, so they can't complain about being accountable for everything while owning nothing. Nevertheless, it pays huge dividends to think like a product manager. Dive deeply into the technologies that underpin your products and your company's ecosystem. Listen closely to experts and use your amygdala to show empathy for their concerns. When you have to make a decision that upsets certain factions, your strong relationships—"she's one of us"—will soften the blow.

Going "Risk on" During Uncertainty and Disruption

Financial theory says that in times of exceptional volatility, you should become extra cautious and adopt a "risk off" mindset. But Systems Leaders generally have the opposite impulse. The more disruptive their situation, the more they go "risk on" and confront the source of the challenge, rather than passively waiting to see how things play out in their company or industry. They learn how to manage their own anxiety and that of their teams. The Systems Leaders we've met in this book, from both disruptors like Stripe and incumbents like John Deere, have applied their prefrontal cortexes and summoned their courage for untested, risky strategies.

One tactic for leading through uncertainty is to watch how you spend your time, because your people are definitely watching. Your actions send a clear signal to the organization about what you consider important, regardless of what you might say in a speech or email blast. Intel's iconic CEO Andy Grove proved this in his classic book *Only the Paranoid Survive*, when he reprinted a week from the desk calendar of the CEO of a large multinational during a significant corporate inflection point. This leader allowed his time to be filled with lots of nonessential meetings and factory tours, while ignoring the crisis at hand.[6]

Another tactic to be mindful of is the difference between skill and luck. If you look at your career history, were all of your past successes really dependent on your talents and hard work? Or were you just in the right place at the right time for some key opportunities? Acknowledging the role of luck won't diminish your accomplishments, but it will inoculate you against hubris. As Warren Buffett famously said, "You never know who's swimming naked until the tide goes out." That applies to lucky business leaders as well as lucky wealth managers.

Now let's conclude by looking at two Systems Leaders who exemplify all of these mindsets and attributes.

Katrina Lake: Shaking Up the Fashion Retail Business

Katrina Lake, the founder and Executive Chairperson of online retailer Stitch Fix, is an expert on disruptive change. She first took on a crowded market in 2011 by launching a new kind of personal shopping advice service. Instead of going to a fancy boutique for help in picking out clothes, Stitch Fix customers could simply fill out a survey about their tastes and then let a human stylist, supported by an AI algorithm, make suggestions. The stylist would send a five-item "fix" and the customer could decide how many to keep and how many to send back in a prepaid, preaddressed return envelope. As of early 2021, the company has sold $6 billion worth of clothing in its first decade, entirely sight unseen, and its average customer spends $500 in the first year.[7]

As the *New York Times* noted in May 2017, "The retail landscape is littered with the casualties of changing consumer behavior. Shoppers are bargain hunting online, department stores are struggling, and once-mainstay brands are closing out permanently. Then there is Stitch Fix, a mail-order clothing service that offers customers little choice in what garments they receive, and shies away from discounts for brand name dresses, pants, and accessories. Despite a business model that seems to defy conventional wisdom, Stitch Fix continues to grow."[8]

Although Lake was initially rejected by about 50 skeptical venture capitalists, the company had a successful IPO in November 2017, making her the youngest woman ever to take a start-up public. She has become an icon in Silicon Valley for building an innovative disruptor in the face of fierce competition. She displays the appealing blend of self-confidence and self-awareness that most Systems Leaders share, which immediately became apparent when she visited my class in April 2019 and again in January 2021.

Lake can speak with sophistication and depth about all the major aspects of her business, including fashion, big data, AI, branding, marketing, and workplace culture. She obsesses about the big picture of Stitch Fix's ecosystem as well as the smallest details of its products and services. As Lake and her team have expanded the company to serve new markets and demographics (such as men and children), she is determined to maintain its biggest competitive advantage: a unique blend of analytics, fashion, and customer service, driving a unique shopping experience.

Lake pointed out that the Stitch Fix system enables customers to give extremely detailed feedback on the clothes that they both *do* and *do not* choose to purchase, with specific questions about fit (allowing customers to provide input on items such as the placement of the first button in a shirt or blouse, where the back pockets sit on a body for a pair of jeans, etc.), in a manner that no physical retailer could match. Not even Amazon would have this level detail if it chose to offer a similar clothing service. Stitch Fix uses all this data not only to make better suggestions to customers, but also to feed information back to 1,000+ clothing brands so they can improve their products.

Stitch Fix blends a horizontally scalable business with enough customization to hold onto customers over time. The uniquely personalized recommendations made by the company's 3,000+ stylists get more and more accurate as people continue to use the service and provide more feedback. This combination of scale and intimacy make it nearly impossible for any clothing retailer to copy the Stitch Fix model without a massive restructuring of their businesses.

Rather than rest on that competitive advantage, Lake always seeks improvement on all fronts. She believes that personal growth correlates directly to company growth; if a company has grown by 40 percent, its people need to ask themselves if they've also grown by 40 percent. Other questions she asks herself and her leadership team every couple of years: "If you were filling your own job today, would you rehire yourself? Are you the best person for the role now, rather than when you first got the job? If you're no longer the best person, what are you going to do about it?" These conversations are often uncomfortable, especially if someone has been great at whatever got them to their current position, but now needs new skills for a changing business. But they're a powerful way to drive professional development.

When Lake stressed the importance of hiring a diverse team, she framed it in an unusual way. Instead of merely seeking demographic diversity, she also evaluates potential new hires on whether they will become a "cultural fit" or (preferably) a "cultural add." She believes that any organization that brings in only new people who reflect the existing culture and values—even if they reflect diversity of gender, ethnicity, age, and so on—will risk group-think and blind spots.

Stitch Fix is a hybrid of Brains and Brawn, blending innovative algorithms, skillful use of big data, the empathy of its human stylists, and the strong spine of its logistics as it sends millions of pieces of clothing back and forth. The company's rapid growth stems in large part from Lake's willingness to go "risk on" rather than avoiding hard decisions, and the company has thrived with their model during the pandemic as other retail brands have struggled. She knows that moving toward disruption is the best way to avoid becoming a passive receiver of new technologies and trends. It will also give Stitch Fix stamina to help ward off future disruptions that can't even be imagined yet.

As I approached the end of writing this book, Lake came back to my class at Stanford for a second visit. This conversation with students was a challenge, with some in the class being big fans of the company, while others were skeptical of Stitch Fix's long-term differentiated potential. Lake remained resolute and passionate about the many opportunities available for the company's future, but shortly after the session took place, she changed her role from CEO to Executive Chairperson. The continuing evolution of the fashion retail segment continues to confront even successful disruptors such as Lake and her team. Systems Leaders can never declare a permanent victory, because competitors, markets and customers never stop changing, sometimes in unexpected directions. Nothing can detract from Lake's success in building a groundbreaking company, but every new day presents new potential threats, whether from Amazon or a previously unknown start-up.

Julie Sweet: Reinventing a Brawny Consulting Giant

Accenture has come a long way since the early 1950s, with origins that trace back to the accounting firm Arthur Andersen. In 1989, Arthur Andersen and Andersen Consulting were established as separate business units and legal entities with a shared owner, with a profit-sharing arrangement that led to tensions between them. The two formally broke ties in 2000 after an arbitration settlement, and Andersen Consulting took on its new name in 2001—just in time to avoid being tarnished by the Enron accounting scandal, which destroyed Arthur Andersen.[9]

Two decades later, Accenture is a giant player in technology-driven consulting, with $44.3 billion in annual revenue generated by its 514,000 employees, who are located in 51 countries and serve clients in 120 countries.[10] If any company needs help figuring out its IT strategy, cloud services, global systems integration, information security, or even supporting vertical areas such as digital advertising or building more stable supply chains and reinventing manufacturing and operations, there's a good chance it will reach out to Accenture. But the road to that strong position has been tough.

Julie Sweet spoke to my class in February 2019, a few months before she was promoted from North American CEO to worldwide CEO. She had joined Accenture as general counsel in 2010; her legal background gave her a rare and valuable perspective in a company filled with engineers and MBAs. During her first decade at the firm, Sweet played an integral role as a member of the global management team, running Accenture's largest market starting in 2015 and contributing to a dramatic expansion and transformation of its services—from primarily a back-end integrator of existing technologies to a pioneer of cutting-edge artificial intelligence, security, cloud storage, quantum computing, and even advertising technology. In Silicon Valley jargon, Accenture has "moved up the technical stack" to offer its clients more sophisticated and valuable services.

Sweet now leads Accenture's ongoing evolution by combining the essential skills of a Systems Leader: predicting and preparing for the future, adopting a product manager mindset, managing the context of her changing ecosystem, and staying calm in the face of tough competition. She has leveraged Accenture's brawny size and scale (muscles) to expand into many new kinds of services, operating glocally in those 120 countries. She blends a strong focus on Accenture's core mission of serving clients with an openness to changing anything else—including its org chart, success metrics, and compensation practices. She continually expands her knowledge of new domains, such as advertising, to be able to serve new kinds of clients. And she's been willing to part ways with senior leaders who weren't willing to adapt and grow during Accenture's reinvention.

As Sweet told my class in 2019, "Everything about the services we provide to our clients has changed. Eight years ago, we were less than 10 percent doing digital, cloud, and security. Today it's over 60 percent. And in order to drive that, we've fundamentally transformed all of Accenture. The most fundamental change is the mindset. Eight years ago, we were very proud of being fast followers and light on investment. Today, we're an innovation-led company and we deeply invest in skills and capabilities."[11]

Accenture has found creative ways to redevelop talent within its existing workforce. For instance, instead of hiring tens of thousands of new employees to deliver more advanced services, Accenture started challenging employees to automate their own jobs. They went through training programs to master new skills, then graduated by showing how to automate their old jobs before being promoted into new roles. By gamifying this process, Sweet told us, Accenture has since retrained more than 300,000 workers in digital, cloud, and security, and continues to push continuous learning while retaining institutional knowledge.

Another great example of driving change is how Accenture became an unlikely leader in digital advertising. As the *Wall Street Journal* reported in 2018, consumer products giants such as Unilever have shifted their advertising focus from *Mad Men*–style creative campaigns toward data-driven analytics and sophisticated online targeting. Accenture set up an interactive practice to offer those services with a focus on designing and running great experiences, and to compete with major ad agencies. As the head of its interactive marketing group told the *Journal*, Accenture might not be the place to go for a clever car commercial, but it has the expertise to help an automaker reinvent its entire car-buying experience.[12]

Sweet explained, "You have to put together a deep understanding of technology with the use of artificial intelligence and analytics to understand the customer. It's not simply one skill set. And that's what makes Accenture so unique."[13] She also stressed the diversity of talent required to branch out into new markets. "Accenture Interactive is now the largest digital ad agency in the world. Those individuals tend to work in studios. They work very differently. We're quite proud of the fact that we have a 'culture of cultures' that come together to serve our clients."[14]

Sweet also has a strong inner ear for balancing ownership and partnership. The firm depends on maintaining healthy relationships with everyone from software giants like SAP, Oracle, and Microsoft to smaller players like Appian, a low-code platform that automates operations—which in the life sciences industry enables companies to focus on biopharma innovation. Accenture comments on its website about partnering "with a vast set of leading ecosystem partners to help push the boundaries of what technology can enable for your business."[15] Links to hundreds of companies follow. Organizing this huge ecosystem requires strong hand-eye coordination and a keen appreciation for context. Accenture constantly has to decide which areas it should compete in and which it should leave to its partners. Sweet believes that the best way to serve Accenture's clients is to bring them the best possible technology, even if it comes via a third-party.

In October 2020, *Fortune* ranked Sweet number one on its annual list of the most powerful women in business, noting that Accenture's profit had risen 7 percent in her first year as CEO and that "Sweet steered Accenture's more than half a million employees in 51 countries through the pandemic, a crisis that has made the firm's skills more essential than ever. . . . As COVID-19 hit, the company tapped into that expertise to help connect the UK's 1.2 million National Health Service workers remotely and to partner with Salesforce on contact tracing and vaccine management technology."[16]

If Accenture could thrive even during a global pandemic, its future as a hybrid Brains and Brawn company seems bright indeed.

The New World of Digital *and* Physical

I'm completing this book at the beginning of 2021, after a year that has turned all the popular clichés about disruption, uncertainty, and rapid change into laughable understatements. Last January, I wondered whether the headlines about a new virus in China would amount to anything significant. By December, I felt like a veteran of distance learning, routinely delivering virtual lectures and conducting workshops from my home office to executives and students as far away as Jakarta, Kuala Lumpur, Rio de Janeiro, London, Riyadh, Stockholm, and Chicago. I've continued to upgrade my home office with a high-resolution 4K camera, studio lighting, and an improved sound system.

While I can't predict exactly what the "new normal" will fully encompass once the pandemic is behind us, I do know that there will be no going back to a world of solely in-person presentations and flying around for speeches and meetings. Today, I am able to communicate and deliver compelling, interactive education experiences using technology to cross thousands of miles. These new solutions are too effective and efficient to disappear completely. Going forward, I expect to be doing a blend of both in-person and online meetings and events, choosing the appropriate format as needed.

My future, like yours, will surely be a hybrid of the best aspects of digital and physical, virtual and in-person, innovation and tradition, Brains and Brawn. I wish you the very best as you adapt to that future, and as you continue your journey as a Systems Leader.

THE SYSTEMS LEADER'S NOTEBOOK

The Brain Competencies:

The Left Hemisphere: Using Analytics

▶ Build up your data by measuring every possible interaction. You won't necessarily know which variables are significant to your business until you analyze many of them.

▶ Use size to your advantage. Disruptors might seek to scale quickly by building data moats; incumbents can use their large data sets to aggressively defend their turf.

▶ Be patient, knowing that the transformation of existing industries rarely happens overnight. Don't assume that big data will reveal immediate insights. You might need months or years before data collection and analysis really pays off.

The Right Hemisphere: Harnessing Creativity

- ▶ Study the forces shaping technological invention and innovation, and try to find new ideas at the intersections of existing ideas. Look for previously unnoticed connections to other industries or markets.
- ▶ Focus your creativity on improving customer outcomes, especially for how your product or service can improve the income statement, balance sheet, or quality of life of your customers.
- ▶ In times of volatility, resist the temptation to play it safe. Instead, rush *toward* the disruption; embrace it to discover how it might work for you. The opposite of creativity is standardization. In times of great uncertainty, urge your people to be even more creative than usual.

The Amygdala: Tapping the Power of Empathy

- ▶ Even when you focus on customer outcomes, be aware that while their goals may remain consistent, how they choose to achieve those goals might change.
- ▶ Inspire change not necessarily by being extremely dynamic or flashy, but by providing clear and concise messaging both inside and outside of the organization. Articulate your company's mission in a way that motivates employees and partners. Show empathy even to departments or groups that usually don't get much respect.
- ▶ Treat governments as a key part of your ecosystem, worthy of a great deal of attention and empathy, even if you have to deal with political parties or bureaucracies with whom you personally disagree.

The Prefrontal Cortex: Managing Risk

- ▶ Nudge your people toward welcoming risks and uncertainty as a window of opportunity. Show them how they can personally contribute to an exciting new mission or goal, and why the risks the company is taking are better than accepting the status quo.
- ▶ Be mindful of your own biases, which naturally emerge from your personal journey and surroundings. People are shaped by whatever behaviors have been rewarded in the past, reinforcing our urge to repeat old habits instead of embracing change.
- ▶ Become conversant in whatever new tools and technologies are reshaping your industry, including your customers and their organizations. Expecting your subordinates to explain these changes will only lead to a superficial understanding of their implications. Get firsthand experience whenever possible.

The Inner Ear: Balancing Ownership and Partnership

▶ Analyze your industry's changing landscape to decide on partners who are not just appropriate for the present but can help you expand in the future. Consider the possibility that your industry doesn't have to be "zero sum" and multiple parties can win. Always create space where others can win in their efforts, too.

▶ Focus on the best interests of your real customers, the ones actually paying for goods and services. This is especially important when you might be tempted to share information entrusted to you with partners who don't have a right to it. Never betray the trust of your customers to benefit your partners.

▶ Whenever possible, think of your suppliers as partners to be helped on a win-win basis, not as costs to be minimized.

The Brawn Competencies:

The Spine: Logistics

▶ Don't fight the inevitable: customers increasingly want to shop online, and e-commerce activity is accelerating. If you have physical locations, focus on combining digital capabilities with logistical excellence to deliver great customer experiences.

▶ Use software to add service opportunities in combination with physical products.

▶ Not every product can be easily shipped and delivered via e-commerce. Look for ways in which the nature of your products and solutions can serve as a barrier to entry to other companies (especially Amazon, which can't sell and deliver *everything*).

Hands: The Craft of Making Things

▶ Lean into platform transitions with the goal of moving the frontier of your industry's perceived value/delivered cost curve. If possible, don't wait for your competitors to drive change first and force you to play catch-up.

▶ Know the impact of your products on the income statement and balance sheet of each major customer or market segment. Think about how you can customize your products accordingly, based on your deep understanding of those customers or markets.

▶ Be flexible in your business model, if you serve multiple market segments. Just as Desktop Metal realized that it needed to develop both office-sized *and* industrial-sized machines, think about different solutions you can offer at different price points.

Muscles: Leveraging Size and Scale

▶ Redefine your core competency around technologies and products that enable widespread reach, whether via data, product distribution, or manufacturing.

▶ Put your employees as close as possible to your customers. Even in a world that increasingly depends on digital communication and collaboration, understanding local markets requires humans to live and work among the people who use what you sell.

▶ Overcommunicate when your teams are operating at scale. Making a new strategy or vision stick requires extremely clear messaging, repeated frequently, customized for different factions of a large organization. You can't change an entrenched culture with just a few emails.

Hand-Eye Coordination: Organizing an Ecosystem

▶ Develop an industry influence map and dependence/influence tables to help your team understand how various constituents interact with each other in your industry, and who really has power over others.

▶ Be very clear about distinguishing when your company is essentially dabbling in a space (like Google's Pixel) and when something is critical to your success (like Walmart's low prices). This distinction will affect how much pressure you may need to put on your ecosystem partners.

▶ Be mindful of any governmental regulations that may restrict your strategic and tactical options, especially as you grow big enough to attract the scrutiny of regulators. Like it or not, government agendas may shape your competitive landscape—stay in front of government regulation.

Stamina: Surviving for the Long Run

▶ Make customer outcomes the primary driver of your company's behavior. By understanding the impact of your products and services on your *customer's* business or personal life, you can deploy resources correctly and effectively.

▶ Make sure that your company's mission is clear and easily understood throughout the organization, and that it works as a set of guiding principles through good and bad times. If not, change it.

▶ Drive change deliberately and thoughtfully. Even when dealing with potentially existential threats, show confidence in the company's overall path. Paradoxically, to be seen as an institution that will endure over time, you must constantly act as though change and evolution are the norm, not a reason to panic.

ACKNOWLEDGMENTS

This book is the culmination of years of work, persistent exploration, collaboration with hundreds of people, and perhaps most of all, the good fortune to be surrounded by great individuals.

I am indebted to my teammates at the Stanford Graduate School of Business for their intelligence and rigor around all things business. The university has been unbelievably supportive in providing resources and a foundation to work with others who seem to have infinite competencies and talent. In particular, Professor Robert Burgelman has been a mentor for almost three decades, and I am grateful for all he has taught me. My co-teachers and partners for much of the material in this book include Max Wessel and Aaron Levie, who inspired the initial ideas and directions in our course The Industrialist's Dilemma. I have been blessed to teach my Systems Leadership class with Jeff Immelt, who not only shared so much of what he learned in his career, but who also provided invaluable support—mental, intellectual, emotional, and otherwise.

Over the years I've had countless guests and visitors to my courses, including not only those mentioned in this book, but also hundreds of others who shared their insights, wisdom, and generosity with our school. I've been lucky to instruct thousands of students who inspire me every day with their big brains, their bigger hearts, and their desire to do both good and well in the world. Teaching at Stanford is akin to teaching at the United Nations: every moment surrounded by brilliant men and women who come from every continent and country.

I have the best job ever.

Stephen Issacs, Donya Dickerson, and the team at McGraw Hill have been vital in their support and coaching in the writing of this book. I owe them a debt of gratitude for patiently working with me as a first-time author.

Will Weisser helped me find my voice and write a manuscript that was understandable and more closely resembled how I actually speak. If anything in the content is simple and easy to understand, it is entirely due to his relentlessly driving me to be clearer in my messages. If anything is unclear, it is my fault. I look forward to our continued collaborations in the future.

Catherine Fredman was kind enough to provide a sharp pen and critical eye that pushed me to be better and more consistent throughout the writing process. I hope someday to have half of her capabilities in fine-tuning the written word. When I write I now hear her voice in my head providing input even before I send her something to review.

Leah Spiro took me under her wing and taught me the ins and outs of proposing, writing, and thinking about a book. I am grateful for her infinite support and her dedication to sticking with me through the ups and downs of making this manuscript a reality.

Finally, and most important, I could only have completed this book with the love and support of my family: Debbie, Kelly, Evan, and Samantha. Without them I have nothing.

NOTES

Chapter 2

1. Much of the background information on Daimler in this chapter is adapted from the Stanford GSB case study E-642 "Daimler: Reinventing Mobility" by Amadeus Orleans and Robert E. Siegel, copyright 2017 by the Board of Trustees of the Leland Stanford Junior University.
2. https://www.mercedes-benz.com/en/classic/museum/ (1/6/21).
3. Greg Schneider and Kimberly Edds, "Fans of GM Electric Car Fight the Crusher," *Washington Post*, March 10, 2005.
4. "The Electric Car Revolution Is Accelerating," *Bloomberg Businessweek*, July 6, 2017.
5. https://twitter.com/elonmusk/status/912036765287845888 (1/6/21).
6. https://twitter.com/Daimler/status/912349809662496768 (1/6/21).
7. "All Tesla Cars Being Produced Now Have Full Self-Driving Hardware," Tesla Press Release, October 19, 2016.
8. "GM and Cruise Announce First Mass-Production Self-Driving Car," TechCrunch, September 11, 2017.
9. https://www.car2go.com/US/en/ (1/6/21).
10. https://www.businessinsider.com/mytaxi-has-just-dropped-its-prices-by-50 -after-tfl-took-ubers-licence-2017-9 (1/6/21).
11. https://www.mercedes-benz.com/en/innovation/connected/car-to -x-communication/ (1/7/21).
12. https://www.statista.com/statistics/233743/vehicle-sales-in-china/ (1/25/21).
13. https://www.iea.org/reports/global-ev-outlook-2020 (1/25/21).
14. https://insideevs.com/news/394229/plugin-electric-car-sales-china-2019/ (1/25/21).
15. Orleans and Siegel, Interview with Nicholas Speeks.
16. Orleans and Siegel, Interview with Dr. Uwe Ernstberge.
17. Orelans and Siegel, Interview with Markus Schäfer.
18. "Workers at Daimler in Germany Fight for Their Future Jobs," IndustriALL Global Union, June 29, 2017.
19. Interview with Wilko Stark.

20. https://www.forbes.com/sites/bradtempleton/2020/06/26/amazon-buys-self
    -driving-company-zoox-for-12b-and-may-rule-the-world/?sh=1ac8e109769c
    (1/26/21).
21. https://www.axios.com/apple-car-what-we-know-421ac809-2560-4609-8f66
    -809dd5f80d71.html (1/26/21).
22. https://www.ft.com/content/047507bb-d5b8-44cb-bc20-06efb983eac7
    (1/26/21).
23. Much of the background information on 23andMe in this chapter is adapted
    from the Stanford GSB case study E-688 "23andMe: A Virtuous Loop" by
    Jeffrey Conn and Robert E. Siegel, copyright 2019 by the Board of Trustees of
    the Leland Stanford Junior University.
24. Conn and Siegel, Interview with Anne Wojcicki.
25. Conn and Siegel, Interview with Anne Wojcicki.
26. https://www.fda.gov/news-events/press-announcements/fda-allows-marketing
    -first-direct-consumer-tests-provide-genetic-risk-information-certain
    -conditions (1/7/21).
27. Heather Murphy, "Don't Count on 23andMe to Detect Most Breast Cancer
    Risks, Study Warns," New York Times, April 16, 2019, https://www.nytimes
    .com/2019/04/16/health/23andme-brca-gene-testing.html (1/7/21).
28. Conn and Siegel, Interview with Anne Wojcicki.
29. Conn and Siegel, Interview with Roelof Botha, June 28, 2019.
30. "Lark Health and 23andMe Collaborate to Integrate Genetic Information in
    Two New Health Programs," 23andMe website, January 8, 2019.
31. Conn and Siegel, Interview with Dr. Emily Conley.
32. Conn and Siegel, Interview with Anne Wojcicki.

Chapter 3

1. Dana Mattioli, "Amazon Scooped Up Data from Its Own Sellers to Launch
   Competing Products," Wall Street Journal, April 23, 2020.
2. Nicholas Confessor, "Cambridge Analytica and Facebook: The Scandal and
   the Fallout So Far," New York Times, April 4, 2018.
3. Much of the background information on Schwab in this chapter is adapted
   from the Stanford GSB case study SM-282 "Charles Schwab Corp in 2017,"
   by Julie Makinen and Robert E. Siegel, copyright 2017 by the Board of
   Trustees of the Leland Stanford Junior University.
4. John Kador, Charles Schwab: How One Company Beat Wall Street and
   Reinvented the Brokerage Industry (Hoboken, NJ: John Wiley & Sons, Inc.,
   2002), p. 54.
5. Ibid.
6. Makinen and Siegel, Interview with Walt Bettinger, August 17, 2017.
7. Makinen and Siegel, Interview with Walt Bettinger, August 17, 2017.

8. Interview with Walt Bettinger, June 17, 2020.

9. Lisa Beilfuss, "How Schwab Ate Wall Street," *Wall Street Journal*, April 28, 2019.

10. https://www.aboutschwab.com/who-we-are (1/8/21).

11. Document from Charles Schwab Corp.

12. Interview with Walt Bettinger, June 17, 2020.

13. Interview with Walt Bettinger, June 17, 2020.

14. Makinen and Siegel, Interview with Walt Bettinger, August 17, 2017.

15. Alexander Osipovich and Lisa Beilfuss, "Why 'Free Trading' on Robinhood Isn't Really Free," *Wall Street Journal*, November 9, 2018.

16. Interview with Walt Bettinger, June 17, 2020.

17. Maggie Fitzgerald, "Charles Schwab Says Broker's Move to Zero Commissions Was an Ultimate Goal for the Firm," CNBC.com, October 7, 2019.

18. Makinen and Siegel, Interview with Walt Bettinger, August 17, 2017.

19. Makinen and Siegel, Interview with Joe Martinetto.

20. Makinen and Siegel, Interview with Joe Martinetto.

21. https://www.cnbc.com/2021/01/28/robinhood-interactive-brokers-restrict-trading-in-gamestop-s.html (3/28/21).

22. Interview with Walt Bettinger, June 17, 2020.

23. Makinen and Siegel, Interview with Tim Heier.

24. Makinen and Siegel, Interview with Tim Heier.

25. https://www.wsj.com/articles/charles-schwab-to-buy-td-ameritrade-for-26-billion-11574681426 (1/8/21).

26. Makinen and Siegel, Interview with Mike Hecht.

27. Makinen and Siegel, Interview with Joe Martinetto.

28. Makinen and Siegel, Interview with Joe Martinetto.

29. Makinen and Siegel, Interview with Tim Heier.

30. Theresa W. Carey, "Robo-Advisors 2019: Still Waiting for the Revolution," Investopedia, September 24, 2019.

Chapter 4

1. https://www.lego.com/en-us/aboutus/lego-group/the-lego-group-history/ (1/9/21).

2. https://www.legoland.com/about/ (1/9/21).

3. https://www.nytimes.com/2009/09/06/business/global/06lego.html (1/9/21).

4. https://www.boxofficemojo.com/release/rl643728897/ (1/9/21).

5. Gabe Cohn, "What's on TV Wednesday: Lego Masters," *New York Times*, February 5, 2020.

6. https://www.lego.com/en-us/aboutus/news/2020/march/annual-results/ (1/9/21).

7. David Pogue, "Software as a Monthly Rental," *New York Times*, July 3, 2013.

8. Phil Knight, *Shoe Dog*, Simon & Schuster, 2016.

9. https://news.nike.com/news/nike-inc-reports-fiscal-2019-fourth-quarter-and -full-year-results (1/9/21).

10. https://www.aligntech.com/about (1/9/21).

11. Anne Coughlin, Julie Hennessey, and Andrei Najjar, "Invisalign: Orthodontics Unwired," Case number KEL032, Kellogg School of Management, 2004.

12. https://www.aligntech.com/about (1/2/21).

13. Much of the background information on Align in this chapter is adapted from the Stanford GSB case study E-686 "Align Technology: Clearing the Way for Digital" by Patrick Robinson and Robert E. Siegel, copyright 2019 by the Board of Trustees of the Leland Stanford Junior University.

14. https://www.aligntech.com/about (1/9/21).

15. Robinson and Siegel, Interview with Emory Wright.

16. Align Technology public statement.

17. http://investor.aligntech.com/news-releases/news-release-details/align -technology-named-class-action-lawsuit-company-believes (1/9/21).

18. Interview with Joe Hogan, August 14, 2020.

19. Interview with Joe Hogan, August 14, 2020.

20. Robinson and Siegel, Interview with Shannon Henderson.

21. Interview with Joe Hogan, August 14, 2020.

22. https://medium.com/systemsleadership/adapting-business-models-joe-hogan -ceo-align-technologies-fee6b4720f58 (1/9/21).

23. Robinson and Siegel, Interview with Joe Hogan, May 10, 2019.

24. Robinson and Siegel, Interview with Joe Hogan, May 10, 2019.

25. IBISWorld Industry Report 62121, "Dentists in the US" (December 2018).

26. Robinson and Siegel, Interview with Raphael Pascaud.

27. Robinson and Siegel, Interview with Raphael Pascaud.

28. Robinson and Siegel, Interview with Shannon Henderson, May 10, 2019.

29. Robinson and Siegel.

30. Robinson and Siegel, Interview with Raphael Pascaud, May 10, 2019.

31. Robinson and Siegel, Interview with Raphael Pascaud, May 10, 2019.

32. Robinson and Siegel, Interview with Raphael Pascaud, May 10, 2019.

33. Megan Rose Dickey, "Teeth-Straightening Startup SmileDirectClub Is Now Worth $3.2 Billion," *TechCrunch*, November 2018, https://techcrunch.com /2018/10/10/teeth-straightening-startup-smiledirectclub-is-now-worth-3-2 -billion (1/9/21).

34. Interview with Shannon Henderson, May 10, 2019.

35. https://www.forbes.com/sites/laurendebter/2019/09/11/smiledirectclub-ipo/ #325b42ba6aca (1/9/21).

36. http://investor.aligntech.com/news-releases/news-release-details/align -technology-announces-fourth-quarter-and-fiscal-2019 (1/9/21).

Chapter 5

1. https://www.merriam-webster.com/dictionary/empathy (1/11/21).
2. https://fleishmanhillard.com/wp-content/uploads/meta/resource-file/2019/what-could-empathy-look-like-1550775510.pdf (1/11/21).
3. https://fleishmanhillard.com/wp-content/uploads/meta/resource-file/2019/what-could-empathy-look-like-1550775510.pdf (1/11/21).
4. https://thepointsguy.com/guide/southwest-underrated-airline/ (1/11/21).
5. https://thepointsguy.com/guide/southwest-underrated-airline/ (1/11/21).
6. https://skift.com/2014/06/17/why-southwest-air-skips-the-safety-videos-in-favor-of-free-styling-flight-attendants/(1/11/21).
7. https://www.forbes.com/sites/stanphelps/2014/09/14/southwest-airlines-understands-the-heart-of-marketing-is-experience/#2436cdae2bda (1/11/21).
8. https://www.forbes.com/sites/stanphelps/2014/09/14/southwest-airlines-understands-the-heart-of-marketing-is-experience/#2436cdae2bda (1/11/21).
9. https://www.jitbit.com/news/201-hire-customer-support-like-southwest-hires-flight-attendants/ (1/11/21).
10. https://ffbsccn.wordpress.com/2010/08/27/the-key-to-business-success-in-one-sentence-from-herb-kelleher-via-tom-peters/ (1/11/21).
11. https://www.fastcompany.com/1681023/how-patagonia-makes-more-money-by-trying-to-make-less (1/11/21).
12. https://www.fastcompany.com/1681023/how-patagonia-makes-more-money-by-trying-to-make-less (1/11/21).
13. https://www.fastcompany.com/1681023/how-patagonia-makes-more-money-by-trying-to-make-less (1/11/21).
14. https://wornwear.patagonia.com (1/11/21).
15. https://contently.com/2019/05/20/empathetic-marketing-fake-empathy/ (1/11/21).
16. https://contently.com/2019/05/20/empathetic-marketing-fake-empathy/ (1/11/21).
17. https://archive.thinkprogress.org/patagonia-employees-can-stay-home-on-thanksgiving-day-f554ea75c6ae/ (1/11/21).
18. https://www.inc.com/scott-mautz/how-can-patagonia-have-only-4-percent-worker-turnover-hint-they-pay-activist-employees-bail.html (1/11/21).
19. Thomas A. Kochan and Richard Schmalensee (2003), *Management: Inventing and Delivering Its Future*, MIT Press, p. 117.
20. https://www.fastcompany.com/3004953/how-sas-became-worlds-best-place-work (1/11/21).
21. https://about.kaiserpermanente.org/who-we-are/leadership-team/board-of-directors/bernard-j-tyson.
22. Interview with Bernard Tyson, February 11, 2016, https://youtu.be/mxUMZJd2zN4 (1/11/21).
23. Interview with Bernard Tyson, February 11, 2016, https://youtu.be/mxUMZJd2zN4 (1/11/21).

24. Interview with Bernard Tyson, February 11, 2016, https://youtu.be/mxUMZJd2zN4 (1/11/21).

25. https://www.mentalfloss.com/article/53525/11-actors-you-might-not-realize-do-commercial-voiceovers (1/11/21).

26. https://thrive.kaiserpermanente.org/care-experience/healthy-adults (1/11/21).

27. https://thrive.kaiserpermanente.org/care-experience/healthy-adults (1/11/21).

28. Interview with Bernard Tyson, February 11, 2016, https://youtu.be/mxUMZJd2zN4 (1/11/21).

29. https://www.salesforce.com/video/3402968/ (1/11/21).

30. https://kpproud-midatlantic.kaiserpermanente.org/kpmas-good-health-great-hair-third-year (1/11/21).

31. https://www.salesforce.com/video/3402968/ (1/11/21).

32. Interview with Bernard Tyson, February 11, 2016, https://youtu.be/mxUMZJd2zN4 (1/11/21).

33. Interview with Bernard Tyson, February 11, 2016, https://youtu.be/mxUMZJd2zN4 (1/11/21).

34. https://www.wsj.com/articles/kaiser-permanente-cultivates-the-digital-doctor-patient-relationship-1527559500 (1/11/21).

35. Interview with Bernard Tyson, February 11, 2016, https://youtu.be/mxUMZJd2zN4 (1/11/21).

36. https://www.wsj.com/articles/kaiser-permanente-cultivates-the-digital-doctor-patient-relationship-1527559500 (1/11/21).

37. Interview with Bernard Tyson, February 11, 2016, https://youtu.be/mxUMZJd2zN4 (1/11/21).

38. Interview with Bernard Tyson, February 11, 2016, https://youtu.be/mxUMZJd2zN4 (1/11/21).

39. Interview with Bernard Tyson, February 11, 2016, https://youtu.be/mxUMZJd2zN4 (1/11/21).

40. https://www.salesforce.com/video/3402968/ (1/11/21).

41. https://www.salesforce.com/video/3402968/ (1/11/21).

42. Interview with Bernard Tyson, February 11, 2016, https://youtu.be/mxUMZJd2zN4 (1/11/21).

43. Interview with Bernard Tyson, February 11, 2016, https://youtu.be/mxUMZJd2zN4 (1/11/21).

Chapter 6

1. https://www.salesforlife.com/blog/no-one-ever-got-fired-for-buying-ibm/ (1/13/21).

2. Much of the background information on Stripe in this chapter is adapted from the Stanford GSB case study E-601 "Stripe: Increasing the GDP of the Internet," by Ryan Kissick and Robert E. Siegel, copyright 2016 by the Board of Trustees of the Leland Stanford Junior University.

3. Kissick and Siegel.
4. https://www.fastcompany.com/1813087/inside-stripe-paypal-competitor-backed-paypal-founders-peter-thiel-elon-musk (1/13/21).
5. Kissick and Siegel.
6. Kissick and Siegel.
7. https://social.techcrunch.com/2019/09/05/stripe-launches-stripe-capital-to-make-instant-loan-offers-to-customers-on-its-platform/ (1/13/21).
8. https://techcrunch.com/2020/12/03/stripe-announces-embedded-business-banking-service-stripe-treasury/ (1/12/21).
9. https://hbr.org/2017/05/why-some-digital-companies-should-resist-profitability-for-as-long-as-they-can (1/12/21).
10. www.JohnDeere.com (1/13/21).
11. https://www.wired.com/story/why-john-deere-just-spent-dollar305-million-on-a-lettuce-farming-robot/ (1/13/21).
12. Much of the background information on AB InBev in this chapter is adapted from the Stanford GSB case study E-643 "AB InBev: Brewing an Innovation Strategy," by Amadeus Orleans and Robert E. Siegel, copyright 2017 by the Board of Trustees of the Leland Stanford Junior University.
13. Orleans and Siegel, Interview with Carlos Brito, 2017.
14. https://firstwefeast.com/features/illustrated-history-of-craft-beer-in-america (1/12/21).
15. Orleans and Siegel.
16. Orleans and Siegel, Interview with Carlos Brito, 2017.
17. Orleans and Siegel, Interview with Pedro Earp, 2017.
18. AB InBev's 2015 Annual Report, p. 4.
19. Orleans and Siegel, Interview with Pedro Earp, 2017.
20. Orleans and Siegel, Interview with Pedro Earp, 2017.
21. Interview with Pedro Earp, September 13, 2020.
22. Orleans and Siegel, Interview with Michel Doukeris, 2017.
23. Orleans and Siegel, Interview with Alex Nelson, 2017.
24. Orleans and Siegel, Interview with Alex Nelson, 2017.
25. Orleans and Siegel, Interview with David Almeida, 2017.
26. https://finance.yahoo.com/news/ab-inbev-bud-beats-q2-154403266.html (1/13/21).
27. https://www.ab-inbev.com/who-we-are/people.html (1/13/21).
28. Interview with Carlos Brito, September 14, 2020.
29. Interview with Pedro Earp, September 13, 2020.

Chapter 7

1. https://edgeeffects.net/fordlandia/ (1/14/21).
2. https://www.christenseninstitute.org/interdependence-modularity/ (1/14/21).

3. https://customerthink.com/peter_drucker_jack_welch_and_outsourcing/ (1/14/21).

4. https://www.atmmarketplace.com/blogs/the-outsourcing-debate (1/14/21).

5. Interview with Dr. Emily Conley.

6. https://www.techradar.com/news/best-apple-carplay-apps (1/14/21).

7. https://money.cnn.com/2001/04/11/companies/amazon/?s=2 (1/14/21).

8. https://highexistence.com/50-elon-musk-quotes/ (1/14/21).

9. https://highexistence.com/50-elon-musk-quotes/ (1/14/21).

10. https://cleantechnica.com/2020/06/18/elon-musk-uses-economies-of-scale -vertical-integration-to-revolutionize-auto-industry/ (1/14/21).

11. https://www.tesla.com/gigafactory (1/14/21).

12. https://electrek.co/2016/02/26/tesla-vertically-integrated/ (1/14/21).

13. https://www.forbes.com/sites/enriquedans/2020/06/05/for-elon-musk -economies-of-scale-are-not-rocket-science-or-arethey/#525f873a5316 (1/14/21).

14. https://www.latimes.com/business/technology/la-fi-himi-apoorva-mehta -20170105-story.html (1/14/21).

15. https://www.latimes.com/business/technology/la-fi-himi-apoorva-mehta -20170105-story.html (1/14/21).

16. Fortune interview https://www.youtube.com/watch?v=HxaPgNrceos (1/14/21).

17. https://www.bloomberg.com/news/articles/2020-06-11/instacart-valuation -hits-13-7-billion-in-pandemic-investment (1/14/21).

18. https://www.wsj.com/articles/online-orders-force-supermarkets-to-rethink -their-stores-1538532420 (1/14/21).

19. September 2018 Recode interview, https://www.youtube.com/watch?v= kDUxjO1Hd4g (1/14/21).

20. https://hbr.org/2020/07/delivery-apps-need-to-start-treating-suppliers-as -partners (1/14/21).

21. https://www.eater.com/2020/4/28/21239754/instacart-brings-in-10-million -profit-in-april-coronavirus-deliveries (1/14/21).

22. https://hbr.org/2020/07/delivery-apps-need-to-start-treating-suppliers-as -partners (1/14/21).

23. https://www.foxbusiness.com/money/instacart-shopper-income-manahawkin -nj (1/14/21).

24. https://www.businessinsider.com/instacart-hiring-spree-coronavirus-working -conditions-worse-for-everyone-report-2020-5 (1/14/21).

25. Fortune interview https://www.youtube.com/watch?v=HxaPgNrceos (1/14/21).

26. Fortune interview https://www.youtube.com/watch?v=HxaPgNrceos (1/14/21).

27. https://nypost.com/2017/03/08/instacart-now-valued-at-3-4b-after-major -investment/ (1/14/21).

28. https://www.cnbc.com/2017/11/28/instacart-albertsons-delivery-partnership
    -takes-on-amazon-whole-foods.html (1/14/21).

29. https://www.grocerydive.com/news/grocery--grocery-executive-of-the-year
    -apoorva-mehta-ceo-of-instacart/534438/ (1/14/21).

30. https://www.recode.net/2018/10/16/17981074/instacart-600-million-funding
    -7-billion-d1-capital-partners (1/14/21).

31. https://www.cnbc.com/2020/08/11/walmart-and-instacart-partner-in-fight
    -against-amazons-whole-foods.html (1/14/21).

32. https://www.supermarketnews.com/online-retail/walmart-bring-two-hour
    -express-delivery-2000-stores (1/14/21).

33. https://www.wsj.com/articles/online-orders-force-supermarkets-to-rethink
    -their-stores-1538532420 (1/14/21).

34. https://investorplace.com/2020/08/hottest-upcoming-ipos-to-watch-instacart
    -airbnb/ (1/14/21).

35. https://www.wsj.com/articles/grocers-embrace-food-delivery-but-they-still
    -dont-love-it-11592056800 (1/14/21).

36. https://www.digitalcommerce360.com/2019/03/08/amazon_grocery_stores
    _market_strategy_dominance/ (1/14/21).

Chapter 8

1. https://mashable.com/shopping/warby-parker-affordable-designer-glasses/
   (1/15/21).

2. https://mashable.com/shopping/warby-parker-affordable-designer-glasses/
   (1/15/21).

3. https://www.inc.com/magazine/201706/tom-foster/warby-parker-eyewear
   .html (1/15/21).

4. https://www.inc.com/magazine/201706/tom-foster/warby-parker-eyewear
   .html (1/15/21).

5. https://www.inc.com/magazine/201706/tom-foster/warby-parker-eyewear
   .html (1/15/21).

6. Interview with Hubert Joly, March 2019, https://youtu.be/1SUvA5XQCVg
   (1/15/21).

7. Interview with Hubert Joly, March 2019, https://youtu.be/1SUvA5XQCVg
   (1/15/21).

8. Interview with Hubert Joly, March 2019, https://youtu.be/1SUvA5XQCVg
   (1/15/21).

9. https://www.wsj.com/articles/best-buys-future-is-still-made-of-brick
   -11598371372 (1/15/21).

10. https://www.marketplace.org/2017/12/20/home-depot-may-be-e-commerce
    -model-retail-industry (1/15/21).

11. https://www.mmh.com/article/the_home_depot_builds_an_omni_channel
    _supply_chain (1/15/21).

12. https://www.mmh.com/article/the_home_depot_builds_an_omni_channel_supply_chain (1/15/21).

13. https://www.mmh.com/article/the_home_depot_builds_an_omni_channel_supply_chain (1/15/21).

14. https://www.marketplace.org/2017/12/20/home-depot-may-be-e-commerce-model-retail-industry (1/15/21).

15. https://www.wsj.com/articles/home-depot-sets-1-2-billion-supply-chain-overhaul-1528739061 (1/15/21).

16. https://ir.homedepot.com/news-releases/2020/08-18-2020-110014886 (1/15/21).

17. Interview with Brian Cornell, April 2019 https://youtu.be/AzCQ56KJHy4 (1/15/21).

18. Some of the background information on Target and this quote is adapted from the Stanford GSB case study SM-308 "Target: Creating a Data-Driven Product Management Organization," by David Kingbo and Robert E. Siegel, copyright 2018 by the Board of Trustees of the Leland Stanford Junior University.

19. Interview with Brian Cornell, April 2019 https://youtu.be/AzCQ56KJHy4 (1/15/21).

20. https://www.wsj.com/articles/targets-answer-to-discounters-is-an-even-cheaper-store-brand-1538827200 (1/15/21).

21. https://www.inc.com/justin-bariso/amazon-almost-killed-target-then-target-did-impossible.html (1/15/21).

22. Interview with Brian Cornell, April 2019 https://youtu.be/AzCQ56KJHy4 (1/15/21).

Chapter 9

1. https://additivemanufacturing.com/basics/ (1/16/21).

2. Robert A. Burgelman, *Strategic Management*, Stanford University, 2015, Elsevier, pages 511–513.

3. https://investor.aligntech.com/news-releases/news-release-details/align-technology-announces-invisalign-g8-new-smartforce (3/25/21).

4. https://media.daimler.com/marsMediaSite/en/instance/ko/The-production-network-The-worldwide-plants.xhtml?oid=9272049 (1/16/21).

5. https://media.daimler.com/marsMediaSite/en/instance/ko/Industrie-40--Digitalisation-at-Mercedes-Benz-The-Next-Step-in-the-Industrial-Revolution.xhtml?oid=9272047 (1/16/21).

6. https://media.daimler.com/marsMediaSite/en/instance/ko/Industrie-40--Digitalisation-at-Mercedes-Benz-The-Next-Step-in-the-Industrial-Revolution.xhtml?oid=9272047 (1/16/21).

7. https://media.daimler.com/marsMediaSite/en/instance/ko/Industrie-40--Digitalisation-at-Mercedes-Benz-The-Next-Step-in-the-Industrial-Revolution.xhtml?oid=9272047 (1/16/21).

8. https://www.wsj.com/articles/samsung-harman-getting-in-an-automotive-groove-1479123162 (1/17/21).
9. https://www.wsj.com/articles/samsungs-drugmaking-future-includes-a-2-billion-super-plant-bigger-than-the-louvre-11599125658 (1/17/21).
10. https://medium.com/systemsleadership/innovating-in-business-and-technology-young-sohn-president-and-chief-strategy-officer-samsung-bac4e6d1070f (1/17/21).
11. https://medium.com/the-industrialist-s-dilemma/the-transformation-of-an-industrial-and-digital-giant-young-sohn-corporate-president-and-chief-617540d860b2 (1/17/21)
12. https://www.desktopmetal.com/about-us (1/17/21).
13. https://www.desktopmetal.com/about-us/team/ric-fulop-1 (1/17/21).
14. https://www.forbes.com/sites/amyfeldman/2018/09/27/the-next-industrial-revolution-how-a-tech-unicorns-3-d-metal-printers-could-remake-manufacturing/?sh=400a646713be (1/17/21).
15. https://medium.com/ipo-2-0/desktop-metal-the-next-10-billion-company-2dc85bcde194 (1/17/21).
16. Desktop Metal investor conference call transcript, August 2020.
17. https://medium.com/ipo-2-0/desktop-metal-the-next-10-billion-company-2dc85bcde194 (1/17/21).
18. Desktop Metal investor conference call transcript, August 2020.
19. https://www.desktopmetal.com/about-us (1/17/21).
20. https://medium.com/ipo-2-0/desktop-metal-the-next-10-billion-company-2dc85bcde194 (1/17/21).
21. https://www.forbes.com/sites/amyfeldman/2018/09/27/the-next-industrial-revolution-how-a-tech-unicorns-3-d-metal-printers-could-remake-manufacturing/?sh=3b49447613bc (1/17/21).
22. Desktop Metal investor presentation slide deck, August 2020.
23. https://www.forbes.com/sites/amyfeldman/2018/09/27/the-next-industrial-revolution-how-a-tech-unicorns-3-d-metal-printers-could-remake-manufacturing/?sh=3b49447613be (1/17/21).
24. https://www.forbes.com/sites/amyfeldman/2018/09/27/the-next-industrial-revolution-how-a-tech-unicorns-3-d-metal-printers-could-remake-manufacturing/?sh=3b49447613be (1/17/21).
25. https://www.forbes.com/sites/amyfeldman/2018/09/27/the-next-industrial-revolution-how-a-tech-unicorns-3-d-metal-printers-could-remake-manufacturing/?sh=3b49447613be (1/17/21).
26. Trine conference call with investors, August 2020.
27. Trine conference call with investors, August 2020.
28. Desktop Metal investor presentation slide deck, August 2020.
29. Trine conference call with investors, August 2020.
30. https://medium.com/ipo-2-0/desktop-metal-the-next-10-billion-company-2dc85bcde194 (1/17/21).

Chapter 10

1. https://finance.yahoo.com/news/ab-inbev-bud-beats-q2-154403266.html.
2. https://www.cnn.com/about (1/18/21).
3. https://www.wsj.com/articles/life-at-cnn-skeleton-staff-record-ratings-and
   -vanishing-ads-11586984881 (1/18/21).
4. https://www.wsj.com/articles/cnn-president-jeff-zucker-faces-what-might-be
   -his-last-lap-11603487817 (1/18/21).
5. https://annualreport.visa.com/financials/default.aspx (1/18/21).
6. Interview with Charlie Scharf, February 18, 2016.
7. Interview with Charlie Scharf, February 18, 2016.
8. Interview with Charlie Scharf, February 18, 2016.
9. https://medium.com/the-industrialist-s-dilemma/outpacing-change-charlie
   -scharf-ceo-visa-c1156a94d00c (1/18/21).
10. Interview with Charlie Scharf, February 18, 2016.
11. Some of the background information on Michelin is adapted from the Stanford GSB case study SM-315 "Michelin Group: Embracing Culture While Adapting to Change" by Jocelyn Hornblower and Robert E. Siegel, copyright 2019 by the Board of Trustees of the Leland Stanford Junior University.
12. "The Michelin Group Presents its Global Reorganization Project to Better Serve its Customers," Michelin press release, https://www.michelin.com/eng/media-room/press-and-news/press-releases/Group/The-Michelin-Group-presents-its-global-reorganization-project-to-better-serve-its-customers (1/17/21).
13. Sunil Gupta and Christian Godwin, Harvard Business School case study #9-520-061, "Michelin: Building a Digital Service Platform," March 2020.
14. Hornblower and Siegel, Interview with Scott Clark, August 30, 2018.
15. Hornblower and Siegel, Interview with Eric Duverger, August 30, 2018.
16. Hornblower and Siegel, Interview with Eric Duverger, August 30, 2018.
17. Hornblower and Siegel, Interview with Florent Menegaux, August 30, 2018.
18. Hornblower and Siegel, Interview with Eric Duverger, August 30, 2018.
19. Tire Business Magazine, August 2017, https://www.tirebusiness.com/this-week-issue/archives?year=2017 (1/18/21).
20. Hornblower and Siegel, Interview with Yves Chapot, July 16, 2018.
21. Hornblower and Siegel, Interview with Scott Clark, August 30, 2018.
22. Interview with Florent Menegaux, April 11, 2019, https://youtu.be/UN2WBLzh3Ts (1/18/21).
23. Hornblower and Siegel, Interview with Florent Menegaux, August 30, 2018.
24. Sunil Gupta and Christian Godwin, Harvard Business School case study #9-520-061, "Michelin: Building a Digital Service Platform," March 2020.
25. Hornblower and Siegel, Interview with Terry Gettys, July 16, 2018.
26. Hornblower and Siegel, Interview with Sonia Artinian-Fredou, July 16, 2018.

27. Interview with Florent Menegaux, April 11, 2019, https://youtu.be /UN2WBLzh3Ts (1/18/21).

28. Hornblower and Siegel, Interview with Florent Menegaux, August 30, 2018.

29. https://webarchive.fivesgroup.com/news-press/news/the-michelin-group-and -fives-join-forces-and-create-fives-michelin-additive-solutions-to-become -a-major-metal-3d-printing-player.html (1/18/21).

30. Interview with Ralph DiMenna, Director of Services and Solutions, December 4, 2020.

31. Hornblower and Siegel, Interview with Florent Menegaux, August 30, 2018.

32. Hornblower and Siegel.

33. Sunil Gupta and Christian Godwin, Harvard Business School case study #9-520-061, "Michelin: Building a Digital Service Platform," March 2020.

34. Hornblower and Siegel, Interview with Eric Duverger, August 30, 2018.

35. Hornblower and Siegel, Interview with Terry Gettys, July 16, 2018.

36. Interview with Florent Menegaux, April 11, 2019, https://youtu.be /UN2WBLzh3Ts (1/18/21).

Chapter 11

1. https://www.independent.co.uk/news/obituaries/ray-noorda-422415.html (1/18/21).

2. L. Bourne and D. H.Walker (2005), "Visualising and Mapping Stakeholder Influence," *Management Decision*, 43(5), 649–660.

3. https://www.quirks.com/articles/mapping-the-chain-of-influence-on -consumer-choice (1/18/21).

4. R. A. Burgelman, *Strategy Is Destiny: How Strategy Making Shapes a Company's Future*, The Free Press, 2002.

5. https://chancellor.ucsf.edu/leadership/chancellors-cabinet/mark-laret (1/18/21).

6. https://www.ucsf.edu/sites/default/files/UCSF_General_Fact_Sheet.pdf (1/18/21).

7. https://www.beckershospitalreview.com/news-analysis/ceo-mark-laret -discusses-ucsf-medical-centers-rise-from-near-financial-ruin-to-recent-success -new-mission-bay-hospital.html (1/18/21).

8. Interview with Mark Laret, May 29, 2018, https://youtu.be/xHwd45qEoL8 (1/18/21).

9. Interview with Mark Laret, May 29, 2018, https://youtu.be/xHwd45qEoL8 (1/18/21).

10. https://www.cnbc.com/2020/11/05/california-prop-22-win-improves -doordash-instacart-ipo-prospects.html (1/18/21).

11. https://archive.fortune.com/galleries/2012/news/companies/1203/gallery .greatest-entrepreneurs.fortune/12.html (1/18/21).

12. https://www.fastcompany.com/47593/wal-mart-you-dont-know (1/18/21).

13. https://www.cips.org/supply-management/news/2017/march/wal-mart-to
-squeeze-suppliers-to-win-discount-chain-price-war-/ (1/18/21).

14. https://www.cips.org/supply-management/news/2017/march/wal-mart-to
-squeeze-suppliers-to-win-discount-chain-price-war-/ (1/18/21).

15. https://corporate.walmart.com/our-story/our-business (12/5/20).

16. https://www.android.com/everyone/facts/ (1/18/21).

17. https://www.theverge.com/2019/5/7/18528297/google-io-2019-android
-devices-play-store-total-number-statistic-keynote (1/18/21).

18. https://www.kamilfranek.com/how-google-makes-money-from-android/
(1/18/21).

19. https://www.nytimes.com/2015/05/28/technology/personaltech/a-murky-road
-ahead-for-android-despite-market-dominance.html (1/18/21).

20. Some of the background information on Android is adapted from two
Stanford GSB case studies: SM-176C "Google and Android in 2015: Looking
Towards the Future" by Michael Seltzer, Robert E. Siegel, and Robert A.
Burgelman, August 2015, copyright 2015 by the Board of Trustees of the
Leland Stanford Junior University, and SM-176D "Google and Android in
2018: A Changing World Order" by Cameron Lehman, Robert E. Siegel, and
Robert A. Burgelman, November 2018, copyright © 2018 by the Board of
Trustees of the Leland Stanford Junior University.

21. Lehman, Siegel, and Burgelman, Interview with Bob Borchers on June 1,
2018.

22. Lehman, Siegel, and Burgelman, Interview with Bob Borchers on June 1,
2018.

23. Lehman, Siegel, and Burgelman, Interview with Bob Borchers on June 1,
2018.

24. Lehman, Siegel, and Burgelman, Interview with Sagar Kamdar on June 1,
2018.

25. https://www.statista.com/statistics/271539/worldwide-shipments-of-leading
-smartphone-vendors-since-2007/ (1/18/21).

26. *Business Insider*, "Samsung's Plan to Distance Itself from Android Is Finally
Taking Shape," May 1, 2015, http://www.businessinsider.com/samsung
-unleashes-tizen-store-to-the-world-2015-5 (1/18/21).

27. DroidViews, "Easily Root Amazon Fire Phone," February 3, 2015, http://www
.droidviews.com/easlily-root-amazon-fire-phone-using-towelroot (1/18/21)

28. Seltzer, Siegel, and Burgelman, Interview with Jamie Rosenberg on February
24, 2015.

29. https://www.news18.com/news/tech/smartphone-users-in-india-crossed-500
-million-in-2019-states-report-2479529.html (1/18/21).

30. Seltzer, Siegel, and Burgelman, Interview with Jamie Rosenberg on February
24, 2015.

31. Lehman, Siegel, and Burgelman, Interview with Paul Gennai on June 1, 2018.
32. Lehman, Siegel, and Burgelman, Interview with Paul Gennai on June 1, 2018.
33. Seltzer, Siegel, and Burgelman, Interview with Sundar Pinchai on April 28, 2015.
34. Seltzer, Siegel, and Burgelman, Interview with Sundar Pinchai on April 28, 2015.
35. Lehman, Siegel, and Burgelman, Interview with Sagar Kamdar on June 1, 2018.
36. Lehman, Siegel, and Burgelman, Interview with Sabrina Ellis on June 1, 2018.
37. https://arstechnica.com/gadgets/2020/06/idc-google-outsells-oneplus-with-7-2
   -million-pixel-smartphones-in-2019/ (1/18/21).
38. Lehman, Siegel, and Burgelman, Interview with Sabrina Ellis on June 1, 2018.
39. https://www.nytimes.com/2018/07/18/technology/google-eu-android-finc
   .html (1/18/21).
40. https://blog.google/around-the-globe/google-europe/android-has-created-more
   -choice-not-less/ (1/18/21).
41. https://www.android.com/everyone/facts/ (1/18/21).

Chapter 12

1. https://www.history.com/this-day-in-history/national-geographic-society
   -founded (1/19/21).
2. https://www.nationalgeographic.org/about-us/ (1/19/21).
3. https://www.nationalgeographic.org/about-us/ (1/19/21).
4. https://www.nationalgeographic.com/mediakit/assets/img/downloads/2020
   /NGM_2020_Media_Kit.pdf (1/19/21).
5. https://nationalgeographicpartners.com/about/ (1/19/21).
6. https://www.forbes.com/sites/adamhartung/2012/05/12/oops-5-ceos-that
   -should-have-already-been-fired-cisco-ge-walmart-sears-microsoft/?sh=
   64383dd827c0 (1/19/21).
7. https://www.wsj.com/articles/microsofts-resurgence-under-satya-nadella
   -11549022422 (1/19/21).
8. https://interestingengineering.com/the-fascinating-history-of-netflix (1/19/21).
9. https://entertainmentstrategyguy.com/2019/10/03/why-most-netflix-charts
   -start-in-2012-a-history-of-netflix-subscribers/ (1/19/21).
10. https://www.huffpost.com/entry/qwikster-dead-netflix-kills_n_1003098
    (1/19/21).
11. https://entertainmentstrategyguy.com/2019/10/03/why-most-netflix-charts
    -start-in-2012-a-history-of-netflix-subscribers/ (1/19/21).
12. https://mediadecoder.blogs.nytimes.com/2011/03/18/netflix-gets-into-the-tv
    -business-with-fincher-deal/?searchResultPosition=29 (1/19/21).

13. https://www.wsj.com/articles/netflix-adds-16-million-new-subscribers-as-home
    -bound-consumers-stream-away-11587501078 (1/19/21).
14. "Our History," *Johnson and Johnson,* https://www.jnj.com.ph/about-jnj
    /company-history/timeline (1/19/21).
15. Hannah Blake, "A History of Johnson & Johnson," *Pharmaphorum,* June
    26, 2013, https://pharmaphorum.com/articles/a-history-of-johnson-johnson/
    (1/19/21).
16. https://www.drugreport.com/brands-owned-by-johnson-and-johnson/
    (1/19/21).
17. "Johnson and Johnson Form 10-K," *Johnson and Johnson,* February 20,
    2019, https://johnsonandjohnson.gcs-web.com/sec-filings/sec-filing/10
    -k/0000200406-19-000009 (1/19/21).
18. https://www.upcounsel.com/how-long-does-a-drug-patent-last (1/19/21).
19. https://www.jnj.com/credo/ (1/19/21).
20. https://www.jnj.com/sites/default/files/pdf/our-credo.pdf (1/19/21).
21. Interview with Alex Gorsky, February 15, 2018, https://youtu.be/PG1
    -eiF7okM (1/19/21).
22. Interview with Alex Gorsky, February 15, 2018, https://youtu.be/PG1
    -eiF7okM (1/19/21).
23. Background information courtesy of Johnson & Johnson.
24. Karla Lant, "Scientists Modify Viruses with CRISPR to Kill Antibiotic-
    Resistant Bacteria," *Futurism,* June 24, 2017, https://futurism.com/scientists
    -modify-viruses-with-crispr-to-kill-antibiotic-resistant-bacteria (1/19/21).
25. "T Cell," *Encyclopedia Britannica*, https://www.britannica.com/science/T-cell
    (1/19/21).
26. Background information courtesy of Johnson & Johnson.
27. Interview with Alex Gorsky, February 15, 2018, https://youtu.be/PG1
    -eiF7okM (1/19/21).
28. Interview with Alex Gorsky, February 15, 2018, https://youtu.be/PG1
    -eiF7okM (1/19/21).
29. https://www.reuters.com/article/us-usa-crime-shkreli/pharma-bro-shkreli
    -sentenced-to-seven-years-for-defrauding-investors-idUSKCN1GL1EA
    (2/5/21).
30. "2018 Edelman Trust Barometer, Trust in Healthcare: Global," *Edelman,*
    June 2018, https://www.edelman.com/sites/g/files/aatuss191/files/2018-10
    /Edelman_Trust_Barometer_Global_Healthcare_2018.pdf (3/25/20).
31. Peter Loftus, "Johnson & Johnson's Legal Challenges Mount," *Wall Street
    Journal,* October 14, 2019, https://www.wsj.com/articles/johnson-johnsons
    -legal-challenges-mount-11571055242 (1/19/21).
32. "Sweeping Plan to Lower Drug Prices Introduced in Senate and House,"
    Bernie Sanders U.S. Senator, January 10, 2019, https://www.sanders.senate.gov
    /newsroom/press-releases/sweeping-plan-to-lower-drug-prices-introduced-in
    -senate-and-house (1/31/20).

33. Jessie Hellmann, "Support Drops for 'Medicare for All' but Increases for Public Option," *The Hill,* October 15, 2019, https://thehill.com/policy /healthcare/465786-support-drops-for-medicare-for-all-but-increases-for -public-option (1/19/21).

34. "Largest Health Insurance Companies of 2020, *ValuePenguin by LendingTree,* January 2020, https://www.valuepenguin.com/largest-health-insurance -companies (1/19/21).

35. "Largest-ever analysis of baby powder and ovarian cancer finds no link between the two," *Los Angeles Times,* January 7, 2020, https://www.latimes .com/science/story/2020-01-07/largest-ever-analysis-baby-powder-ovarian -cancer (1/19/21).

36. Katie Thomas, "$8 Billion Verdict in Drug Lawsuit Is Reduced to $6.8 Million," *New York Times,* January 17, 2020, https://www.nytimes.com/2020 /01/17/health/jnj-risperdal-verdict-reduced.html (1/19/21).

37. Josh Nathan-Kazis, "J&J Stock Gets Another Thumbs Up. Analyst Says Legal Worries Are 'Priced In.'," *Barron's,* December 19, 2019, https://www.barrons .com/articles/johnson-johnson-stock-opioids-talc-ligitation-51576770923 (1/19/21).

38. Interview with Alex Gorsky, February 15, 2018, https://youtu.be/PG1 -eiF7okM (1/19/21).

Chapter 13

1. https://medium.com/systemsleadership/optimizing-market-structure-carl-ice -cco-bnsf-railway-924142008521 (1/21/21).

2. https://www.lexico.com/en/definition/context (1/20/21).

3. https://www.wsj.com/articles/china-once-germanys-partner-in-growth-turns -into-a-rival-11600338663 (1/20/21).

4. https://www.nokia.com/blog/study-ai-machine-learning/ (1/21/21).

5. Goldberg, et al., "Fitting In or Standing Out? The Tradeoffs of Structural and Cultural Embeddedness." *American Sociological Review*, October 31, 2016.

6. Andy Grove, *Only the Paranoid Survive*, Currency / Doubleday, 1996, page 126.

7. Interview with Katrina Lake, January 21, 2021.

8. https://www.nytimes.com/2017/05/10/business/dealbook/as-department -stores-close-stitch-fix-expands-online.html (1/20/21).

9. https://www.accenture.com/us-en/accenture-timeline (1/21/21).

10. https://newsroom.accenture.com//content/1101/files/Accenture_Factsheet_Q1 _FY21_FINAL.pdf (1/21/21).

11. Interview with Julie Sweet, February 14, 2019, https://youtu.be /BxYdT84S3pw (1/20/21).

12. https://www.wsj.com/articles/tech-consultants-are-the-new-mad-men -1541765256 (1/20/21).

13. Interview with Julie Sweet, February 14, 2019, https://youtu.be /BxYdT84S3pw (1/20/21).
14. Interview with Julie Sweet, February 14, 2019, https://youtu.be /BxYdT84S3pw (1/20/21).
15. https://www.accenture.com/us-en/services/technology/ecosystem (1/20/21).
16. https://fortune.com/most-powerful-women/2020/julie-sweet/ (1/20/21).

INDEX

ABOUT THE AUTHOR

Robert E. Siegel is a Lecturer in Management at the Stanford Graduate School of Business and a venture investor based in Silicon Valley.

At Stanford he teaches multiple courses on strategy and innovation in both large and small companies, focusing on the opportunities and challenges created by technological innovation. Specifically, he explores how companies combine digital and physical solutions for their customers, and the corresponding impact on product development, organizational design, and leadership. He also teaches product management and development best practices, financial management for entrepreneurs, and related topics.

As a venture investor, Siegel analyzes growing start-ups and has been involved in hundreds of millions of dollars in VC funding. He previously held leadership roles at large organizations such as GE and Intel, and was a multi-time start-up entrepreneur. He also sits on numerous boards of directors. He served as lead researcher for Andy Grove's best-selling book *Only the Paranoid Survive* and contributes frequently to business and academic publications.

Siegel holds a BA from UC Berkeley and an MBA from Stanford University. He and his wife have three grown children and live in Portola Valley, California.